D1034858

SONG AND WORDS

A History of The Curwen Press

SONG AND WORDS

A HISTORY OF THE CURWEN PRESS

BY

HERBERT SIMON

LONDON · GEORGE ALLEN & UNWIN LTD

RUSKIN HOUSE · MUSEUM STREET

FIRST PUBLISHED IN 1973

This book is copyright under the Berne Convention. All rights reserved. Apart from any fair dealing for the purpose of private study, research, criticism or review, as permitted under the Copyright Act, 1956, no part of this publication may be reproduced, stored in a retrieval system, or transmitted, in any form or by any means, electronic, electrical, chemical, mechanical, optical, photocopying, recording or otherwise, without the prior permission of the copyright owner. Enquiries should be addressed to the Publishers.

© *Herbert Simon 1973*

ISBN 0 04 6550119

PRINTED IN GREAT BRITAIN
in 12 point Monotype Caslon
AT THE CURWEN PRESS LTD
PLAISTOW, LONDON

Z
232
·C98S55

CONTENTS

YOUNGSTOWN STATE UNIVERSITY
LIBRARY

326404

THE PLATES

FOREWORD

This book attempts to record the history of a small music publishing and printing business. The Curwen firm was never large but in the nineteenth century it had an immense influence on popular musical education. In the present century it has taken a leading part in what has been called the printing renaissance.

The suggestion that a history should be undertaken came from H. J. Ginbey Jnr who felt it would be an act of piety to try and tell the story of the firm. Ginbey, now retired, was the last of our music compositors and as an old friend I could not refuse his invitation.

I have been encouraged in the task by the interest and steadfast support of Basil Harley, the chairman of the firm. Invaluable has been the help of Christopher Curwen, Donald Cameron, the Truscott family and Rosalind Yelin who found some important material in Norwich. Arthur Pluck was able to tell me much about the Curwen Caxton Choir. Gertrude Temkin most generously provided the story of the stencil printing group and has also seen to it that typographic detail has been properly observed. The fault will be entirely mine if there are departures from Plaistow style. Leonard Heather, our head reader, has exercised his exemplary care and has provided an index.

Everyone consulted has been of service and I must, in particular, thank Marcus Brumwell, Desmond Flower and Hans Schmoller. Tom Hughes was the perfect companion on some local expeditions and, additionally, was able to redraw for reproduction some of the early material. David Unwin undertook to read the whole typescript and made many suggestions which have been adopted to advantage.

Finally I am indebted to Mair Sandercock, who despite her busy life as secretary to the chairman, managed, by some miracle, to do all the typing with a cheerfulness which will always be remembered.

HERBERT SIMON

North Street, Plaistow, 1972

I

JOHN CURWEN

INDEPENDENT MINISTER

THE CURWEN PRESS was started in 1863 by the Reverend John Curwen, the minister of the Plaistow Congregational chapel from 1844 to 1864. That he became a printer when he resigned the pastorate at the age of forty-eight was accidental and, in some ways, incidental to his life's work devoted to the Congregational ministry. To understand how J. Curwen & Sons became the leading publishers of the Tonic Sol-fa movement and how the small beginnings at North Street, Plaistow, took root and grew to become one of the larger music printing establishments of the last quarter of the nineteenth century, the career of the founder needs to be followed in some detail.

John Curwen was born in 1816 at Heckmondwike, a small industrial wool town in the West Riding of Yorkshire. When he was twelve, his father was appointed pastor of the Zion Chapel at Frome, Somerset. It was here, when still a schoolboy, that he decided to devote his life to the Congregational ministry. When he was sixteen he was accepted as a student by the Wymondley Independent College. The college which had long been famous for the training of dissenters was in Wymondley a small village in Hertfordshire near Hitchin.

John Curwen had only been in residence a few months when the college was uprooted and transferred to London. In transferring, its status appears to have been upgraded. It changed its name to Coward College and for secular studies the students attended the newly formed University College in Gower Street. The Wymondley Independent College was eventually to become a part of London University.

[1]

On leaving Coward College in 1838 he became assistant minister to the Independent Chapel at Basingstoke; a welcome start but clearly an appointment of a modest kind. In actual fact, owing to a heart-rending double tragedy, the Basingstoke appointment brought him fame. John Curwen, now a young man of twenty-two, got to know a family called Vanner. There were two daughters, Nelly and Fanny. Fanny was the elder and after a short courtship became engaged to John Curwen. But the engagement came to an abrupt end when Fanny died of consumption; her death had been preceded by the equally tragic death of the younger sister Nelly. These events were naturally a great shock to the young and emotional assistant minister. He was very conscious of the charm and beauty of Nelly Vanner during her short life and wrote a book called *The History of Nelly Vanner*.* It was the story of a simple, placid and uneventful life and it was meant to appeal to children. This it did with astonishing success. Published in 1840, *Nelly Vanner* went to fourteen editions and was a best-seller; if John Curwen had done little else in his life, the book would have ensured him some fame. It made a particular appeal to earnest workers in the Sunday schools and Ragged schools and indirectly paved the way for his momentous meeting with Miss Glover of Norwich.

A fellow student and friend at Coward College was the Revd Andrew Reed, who visited Basingstoke after the publication of *Nelly Vanner*. At the time he wrote,

After leaving college I settled at Norwich and he [John Curwen] at Basingstoke. There I paid him a visit and found him carrying out his theories among a very attached people. He had published his beautiful and successful memoirs of Nelly Vanner and I went with him to visit her home. I was delighted to see how her parents loved and honoured my old colleague for his attention to their daughter in her last hours.

John Curwen was an idealist, a practical man and a good organizer. He was convinced that learning to sing and an appreciation of church and secular music could help millions to endure the hardships of life and ameliorate the often savage conditions into which they had been drawn by economic circumstances. He preached his musical gospel through Sunday schools, the various missions, Ragged schools, choral societies and, always dear to his heart, the powerful temperance societies.

*Also published in 1841 by the American Sunday School Union, 146 Chestnut Street, Philadelphia, under the title of *The History of Eleanor Vanner*.

This was long before the passing of the Education Act of 1870 and therefore before the establishment of the School Boards; in an age when sanitation was almost unknown and the growth of towns and cities virtually unplanned, there was a vast body of poorly fed, poorly housed and poorly paid factory workers and it was these unhappy and sometimes feckless people who found some solace and a good deal of real compassion in the environment of the Independent chapel communities.

A better world seemed possible and a less harsh world for the urban poor if singing could be properly learnt and become a happy experience for everyone. John Curwen was convinced that the practice of singing was just as important for a person's welfare as church or chapel attendance. 'Congregations are waiting for young men and maidens to learn to sing that they may praise the Lord. Who shall do this work? I look chiefly to the young men and young women of our Tonic Sol-fa classes.' This is the call to duty in the preface of his monumental *Teacher's Manual of the Tonic Sol-fa Method*.

England was changing rapidly in those early years of the nineteenth century. As John Curwen was growing up the traditional, and mainly agricultural, society was becoming subordinated to manufacturing and urban life. The factories were creating a new kind of working people very different from the agricultural labourer or domestic servant.

Many innocent men and women were forced to pay a high price for Britain to become the workshop of the world. New factories were becoming an accepted part of the landscape in many parts of the Midlands and the North. Imports of raw materials tell the story of change. Imports into the port of Liverpool doubled between 1815 and 1860, and most of the increase was raw cotton and wool for the textile industry of south Lancashire and the West Riding of Yorkshire.

Operatives or 'hands', as the new factory workers were called, worked incredibly long hours under strict discipline in ill ventilated workrooms. Some masters, it is true, were alive to their responsibilities. Outstanding was Robert Owen who built the model factory village at New Lanark in 1799 and Sir Titus Salt who, later in 1853, built the village of Saltaire around his great woollen mill near Bradford.

But the majority of the new owners were keen on getting safely established and making money as quickly as possible. Exploitation

[3]

was not always deliberate; nevertheless thousands of young boys and girls found themselves helpless factory slaves working under taskmasters who could be callous and ferocious.

Singing had, of course, been a part of village life from time immemorial. It became even more in evidence as the industrialization of the country began to gather momentum after 1750. Today, at the beginning of Millers Dale in the beautiful limestone valley of the Derbyshire Wye, there stands Cressbrook cotton-spinning mill dating back to the late eighteenth century, contemporary with Richard Arkwright and his patent water-powered spinning frame. The mill is still in use and close to it are the remains of the apprentice house and chapel. It was one of those communities in a beautiful and isolated Derbyshire dale so carefully described by Frances Trollope in *Michael Armstrong, the Factory Boy*. This book, which vividly exposed the harsh and dreadful treatment of children in the textile mills, was published in the same year as *Nelly Vanner*. Country textile mills were too often inhuman places and the suffering of young people deeply affected John Curwen's kindly and affectionate nature. In his lecture tours in the industrial centres he had every opportunity of seeing at first hand the plight of many unfortunate boys and girls. Cressbrook Mill employed, like all other textile mills at that period, child labour. But Mr Newton, the master of Cressbrook, was humane and took a lively interest in the welfare of his young charges. Mrs Sterndale describes life at Cressbrook in her *Vignettes of Derbyshire.**

Their highest species of enjoyment, the highest that man can enjoy is music: this delightfully intellectual source of pleasure is improved, encouraged and scientifically taught at Cressbrook. Every boy that has a voice, an ear, or a finger capable of participating in the Heavenly science, receives elementary, and practical instruction; and amidst the cotton-spinners of Cressbrook, the outcasts from parental care, the orphans of humanity, the hallelujahs of Handel fill the valley, and I trust rise with acceptable melody to Heaven. There is also a tenderness of feeling displayed in its arrangement, not to be passed over; a gallery has been appropriated as an Orchestra, so that the liberty of the younger children might not be invaded by the restraint that must have been necessarily imposed, or the study and practice of the young musicians interrupted by the gambols of their companions. The girls do not learn music, for reasons highly creditable to the judgment and decorum that accompany the whole system, that of

Vignettes of Derbyshire by Mary Sterndale: G. and W. B. Whittaker, 1824.

[4]

keeping the boys and girls separate; but their room being above that of the boys, the sweet sounds ascend, and they participate in the harmony. I can scarcely imagine anything more striking than what must have occurred, and what may often re-occur to a benighted traveller, crossing the wild way from Tideswell, that overhangs the deep and rocky channel of the Wye, as he descends into this apparently lone vale, to have the dark silence interrupted by a chorus of sweet and youthful voices, in all the harmony of scientific precision, accompanied by the rich notes of the viol, breaking upon his ear in the words of 'Lord, dismiss us with thy blessing', the hymn that closes the musical exercises of the young choristers.

Mrs Sterndale was charmed but was undisturbed by the long hours of work and saw no hardship and possible harm in sex segregation of the young mill-workers. She was impressed, perhaps too easily impressed, by Cressbrook, 'an establishment most honourable to those who are its proprietors, and to those who preside over its prosperity and its comforts, whilst it may confirm the belief that all cotton mills are not the scenes of unnatural labour or harsh severity'. Evidence of royal commissions makes it clear that William Newton at Cressbrook and Samuel Greg at Bollington in Cheshire were exceptional in their care for the happiness of their mill-workers.

At Bollington education and recreation were given prime consideration. The mill which was opened in 1832 started a Sunday school; this was followed by a playground for the young, the institution of a drawing class and then singing classes. Music proved more popular than drawing. Greg writes 'our music and singing engage many of both sexes, young and old, learned and unlearned. We have a small glee class that meets once a week round a cottage fire. There is another more numerous for sacred music that meets every Wednesday and Saturday during the winter and really performs very well.'*

What was going on at Cressbrook and Bollington would have pleased John Curwen immensely. They were, indeed, early pointers to the value of singing in elementary schooling to which John Curwen was to devote his amazing energy and organizing ability. The Curwen ideal was summed up by George Howarth writing in 1842, 'that the experience of the present has shown, and is showing more and more that even the classes who earn their daily bread by the sweat of their brow may find in music a

---

* *A Social History of English Music* by E. D. Mackerness: Routledge & Kegan Paul, 1964.

recreation within their reach, full enjoyment and pregnant with moral and social benefits'. Responsible behaviour, the avoidance of alcohol, and simple enjoyments were the foundations of John Curwen's approach to his work in popular education.

The need for this work was becoming more and more evident with the spread of industrialization. Villages were beginning to change into towns and towns into cities. A great deal of this was happening in south-east Lancashire, north-east Cheshire, the West Riding of Yorkshire, Tyneside, the Black Country, Birmingham and the valleys of south Wales. Curwen undertook his first lecture tour to Sunday school teachers in the autumn of 1841. He visited Leeds, his birth-place Heckmondwike, Halifax, Bradford and most of the West Riding towns speaking on methods for use in Sunday school teaching. The new railway age made a tour of this extent possible but, even so, it must have required considerable endurance. The first trunk line from London, Euston Square, had only recently been opened. To an impecunious pastor with a whole series of towns to visit, some connected by railway but by no means all, the lecturing itinerary must have been an expensive and physically arduous undertaking.

He did not remain long at Basingstoke. In the year of his lecture tour he moved to Stowmarket, and there took up the post of co-pastor in the Independent Chapel.

APPOINTMENT TO PLAISTOW

THE APPOINTMENT to Stowmarket in 1841 proved to be a piece of geographical good fortune which was to have immense influence in shaping John Curwen's pastoral work. He was only a few miles from Norwich and his friend Andrew Reed and it was not long before a meeting with Sarah Glover and her sister Christiana was arranged.

Miss Glover was then fifty-six years old. She had been experimenting for a long time in making singing easier to learn: it is believed that from about 1812 she began training her choir by a system which was eventually to become known as Tonic Sol-fa. But although John Curwen, through the fame of his *History of Nelly Vanner* and his work in the Sunday schools and Temperance Movement, was probably known to Miss Glover, it is clear that until the meeting in Norwich he knew nothing of the Sol-fa system. An account of his first meeting has fortunately been recorded by Andrew Reed:

I took him to see the Misses Glover in their school, and he was at once riveted by the astonishing results produced by them. He never forgot to allude very honourably to them, so as to give them due credit, but it was himself who saw the general adaptation of the system—who resolved to spread and make it known—who perfected it in many respects, who bore the brunt of the opposition encountered by every novelty—who took the mercantile risks on himself—and who, by his unwearied perseverance and pluck, gave it a place all over the world, wherever music is taught, and exalted it into a scientific notation, which more and more competes with the established notation. Thus he found the chief mission of his life to improve the psalmody of our churches and the singing in our schools, and to make it a delightful medium for the easy culture in homes, schools and churches of harmony wedded to moral and religious poetry.

[7]

YOUNGSTOWN STATE UNIVERSITY LIBRARY 326404

I well remember his hilarity and profound interest when he came back to my lodgings saying 'Now, Andrew, I have a good tool to work with' and how we sat up into the small hours with my harmonium, studying the mysteries of sol-fa and trying some of Miss Glover's exercises.

John Curwen has often been credited with the invention of the Sol-fa method; this was not so and he made no claim to being its inventor. Never for a moment did he forget that Sarah Glover was his teacher and that he owed everything to her for introducing him to the new system. He was indeed most scrupulous and when Tonic Sol-fa was a going concern and he was getting an income from printing and publishing he tried, in vain, to persuade Miss Glover to accept royalties. When refusing any payment, she modestly wrote, 'Do not concern yourself to vindicate my originality. Let the question be not who was the first to invent it, but is the thing itself good and true and useful to the world.' The friendship between John Curwen and Sarah Glover was close and there was continuous correspondence which lasted until she died at Malvern in 1867, at the age of eighty-two.

It is astounding what John Curwen was able to accomplish after his conversion to Sol-fa. The young assistant pastor, without private means, was to spread the knowledge of the Tonic Sol-fa system throughout the world, to write a whole series of text books and teachers' manuals, to edit and publish *The Reporter*, which eventually became a monthly journal with a wide circulation, and, in an age when travel was often arduous, to go all over the country demonstrating the new system. This was to be John Curwen's life work for just on forty years until he died, prematurely worn out, in 1880. In the cause of Tonic Sol-fa, he visited almost every important place in the United Kingdom. Aberdeen, Edinburgh, Glasgow, Paisley and Dundee were on his list and, in Wales, Cardiff, Swansea, Merthyr Tydfil and most of the mining valleys; in England there were Bristol, Manchester, Liverpool, Newcastle, the West Riding of Yorkshire, Birmingham, Portsmouth and even smaller places like Halstead, one of the 'Courtauld' manufacturing centres in north Essex. He enjoyed lecturing and, as an evangelist, he felt an urge to address meetings in any part of the United Kingdom which called out to him. His crusade can be compared to that of Richard Cobden and the Anti-Corn Law League.

His first visit to Miss Glover's school in Norwich had made a

[8]

Sarah Glover

deep impression. Lecturing almost thirty-five years later he said
'. . . as I stood on the stairs listening to the music of that upper
room I found it soft and cultivated, such as I had never heard
from school children before. As I opened the door I saw a little
girl pointing to syllables on a diagram, singing as she pointed.
Stepping in, I saw that she had in front of her a gallery of children
who were following her pointing and singing the syllables with
her. I had never been able to get anything like it in all my hard
two years' work!'

John Curwen was in fact listening to what was for him a first
performance of Tonic Sol-fa and the use of the modulator or
Pointing Board. He decided there and then to become a Sol-faist

[9]

and introduce the new system, modified where necessary, into the normal scheme of work in Sunday and elementary schools.

While still attached to the Independent Chapel at Stowmarket, he was zealous as an instructor and encourager of Sunday school teachers. In June 1842 he is at Euston again, this time taking the train to Manchester. His engagements covered Manchester, Salford and Stockport and his audience were mainly teachers in dissenting Sunday schools. Among the leaders of Sunday school work in Manchester was Joseph Thompson, a successful cotton-spinner, and it was not surprising that he paid John Curwen the compliment of presiding at the first lecture. Not only did he honour the lecturer by his chairmanship, but he invited the young minister to be his guest at Chorlton House during his stay.

There is little doubt that the work that John Curwen was doing had the warm approval of Joseph Thompson. Settled in Manchester in 1796, he was an influential business man of deep piety and sterling integrity. He was one of a small group who worked with Richard Cobden in the cause of securing a charter of incorporation for Manchester. A superintendent of a Sunday school, founder and trustee of the Lancashire Independent College (Congregational) at Whalley Range, a keen supporter of

Miss Glover's schoolroom, Norwich

universal education and a cotton-spinner with an understanding of the hardships and difficulties facing the numerous impoverished factory workers; he sounds a paragon and in all probability was one. His cotton-spinning mill gave him opportunity for encouraging self-improvement. Pin Mill at Ardwick had a library for the use of his workers. The catalogue of the library lists nearly 1,200 books offering a rich variety of reading; this at a time when a works' library was very unusual. The firm provided his workers with a printed catalogue of the mill library. Joseph Thompson was interested in music and was said to be a fair performer: his private organ from Chorlton House was eventually presented to the Chorlton Workhouse.

But Mrs Thompson had two unmarried daughters and it would have been natural in those days for her to entertain on their behalf some harmless worldly hopes; she may have had ideas for her girls marrying Manchester manufacturers or merchants and seeing them established in Hazel Grove, then a pretty village, with a garden screened by evergreens and a carriage and pair in which to pay the customary formal visits. She was alarmed when her husband brought home a young but almost penniless lecturer. Was he married? Mr Thompson did not know but thought he must be, as he had a gift of speaking to children and winning their affection in a way which he considered only a man with children of his own could do. But Mrs Thompson's fears were well founded. The young John Curwen, it transpired, was unmarried and before his stay in Manchester was over had fallen in love with Mary, the younger of the two Thompson daughters, and proposed marriage. Mr and Mrs Thompson were dumbfounded: the young minister was charming but impecunious and the vague dreams of Hazel Grove and a carriage and pair were in danger. After stiff and prolonged opposition, the goodness and charm of John Curwen triumphed over the disability of his being a relatively poor man. Parental consent was given and he and Mary Thompson became engaged.

The engagement, however, and the discovery of the teaching methods of Miss Glover were too much of a disturbance in the emotional life of John Curwen. He felt obliged to leave Stowmarket where he had been working happily for less than two years. He decided to spend a year with his father at Reading, partly to recuperate and overcome signs of ill health, probably brought on by being in love. He also needed rest after the

[11]

physical strain of his lecture tours and he wanted a few quiet months to devote to a closer study of Miss Glover's methods. He was able to modify her system and make it 'the most simple of all, the most easy to teach and the most easy to learn'. It was a fruitful year in which he was able to perfect his teaching method and write and publish his first important primer on Tonic Sol-fa, singing for schools and congregations. He was also restored to health, so that when he was invited to become pastor of the Independent Chapel in North Street, Plaistow he had no hesitation in accepting. On 22 May 1844, the Revd John Curwen was ordained.

Three years earlier, at a meeting of Sunday school teachers held in Hull in 1841, the conference, by special resolution, had charged him to make his mission in life the cultivation of music and singing in the service of God. The pastorate was his opportunity, and from the moment of taking up the appointment he began developing the teaching of singing by the Tonic Sol-fa method which was, in an incredibly short time, to expand into a national movement.

The energy and readiness for practical action which John Curwen brought to his educational and pastoral work was amazing. By August 1844, when he had been minister for only three months, a building at right angles to the chapel had been erected and the first public elementary school in Plaistow was established. It was under the charge of Alfred Brown, who was to become a lifelong friend, disciple and supporter.

Brown was interviewed on 1 July 1844 and found Mr Curwen 'a handsome young bachelor, beaming with benevolence and filled with bright hopes for the children of Plaistow'. He dined with the young pastor—no alcohol, they were both ardent members of the Temperance movement—and they took to each other immediately, Brown becoming a faithful servant and chief helper in all the religious and educational work.

It is astonishing how quickly John Curwen got things going and how quickly he managed to raise money for the school building. The building lasted until a bomb fell on it in 1941 and for many years it housed the office staff of The Curwen Press.

One of his congregation, who was a child when the school was opened, wrote later of 'his beaming eyes and cheerful voice and kind manner. . . . I remember with what delight my brother Charles and I attended his children's Bible class, held on a week-day afternoon. It was there that we learnt the elements of the Tonic Sol-fa system from himself, and it has been a help to me in singing from sight through life.'

Not all the inhabitants of Plaistow held John Curwen in such veneration. The daughter of one of the subscribers to the school found her father did not subscribe to Mr Curwen's left-wing views. Although it was granted he was a man of culture and refinement, kind and helpful to everyone, yet Curwen's Anti-State Church Society was extremely distasteful and democratic equality either in church or social life held no charms for him. It says much for this resident of Plaistow that despite his dislike of John Curwen's views, he was nevertheless ready to support and give financial aid to the North Street school.

Independent Chapel and school, North Street, Plaistow

The new school was exactly what was needed for John Curwen to put into practice his ideas as an educationist and to perfect the teaching of singing by the Tonic Sol-fa system. Alfred Brown was fortunately an enthusiastic Sol-faist and thanks to their earnest and devoted teaching, in a very short time congregational singing and chanting became outstandingly good. The school worked hard; on every week-day there were classes in addition to Sunday schools and all pupils were able to receive instruction in singing from the founder and chief director of the Tonic Sol-fa movement. The school was a kind of laboratory for John Curwen; it served as a testing ground for his theories and, as the system gradually developed on a national scale, it was obviously useful to have a

[13]

school which acted as a test-bed for this new approach in teaching. Curwen knew with certainty that his work could bring comfort and pleasure to thousands of homes; the knowledge that this was possible provided the encouragement and determination to follow for the rest of his life the sacred mission with which he had been entrusted.

Solicitude and active social work were never needed more than in the 'hungry forties'. The Factory Act of 1844 was to many a bitter disappointment. It abandoned the compulsory provision of schooling at the factory and lowered the age for employment of children from nine to eight years. It obliged all masters to arrange for time off for elementary education for all between the ages of eight to thirteen for a period of either three whole days a week or six half days. But the difficulty of inspection made the provisions almost a dead letter; the master could ignore the need of education and, in any case, the towns were growing so rapidly that there were insufficient schools and certainly insufficient trained teachers.

The great number of children receiving no formal education can, in part, be accounted for by parental inability or unwillingness to pay. To the poor of the great manufacturing cities contributions for schooling of such modest sums as threepence or sixpence a week were often beyond the family means.

There were many, inside and outside religious communities, who did their utmost to improve the quality of life for the very poor. Among them was John Pounds,* originally a sailor and then a boot-maker working in Portsmouth, who managed to organize free elementary education for the poorest and generally uncared-for children of the town. It was the practical work of John Pounds that led to the formation of free elementary schools, which became known as the 'Ragged schools'. The Ragged school movement took root in the industrial areas of Scotland; the first free school was established in Aberdeen in 1841 and the London Ragged School Union was formed in 1844.

John Curwen was very much aware of the physical and spiritual decline that the rapid growth in the working population had produced. Like John Pounds he was determined to see that every child had the opportunity of some formal education. He was convinced that, through the teaching of choral singing in Sunday schools and day schools, young boys and girls would find a new

*See *History of Education in Great Britain* by S. J. Curtis: University Tutorial Press, 1967.

[14]

interest that would aid them spiritually and help them to find schooling both enjoyable and beneficial. In Curwen's view the whole process of education should be enjoyable and, as he would put it, 'a continual glorification of the will of God'.

He saw clearly that, if he could introduce his improved and modified version of Miss Glover's method, singing could be taught in a simple and straightforward way, and his young pupils could enjoy personal participation in secular or religious choral singing.

His eldest son, John Spencer Curwen, wrote later that his father

originated the Tonic Sol-fa movement and directed it for forty years. He was thus able to impress upon it a character, and to keep it up to the high level of moral and religious purpose upon which he had started it. This required constant vigilance and often great firmness. The Tonic Sol-fa movement touched almost all efforts for the elevation of mankind. By simplifying musical notation, the art in its domestic and religious aspects entered thousands of homes which had before been without music. Thus the method was the indirect means of aiding worship, temperance and culture, of holding young men and women among good influences, of reforming character, of spreading Christianity.

III

TONIC SOL-FA

WHY WAS Tonic Sol-fa 'the most simple of all, the most easy to teach and the most easy to learn'? And how was it that a devoted clergyman and a great believer in education, working in a remote village, was able to make Tonic Sol-fa within the space of twenty years a great national and international movement?

Although Miss Glover's method of teaching was new to the Revd John Curwen it was, in fact, based on principles which were centuries old. What was known as solmization was a method of using easily pronounced syllables to illustrate the musical scale. For intoned responses of the Roman Catholic Church and in plain-song it was found the tune could be more easily taught to choristers by using simple symbols which were not very different from Miss Glover's. The Sol-fa taught in the Norwich Sunday school can be traced back to the teaching methods of Guido d'Arezzo in the eleventh century. Miss Glover's set of symbols, and her picture of the music scale which she called a 'modulator', made it easier for beginners to learn the aural character of a note before it was sung. The system of Tonic Sol-fa as known in England originated with Miss Glover, who introduced the movable 'doh' so that any note could be the tonic one.*

The great advantage of Tonic Sol-fa notation lay in pupils being able to 'sight-read' the tune without having to learn the more difficult staff notation. It was, however, open to criticism that it was mainly a method of teaching choir or choral singing and was not much of a help for instrumental music. It was essentially a system for training community singers and was not

*See *The Oxford Companion to Music* by Percy A. Scholes: Oxford University Press, 1970

a system of teaching piano playing. Clearly this was a restriction which caused misgiving among many distinguished music teachers; to them it savoured too much of a half-way house. New methods invariably stimulate opposition among professionals: it seemed almost criminal that a tune could be learned by following a teacher pointing the way on a modulator or chart. A singer could learn the tunes without having to know anything about the accepted staff notation. But in 1844 playing the piano was a social accomplishment restricted to, and admired by, the well-off members of society. Musical evenings were much favoured and daughters especially were expected to perform with dignity, style and grace. The world in which John Curwen was teaching was very different. It was all too often the near destitute who were without much, if any, formal education and would almost certainly have little chance of access to a piano and pianoforte lessons.

The Sunday schools of the Independent communities, the free schools, mission schools, Ragged schools and schools supported by the Temperance movement were largely the sources of education for the less favoured; and it was here that John Curwen directed his energies. What was essential to John Curwen's plans was to employ a teaching method which could by-pass what he called the five-barred gate of clefs, crochets, quavers, semi-quavers and demi-semi-quavers. In other words, he could, by using his methods, teach singing by sight-reading without having to make his pupils master the more difficult task of sight-reading ordinary staff notation.

John Curwen himself, not possessed of any natural advantage of ear or voice, found sight-reading of ordinary music difficult to master and could not make out the very plainest tune unless it was already familiar. He had to struggle against these disadvantages in the early days of his Sunday school teaching; he was getting results but they needed such a lot of hard work and were so meagre that he might well have despaired if he had not become acquainted with Miss Glover's method.

The essential thing had been to find a method of teaching which was as simple as possible. Miss Glover's Sol-fa fulfilled this need: 'to teach first the simple and beautiful thing MUSIC and to delay the introduction to the ordinary antiquated mode of writing it, until the pupil had obtained a mastery of the thing itself'. Clearly the aim was to teach the tune by sight-reading and then, when sung with the words, the essential beauty of the music could be brought out. Any student who desired it could follow up Sol-fa sight-reading by learning the more difficult 'tune reading' from the normal staff notation.

There were modifications to be made, however, which had to be explained to Sarah Glover. In 1848 John Curwen wrote in his *Grammar of Vocal Music*: 'The editor is desirous not to deceive the public by allowing them to suppose these modifications go forth under Miss Glover's full approval: and, at the same time, he is most anxious that to Miss Glover should be given the fullest credit for that admirable genius, patience and research which have been shown in the construction of her system, and that to her should be yielded the chief praise for whatever success his own work may obtain.' This is typical of Curwen's generosity, modesty and honesty, which made him so much loved and respected and was to be the constant background to all he did in teaching and helping to raise the moral and material welfare of his fellow human beings.

Five years before the publication of the *Grammar of Vocal Music* he had outlined his proposed changes to Miss Glover, who must have been as kind, generous and modest as her convert. Miss Glover replies, 'But though you prefer some alterations, yet you keep to the leading principles of the Sol-fa notation, and my pupils would soon sing from your book and yours from mine.' What could be kinder and more encouraging to the young pastor, who was on the eve of being appointed to the chapel in North Street, Plaistow?

Tonic Sol-fa leaders regarded their initial meeting in 1841 as the foundation year of the movement. Therefore the Tonic Sol-fa jubilee could be celebrated in 1891 and a 'popular record handbook' was produced by John Spencer Curwen and John Graham. Printed, of course, at North Street, Plaistow with the type set in the composing room which was formerly the Independent Chapel, the Jubilee book begins with 'Reminiscences of Miss Glover' by her niece, Mrs Langton Brown. It reveals Miss Glover as an exceptional teacher, an innovator and a devoted worker. It also makes clear that she did not have the resources or physical energy to develop her method on her own; this was done 'most successfully' and with her wholehearted approval by John Curwen.

Mrs Langton Brown's reminiscences are a valuable record of the Sol-fa pioneer and the link with Mr Curwen. Mrs Langton

[18]

Brown was about sixty-seven when she wrote for the Jubilee handbook; her appreciation of her aunt was profound.

At your kind request, I try to pen some recollections of my dear aunt Sarah Anna Glover. My memory of her begins about 1829, when she probably introduced me (a five-year-old) to Sol-fa. I never remember *thinking* of notes but in relation to a Tonic *do* and a Sol-fa *ladder*.

It seems to me that Miss Glover's qualities and training fitted her to be an inventor, a pioneer. Her father, a clergyman, was a musical enthusiast. My aunt, with her sisters, was early in the field, teaching poor children, and bringing out a series of very good spelling lessons. A manuscript dated 1817 records the words of two young children in her class: 'There will not be any school in heaven?' Reply: 'But Miss Glover will look after us there.' A large number of carefully-prepared sermonettes addressed to her scholars remain in evidence of the pains which she afterwards took to train souls as well as voices. She had an aim—to promote the glory of God in worship—which supported her through years of toil, difficulty and discouragement. In endeavouring to carry this out, fresh ideas came to her gradually, and she gave herself to the patient work of arranging and maturing them. No one burdened with the common duties of life could have done this as she did. Sarah's tendency was to brood and theorize; the return of the practical, music-loving Christiana, in 1838, after long absence, as friend and governess in the family of Sir T. Fowell Buxton, of anti-slavery fame, brought the *complement* which her sister's nature required. Miss Glover was small and slight, of much personal charm in youth, with fair complexion and bright hair. Her youth had been passed in intellectual society and pursuits, and although shy and reserved, she took effect upon those about her as only a cultured woman could. Those who knew my aunt only in connection with her system of singing were unconscious of her remarkable ability and taste as a player of the pianoforte, where she showed as much grasp of harmony as delicacy and fire in rendering the meaning of the composer.

My personal association with my aunt's work is limited to the period of a few visits to Norwich. In the winter of 1840–41, I particularly recall her evening class at home of men and young women, the latter chiefly old pupils. The part-singing was enjoyable in spite of the smallness of the room; some had rich, sweet voices, and all practised with good will. In the Black-Boy Yard School the regular instruction had formed a band of very steady young singers, many of whom went forth as Sol-fa teachers.

Miss Glover had always a single eye to the improvement of singing in church, and had neither time nor money to spend in developing secular music, as has been done so successfully by the late Mr Curwen. Her educational absorption (and certain religious influences) had long withdrawn her from general society and her hands were never strengthened by a coherent body of supporters. As proofs of her concentration of mind upon her main object, I may remark that she had long ceased to pay attention to music in general, and that although she had taken pleasure in composing music, she included none of her compositions in her books.

When I visited my aunt in 1850, the *Tetrachordal Manual* was passing through the press. She was unable to exert herself as formerly in teaching, and my own impression was that her old interest in scientific theory was becoming disproportionate, and hindering her practical success. That may, however, have been an effect of declining physical powers. She soon afterwards quitted Norwich for Cromer, and the main work of her life was over; though she never ceased, whether in Reading, Malvern, or Hereford, to occupy herself on behalf of congregational singing, and of her system in particular.

She derived extreme pleasure from hearing the Tonic Sol-fa choirs sing in the Crystal Palace, and from the very kind reception given to her in 1855 by Mr Curwen and the teachers and pupils assembled in Jewin Street.

'Melody of heart' seems to be well understood and valued by Mr Curwen; and it is very satisfactory to observe how careful he is in the selection of words to his pieces of music, to avoid any sentiment of an immoral tendency, and how well he arranges secular and sacred subjects in such a manner that no violent transition of feeling is experienced by the performer or hearer. He always likes to conclude with something of a solemn character. A sweet and holy fellowship seems to pervade the company of Sunday school teachers, masters of schools, and pupils. Cheerfulness, sobriety, and love seem to characterize the meetings, and I believe the little chapel may truly be regarded as an oasis, in a moral sense, in the midst of the wickedness of the metropolis. Heartily do I wish that its amiable and persevering manager may meet with co-operation from those whose purses are better lined than those of his disciples, for he spends more than he can conveniently afford on plans for carrying his harmonious work into execution.

It hardly enters into my province to touch upon the relations between Mr Curwen and my aunt. One had sowed; the other cultivated, and had the joy of reaping. Knowing her as I did, my wonder was that she was able to rejoice so much in the success of a system which, though based upon hers, in effect superseded it. But among the gains which come with age, is the readiness to 'decrease' while others 'increase'. My dear aunt, I am sure, was full of thankfulness that her efforts had not been in vain, and that after long years the praises of God were being sung, and harmony attained, according to her heart's long desires.

IV

THE PLAISTOW EXPERIMENT

EXACTLY A YEAR after officially taking up his appointment in Plaistow, in May 1845, John Curwen married Mary Thompson. They lived, at first, about ten minutes' walk from the chapel, in a small house long since demolished and now part of the site of St Mary's Hospital for Women.

At this time, Plaistow was a quiet little community about five miles from London and not very accessible; one of a string of three villages stretching towards the Thames from the southern boundary of Epping Forest. First was Forest Gate, where there was actually a gate across the road; not a toll-gate, but a gate to prevent cattle straying on to the Romford high road. Next was Upton, which was the home of some remarkable Quaker families. The present West Ham park was the garden to Ham House, one of the residences of Samuel Gurney and later of Sir Thomas Fowell Buxton, who had married Hannah Gurney. By a strange coincidence John Curwen found himself almost a neighbour of the man who was a friend of Christiana Glover and had employed her as a governess in his family. Opposite West Ham park in Upton Lane was Upton House, the birthplace of Joseph Lister; and not far away in Plashet House lived another Gurney sister, Elizabeth Fry.

Nearly opposite the Independent Chapel in North Street was the Friends' Meeting House, built in 1819 and subsequently hidden from view when incorporated in the buildings of the new Board School. It was only briefly visible again in 1969 when the old Board School, then transformed into a College of Further Education, was demolished.

Unfortunately, the remains of the Meeting House have now been demolished and so also has Upton House, which it was hoped

[21]

would be used by a youth club. The fine old house has been replaced by a block of flats called Joseph Lister House.

North Street is a short street, less than a five minute walk from end to end, but it was one of the important streets in old Plaistow. Besides having the Independent Chapel, the school and the Friends' Meeting House, there was also the Temperance Hall.

Temperance Hall, North Street

This hall, which must have gladdened the heart of John Curwen, was pulled down in 1897 to make room for an extension to the machine room of the Tonic Sol-fa printing works. A difficult decision, no doubt, for the two sons of John Curwen, who were just as devoted to the Temperance movement as their father.

At the census of 1841 Plaistow had less than 2,000 inhabitants and consisted mainly of market gardens, old weather-boarded houses and a few elegant, large Georgian mansions. The stretch from what is now the Barking Road to the Thames was wild marshland, much valued for its duck shooting. But by the middle of the century the rural charm was beginning to crumble; the construction of the 'Royal' group of docks on what were once the Plaistow marshes and the arrival of the great manufacturing firms brought change and rapid growth in population, which increased more than five-fold to over 11,000 in 1860. By the time of the death of the Revd John Curwen in 1880, Plaistow had become a huge and rather forlorn looking London suburb with heavy traffic to and from dockland and rows and rows of utterly undistinguished and cheaply built houses, and by 1891 the population was estimated to be 80,000.

This change to a crowded urban community was bound to create plenty of opportunity for Mary Curwen to use her abilities as a social worker and she filled the office of the pastor's wife with a good sense which earned her much goodwill. Although always ready to help, she had a reputation for being shrewd and was not to be taken in by 'hard luck' stories. Bolts of calico and flannel, sent by the family from Manchester, were a comfort to many; her concern and thoughtfulness for others were appreciated so much that she earned the local courtesy title of 'Lady Curwen'.

Mary must have inherited much of the family goodness and piety. She was considered to be a 'poor musician' and it is known she never mastered sight-reading by Tonic Sol-fa. Despite this disability she made the perfect wife for the exuberant and busy John Curwen. A good housekeeper, ever thoughtful of the needy, she was endowed with a practical shrewdness which the Manchester of those days may have reinforced. She was John Curwen's chancellor of the exchequer and, at times, was to find financial aid for the proper fulfilment of his mission.

Surprisingly the publication of *Singing for Schools and Congregations* brought some profit. In the autobiographical section of his great work *The Teacher's Manual*, John Curwen says, 'My first stimulus was from Miss Glover herself. Very naturally I sent to her the profits of my first Sol-fa publication. But she returned them saying that she had never received a pecuniary reward for her work, and did not wish to do so.' This was in 1843, before his marriage; he used the money returned to produce an enlarged edition called *The Grammar of Vocal Music*. This book was published in 1848, three years after his marriage. John Curwen continues,

but I was destined to receive another stimulus—one of a very different kind from the last. By this time I was married, and my brave wife has seen me lay out all our united savings in paying for a big book slowly written and slowly stereotyped. It was the now old *Grammar of Vocal Music*. When it was finished I asked her whether I should bring it out in an expensive form, so as to be repaid early, or in a cheap form with the hope of being repaid at

[23]

some distant date. She comforted me by saying that she did not think it would ever pay but she would like me to do all the good I could with it by making it cheap. For my part, I hoped that my wife and little child would not be allowed to suffer for my love of music, and so made the book 2s 6d instead of 5s.

Mrs Curwen must have had a well developed business instinct: the Tonic Sol-fa movement thrived on the provision of music books and sheet music made cheap by mass production.

The extra room needed for bringing up a family and floor space for a kind of head office for the Tonic Sol-fa movement made John Curwen seek a larger house and one nearer the North Street chapel. He was lucky to become a tenant of Richmond House, a commodious and pleasant Georgian mansion a minute away. The house was demolished with many other fine Plaistow and Upton houses in the early years of this century; the garden became the site of the works of Jeyes Sanitary Compounds (now moved to Thetford) and Richmond House itself has been replaced by a dull looking building bearing the date 1912 on a lintel made of artificial stone.

The move suited John Curwen and he liked the feeling of being next door to the chapel and his newly established school. Richmond House was ideal for bringing up a family and all the children of John and Mary Curwen enjoyed in childhood the pleasures of the large house and beautiful garden. In 1845 they were in rural surroundings; North Street and High Street were still village streets and what is now St Mary's Road was a real country lane.

A routine of work before breakfast was the start of Curwen's working day, the time being generally devoted to writing text books and articles on Tonic Sol-fa; then there was often a welcome visit from Alfred Brown, when the work of the school was discussed over breakfast. And now, in the background, he was grateful for the support of a wife who was devoted to the same causes as he was, who was tireless in working for the improvement of moral standards and who believed, also, in strict temperance.

Mary Curwen's training fitted her to aid her energetic husband and direct his idealism and missionary zeal. She was brought up in an atmosphere where being of service to others was part of the accepted order of life. Her father's interest in widening the horizon of those who had little chance of formal education, and his recognition that all people, in whatever station of life they happened to be, were precious human beings, gave his daughters a sense of purpose and developed in them exceptional gifts for social work.

John Curwen needed all the help, both secular and spiritual, his wife could give. He had undertaken a huge programme of work: not only was he pastor of the Independent Chapel in a rapidly growing community, but he was often away from home on his incredibly arduous journeys. He was, as it were, national organizer of what was rapidly becoming a big national and international movement. All the time he was perfecting his system of teaching in the pilot-school he had established in Plaistow and, by rising early, he found time to write a whole literature on Tonic Sol-fa. In addition to all this, he was sole director of the movement's public relations. He was determined to fulfil the special mission with which he had been charged at Hull in 1841; but it was not always easy. His conscience told him he was the minister in charge of the Plaistow nonconformists.

His own admission of the dilemma in which he was often placed is characteristically frank. 'For some years,' he says, 'I kept this music mission as of third or fourth rate importance. As a young minister I had first my church, second my Sunday school and third my day school. All these came before my duty to music. I was even so jealous of myself that I would not even learn the piano, lest I should be tempted to waste time. But, looking back, I see I have been gradually forced, sometimes by strong encouragements, sometimes by misfortune, and more often by the sharp stimulus of opposition, to put music in the front.'

His work in Plaistow as pastor of the Independent Chapel and leading teacher in his 'Public School' would have filled every minute of the life of most people. But his enthusiasm for bringing music to thousands of homes gave John Curwen the astonishing ability to fill the double role of being the pastor of Plaistow and the dedicated organizer and propagandist of the Tonic Sol-fa system of teaching music.

There was plenty to do in a rapidly growing Plaistow. He was a good teacher and children loved him; with the sustained help of Alfred Brown the North Street school became a pioneer in teaching Tonic Sol-fa and also a pioneer in general teaching methods. He tried to keep people well informed of what was going on in both the religious and secular worlds. His current

[25]

affairs lectures became very popular and covered such topics as the social dangers of 'the Establishment', new fields of emigration, accounts of the gold rush in North America, homoeopathy and the desirability of avoiding excess of alcohol. There were many who had succumbed to drink and Curwen would specially seek them out and see if he could help them to resist temptation. He enjoyed doing what are sometimes called 'good works' and threw his whole energy into helping others. Typical of him, when he heard that the small Ebenezer Chapel in Greengate Street used by the Wesleyans would have to be closed on account, it was alleged, of unpaid ground rent, he offered accommodation in North Street. To accommodate this small congregation he had a gallery built at each end of the chapel. The galleries are still there, for the chapel remains in daily use and is the only part of the original buildings which survived the 1939–45 war. One gallery is being used to store valuable but rarely needed type; the other, to carry on the craft of music engraving and the modern technique of assembling film before the 'printing down' process in the preparation of lithographic plates.

In addition to parish work he was engaged almost daily in developing teaching methods for Tonic Sol-fa. At the start in Plaistow his pupils could not have numbered more than one or two hundred. Curwen saw that it was essential to train teachers and to provide them with text books and song sheets in the new notation. In 1848 he published his *Grammar of Vocal Music* and, as it has already been recorded, he accepted his wife's advice and sold it at a modest price. For many years the mass of Tonic Sol-fa students were from the poorer section of the community; their schools often part-time and free, and in need of publications at the cheapest possible price. John Curwen never ceased extolling the advantages and cheapness of his new system. He was rewarded with remarkable enthusiasm and a very satisfactory increase in teachers and pupils and an increased demand for Sol-fa publications. When on a tour of towns in north Essex, he visited many temperance societies and reformatories. At Halstead he met Miss Greenwood and saw her reformatory girls. He was glad to be told that in the early days, before authority was established, she found she could conquer the girls by Sol-fa singing when every other means of checking lawlessness had failed. A most heartening acknowledgment of the good to be gained from teaching singing by Tonic Sol-fa.

[26]

THE TONIC SOL-FA REPORTER,

AND

MAGAZINE OF VOCAL MUSIC FOR THE PEOPLE.

| No. 3.] | OCTOBER, 1853. | [Price 1d. |

GOD SPEED THE RIGHT. KEY D. M. 66.

MUSIC FROM THE GERMAN. WORDS BY W. H. HICKSON.

For two female and two male voices. Four voices.

s :s	d¹ :-.s	m :m	s :m	m :—	r :-.r	m :—	:
Now to	*heaven our*	*prayers as - cend - ing,*		God	speed the	right?	
Be. that	*prayer a -*	*gain re - peat - ed,*		God	speed the	right!	

s :s	d¹ :-.s	m :m	s :m	d :—	t₁ :-.t₁	d :—	:

s₁ :s₁	d :-.s₁	m₁ :m₁	s₁ :m₁	s₁ :—	s₁ :-.s₁	s₁ :—	:
Pa - tient, firm,	and	per - se - ver - ing,		God	speed the	right!	
Still their on -	ward	course pur - su - ing,		God	speed the	right!	

s₁ :s₁	d :-.s₁	m₁ :m₁	s₁ :m₁	d₁ :—	s₂ :-.s₂	d₁ :—	:

s :s	d¹ :-.s	m :m'	s :m	m :—	r :-.r	m :—	:
In a no -	ble	cause con - tend - ing,		God	speed the	right!	
Ne'er des - pair -	ing	though de - fea - ted.		God	speed the	right!	

s :s	d¹ :-.s	m. :m	s :m	d :—	t₁ :-.t₁	d :—	:

s₁ :s₁	d :-.s₁	m₁ :m₁	s₁ :m₁	s₁ :—	s₁ :-.s₁	s₁ :—	:
Ne'er th'e - vent,	nor	dan - ger fear - ing,		God	speed the	right!	
Ev' ry foe	at	length sub - du - ing,		God	speed the	right!	

s₁ :s₁	d :-.s₁	m₁ :m₁	s₁ :m₁	d₁ :—	s₂ :-.s₂	d₁ :—	:

d¹ :t	l :s	l :s	f :m	r :m	f :r	s :f
Be their zeal	in	heav'n re - cord - ed,	With	suc - cess on	earth re-	
Like the good	and	great in sto - ry,	If	they fail, they	fail	with

m :s	f :m	f :m	r :d	t₁ :d	r :t₁	m :r

d :d	d :d	d :d	d :d	s₁ :s₁	s₁ :s₁	m₁ :f₁
Pains nor toils,	nor	tri - als heed-ing,	And in heav'n's own	time	suc-	
TRUTH! THY CAUSE, WHAT		N'ER DE - LAY IT,	THERE'S NO POWER ON	EARTH	CAN	

d₁ :d₁	d₁ :d₁	d₁ :d₁	d₁ :d₁	s₂ :s₂	s₂ :s₂	s₂ :ᴇ.

From an early *Reporter*
printed by John Childs at Bungay

In 1850 a first gathering of teachers and pupils of Tonic Sol-fa was held at the school in Jewin Crescent, Aldersgate Street. The small room was packed; there were half a dozen principal speakers and it was generally agreed that the new method was a miracle of cheapness—a new thing in musical history. There were practical examples of sight-reading: one of the tunes being sung at first sight. In 1851 there was an even more important event. The first number of a periodical called *The Tonic Sol-fa Reporter and Magazine of Vocal Music for the People* was published.

The Reporter, as it was popularly known, started in a modest way with a circulation of 700 copies. A foolscap quarto, usually consisting of eight pages, was for a long time published at irregular intervals. To gather together the material and undertake the editing was another self-imposed task which must have added a considerable burden on Mr Curwen.

In 1855 *The Reporter* became a regular monthly publication: with the growth of Tonic Sol-fa the necessity for a proper journal had become manifest. The journal was to be a forum for important announcements, articles, reports from London and the provinces and a medium for advertisers. By the time John Curwen resigned his pastorate in 1864 *The Reporter* had become a highly professional magazine and needed not only much editorial attention but also proper channels for publishing and distribution.

Although printing was started in North Street in 1863, at first the machinery was on a very modest scale and *The Reporter* continued to be printed by John Childs & Son of Bungay. The publishing was done by the Tonic Sol-fa Agency, established at 1 Ivy Lane, Paternoster Row; the Agency was conveniently located in the very heart of what was then the publishers' district of London. It had all the professional airs and although Plaistow still provided the absolute editorial control, the business side—and it must have been substantial business—was looked after by Henry Donkin. There is constant reminder that *The Child's Own Hymn Book, The Tonic Sol-fa Reporter* and all Mr Curwen's works 'are now removed from Messrs Ward & Co., 27 Paternoster Row (whose business has passed into other hands) to the above address, where they are published under the management of Mr Henry Donkin. All correspondence should be addressed, and post-office orders made payable to the Manager, Mr Henry Donkin, 1 Ivy Lane, Paternoster Row, E.C.' In modern terms, the Tonic Sol-fa

HARMONIUMS.

By special arrangement with Messrs. Cramer, Wood, and Co., a few specimens of Harmoniums from the manufactory of M. Debain, of Paris, will be kept for sale at the Tonic Sol-fa Agency, 43, Paternoster Row. M. Debain is the inventor of the Improved Harmoniums. He has the longest experience, and is the best established of the foreign makers. His Harmoniums obtained a first-class medal in both of our Great Exhibitions. It was important to introduce to our Tonic Sol-fa friends instruments of reliable manufacture.

For list of Instruments and descriptive paper, "How to select a Harmonium," apply to Mr. Donkin.

The packing and case free.   A liberal allowance to Teachers.   Terms: cash with order.

TONIC SOL-FA AGENCY, 43, PATERNOSTER ROW, E.C.   [253

Now ready,

THE FIRST PIANOFORTE BOOK for Tonic Sol-fa Pupils, founded on CARL GROBE'S "New Method for the Pianoforte," and edited by JOHN CURWEN. Price *two shillings and sixpence.* [254

NOW READY.—The first two numbers of "Harmonium Music," price threepence each.

No. 1 contains the following pieces :—

1. Voluntary	..	*Root.*
2. Voluntary	..	*Root.*
3. Voluntary	..	*Root.*
4. Voluntary	..	*Root.*
5. Adagio from the "Magic Flute"		*Mozart.*
6. Adagio from "Urania"	..	*Himmel.*
7. Voluntary	..	*Rink.*
Chant	..	*Gregorian.*

No. 2 contains :—

8. Chorale	..	*J. S. Bach.*
9. Voluntary	..	*Root.*
10. Voluntary	..	*Root.*
11. Voluntary	..	*Root.*
12. Adagio from "Alceste"	..	*Glück.*
13. Andantino from "Paradise and the Peri"	..	*R. Schumann.*
14. "Songs without words," No. 4		*Mendelssohn.*

Tonic Sol-fa Agency, 43, Paternoster Row, E.C. [255

HARMONIUMS.—Ten stops, full compass, powerful tone, suitable for School or Chapel, £12 12s. Five stops, full compass, £6 6s. Warranted. Repairs and Alterations at Trade Prices.

A. G. Roberts, 18, Mawbey Road, Old Kent Road, near the Nelson. [256

Price Threepence.

THE GERMAN CONCERTINA BOOK
FOR
TONIC SOL-FA PUPILS.
BY JOHN CURWEN.

T. S. Agency, 43, Paternoster Row, E.C. [257

On September 15th.

GERMAN   CONCERTINA   MUSIC,
No. I. 3d.

T. S. Agency, 43, Paternoster Row. E.C. [258

In preparation.

THE STRING BAND BOOK. Edited by JOHN CURWEN. [259

In the Press.

THE REED BAND BOOK, including the Flute, the Fife, and the Drum. Edited by JOHN CURWEN. [260

In the course of October.

THE FIRST FOUR NUMBERS OF "PIANOFORTE MUSIC," consisting of "Popular Melodies," with variations by CHARLES GROBE. Price 3d. each.

T. S. Agency, 43, Paternoster Row, E.C. [261

Printed by JOHN CHILDS AND SON, BUNGAY; and Published at the T. S. Agency, 43, Paternoster Row, London, E.C.—Sept. 1st, 1864.

Tonic Sol-fa Agency advertisement in *The Reporter*

Agency would be described as a wholly owned subsidiary of John Curwen.

The Tonic Sol-fa Agency stated its terms of business with disarming clarity. 'The business will be strictly a ready-money business. No credit will be given under any circumstances. Not a single account will be opened. Private individuals cannot obtain books at trade price, but the discounts named in the Trade Circular will be allowed to Sunday school superintendents and secretaries, and to Tonic Sol-fa Teachers, as well as to the Trade.' There was no doubt whatever that Henry Donkin was to conduct publishing on a strictly 'cash with order' basis. *The Reporter* carries a cartouche at the top of the front page of each issue urging that the Tonic Sol-fa Method of Teaching to Sing is EASY—CHEAP—AND TRUE. And Mr Donkin tries a bit of sales promotion: 'four shillings', he claims, 'will supply you for the year with a copy for yourself and three of your friends. What social singing parties, what constant influence for our great movement would be gained, if such monthly distribution became general.' The Tonic Sol-fa Agency must have been a successful publishing office.

The Reporter with a circulation of 700 copies in 1851 sold well over 10,000 copies monthly ten years later. This was a respectable circulation and it attracted paid (pre-paid of course) advertisements and announcements: 'Mrs Stapleton announces she has just formed Sol-fa morning classes for Ladies on Mondays at Midday. Her elementary Sol-fa class meets on Thursdays. Tuning forks, post free, for eighteen stamps.' Mrs Stapleton held her classes at her home at 18 Providence Row, Finsbury Square.

Then there was for a long time an advertisement of 'A Carte-de-Visite, with Autograph of the Revd John Curwen (the proceeds of the sale to be given for the erection of the new Public School in Plaistow) which can be obtained by sending half-a-crown, in stamps or otherwise, to Miss Curwen, Richmond House, Plaistow, London, E.' This was part of a fund-raising scheme for the building of the new school, opened in 1866, next door to the new Congregational School in Balaam Street. Miss Curwen was Margaret, the eldest child and only daughter of John and Mary Curwen.

A displayed advertisement for various singing classes under the auspices of the London Tonic Sol-fa Temperance Choir ends sternly with the warning 'open to Total Abstainers only'. A faithful advertiser was Mr Liddle of 35 Devonshire Street, Queen Square, London, W.C. He was a manufacturer of military flutes and fifes and offered to Sol-faists a tuning slide for pitching the key-note. Price with instructions for use 4s 6d (post free for 5s).

The 1863 the Tonic Sol-fa School, the precursor of the Tonic Sol-fa College was established. The school issued the different grades of certificates and was managed by W. H. Thodey who worked at Richmond House under the strict supervision of Mr Curwen. All kinds of announcements concerning the school and the awards of certificates appear in *The Reporter*.

The year in which the printing press was established in North Street, Plaistow, was also the year when the cotton workers of Lancashire suffered extreme distress owing to the interruption of supplies of raw cotton from the southern states of America. It was 1863 and the long drawn out struggle between the Federal and Confederate forces was at its height. All thoughtful people in England were conscious of the awful distress that was being forced on Lancashire, but it was only natural that the true nature of the disaster should be understood most deeply by the dissenting bodies who had a very large membership in the northern manu-facturing districts. In *The Tonic Sol-fa Reporter* of January 1863 John Curwen proposes what local ladies could do to aid the Manchester Central Relief Committee.

He addresses himself to 'The Lancashire Ladies':

Dear Tonic Sol-fa Ladies of Lancashire,—can we appeal to you, for help, in vain? We think not. For the case is pressing and the power of relief is in your hands.

The larger part of the Eighty Gentlemen, who pledged themselves to teach in the sewing classes so far as possible, are themselves at work through the day. They would gladly help the sewing classes at night, but the sewing classes do not meet at night! Mr Griffiths has great difficulty in finding teachers for the classes which apply to him! What can be done? The Lanca-shire Ladies will teach; and we shall be proud to present a Modulator to every Lady Teacher, who will spread it on the walls of a sewing school and teach the Tonic Sol-fa Method! Apply to Mr Robert Griffiths, 17 Cross Street, Manchester, for the Modulators and, if he does not find you the sewing schools, try and find them for yourselves. You love the Method, dear Ladies. This method taught you to sing—has given you many happy hours. Now, use it for the good of others. Let your sisters rejoice in it as you have done.

This 'open' letter is typical of John Curwen's approach. He is

[31]

moved almost to tears by the problem but is ready in a kindly, half humorous way to propose practical measures.

Henry Donkin, with his Curwen-backed Tonic Sol-fa Agency, was rapidly expanding. In January 1864 the front page of *The Reporter* announces a move to 43 Paternoster Row and the occupation of the first and second floors over Mr Collins' Bible warehouse. Next month there is a full page announcement of the sale of Harmoniums made by M. Debain of Paris. Packing and case free, a liberal allowance to teachers and terms cash with order. All this indicates expansion and capital investment in Henry Donkin. Terms cash with order even for harmoniums, be it noted. Mr Donkin would have been horrified at any sort of hire-purchase.

The Reporter was issued from 1851 to 1888; afterwards it became *The Musical Herald* and continued under that title until 1921. It was then merged with *The Musical News*, becoming a weekly with the expanded title *The Musical News and Herald*. It continued as a Curwen publication until 1927.

The year 1852 was also one of importance for John Curwen and Tonic Sol-fa; Mr Cassell suggested that Mr Curwen should contribute music lessons to *Cassell's Popular Educator*. This was a wonderful opportunity for introducing Tonic Sol-fa to a vast new audience. *Cassell's Popular Educator* had a large circulation and there must have been thousands who owed their introduction to music through Mr Curwen's contributions to this supremely successful journal. If numbers are a guide, the Tonic Sol-fa movement was achieving dizzy success. From an estimated 200 or 300 pupils in 1845, by 1856 the number of Sol-faists was believed to be over 20,000; two years later, in 1858, the number of pupils was estimated at 65,000.

In 1856 the inevitable happened: John Curwen had a breakdown in health brought on by sheer overwork. He offered to resign the pastorate of the North Street chapel. His proposal caused consternation and the prospect of losing his services could not be contemplated: instead of resignation he was persuaded to take a prolonged rest and he took himself and his family to Germany where they stayed for seven months.

He returned to Plaistow fully restored and ready to resume his pastorate and the leadership of the Tonic Sol-fa movement. His energy and faith in his work were to be put to severe test almost immediately and they emerged triumphant. The Tonic Sol-fa method was not just growing, it was advancing with a rapidity which was astonishing the musical world.

In April 1857 Handel's Messiah was published with Tonic Sol-fa notation. In June a Juvenile Choral Meeting was held at Exeter Hall. This hall, built in 1831, was a favourite centre for non-conformist gatherings; it became, in the mid-nineteenth century, a synonym for religious dissent. Exeter Hall, demolished in 1907 and the site now occupied by the Strand Palace Hotel, was in its heyday used frequently for the larger Tonic Sol-fa meetings. The Juvenile Choral Meeting was a new venture and proved an outstanding success. The Tonic Sol-fa Association decided to raise its sights and booked the Crystal Palace for a monster children's concert. The event took place on 2 September and 3,000 children trained in Tonic Sol-fa formed the mammoth choir.

The audience was tremendous and dense masses invaded every train to Sydenham. The railway company were almost overwhelmed; every spare carriage had to be commandeered and London Bridge could only just cope with the unexpected invasion. When the day finished it was found that more than 30,000 people had attended the concert and there would have been a still greater number if room and transport could have been found for them. A contemporary newspaper told its readers, 'It was left for an almost unknown institution to draw a larger concourse of persons than has ever been attracted in this country to listen to a musical performance.' The singing of the 3,000 Tonic Sol-fa trained children enraptured everyone. A choir of this size singing the Messiah must have been impressive. It established a tradition of choral singing which has persisted ever since. Choral societies all over the country, of which there are many, owe something to this imaginative enterprise on the part of John Curwen and his associates. A triumph for Tonic Sol-fa which was to be repeated over and over again.

The need for training teachers was becoming apparent as the numbers wishing to enjoy the pleasure of singing became greater and greater. Curwen never underestimated the value of proper teacher-training and in 1859 new elementary, intermediate and advanced certificates were introduced. They were to be the credentials of a teacher's competence and, ten years later in 1869, John Curwen at a breakfast meeting in Plaistow outlined his scheme for the establishment of a Tonic Sol-fa College.

[33]

Meanwhile, despite the excitements and ever widening interest in the Tonic Sol-fa movement, Curwen's work as a pastor had to go on. The growth of Plaistow had made the chapel in North Street too small for the congregation; John Curwen faced the new problem with characteristic optimism and readiness to take on his own shoulders a practical solution. A new and larger church was to be built on a site in Balaam Street, about five minutes walk from the North Street chapel. A lot of money was needed and John Curwen set about finding it. He was successful and collected the large sum of £7,000 which was sufficient to pay for the building. The foundation stone was laid in 1858 by the Lord Mayor of London and the church opened in March 1860. As soon as the chapel had been built, Mr Curwen began to collect money for building a school. Again he was successful, raising the considerable sum of £2,000 and a school was built in Balaam Street adjoining the new and rather magnificent Victorian Gothic church.

The new church and school meant more work for an already over-burdened man; a helpful co-pastor was engaged but on the twenty-first anniversary of his appointment to the Independent Chapel in North Street, Mr Curwen decided to resign. His resignation was regretted by all who knew him, for he was held in the greatest affection by young and old, but it was clear that another breakdown in health had to be avoided and it was impossible to go on combining a pastor's work with the ever increasing demands made by Tonic Sol-fa; the burden was becoming intolerable. Mindful of his mission for music teaching given to him by the conference at Hull in 1841, he decided it was his duty to devote the rest of his life to furthering the Tonic Sol-fa movement.

V

TONIC SOL-FA

AND STAFF NOTATION

THE RESIGNATION of the pastorate in 1864 did little to lighten the load of work undertaken by John Curwen. The growth of the Tonic Sol-fa movement went on unabated and relied more and more upon the imaginative management of its acknowledged founder and chief director. When health permitted, Curwen continued lecturing in all parts of the country and he always insisted on taking an active part in training and personally examining, when possible, candidates for teaching certificates. Something of importance seemed to happen every year, confirming the growing support for the movement; in some years there were a series of momentous events. 1863 was specially important, for it was the year of the establishment of the Tonic Sol-fa Press.

Frustration and the inability of some of his printers to set correctly the unusual symbols and signs of Tonic Sol-fa had tempted the Revd John Curwen to consider doing the job himself. (Only John Childs & Son, printers of *The Reporter* from the first issue of 1851, were exempt from Curwen displeasure.) Every proof needed meticulous proof-reading and checking. Besides using the correct signs and symbols, lateral positioning in relation to the words was of extreme importance. Customers' patience was tried by a lack of understanding and, no doubt, by a certain amount of carelessness. Tonic Sol-fa composition was not easy to master and required a lot of practice before 'clean' setting was taken for granted: correcting mistakes was costly and there was room for argument as to where responsibility lay and who was to foot the correction bill.

Another circumstance pushed John Curwen towards printing.

[35]

The North Street chapel was standing empty and available on reasonable terms. This building and later the old school, could provide floor space for a printing works suited to the needs of Tonic Sol-fa publications. He had plenty to print and having control of both manufacture and publishing would be, he thought, an advantage. Numbers were still growing fast and in the year he established his printing press it was estimated there were 186,000 pupils; as the number of pupils increased it could be safely assumed the demand for printed matter would increase.

His health, however, was again in a poor state and he confesses that for a time he could write no books and could hardly lecture without inflicting sore trial on his audience. But he found he could look after machinery and gain renewed strength by attending to all the manifold details of printing and training craftsmen in the special requirements of Tonic Sol-fa type-setting.

In a short autobiographical essay he states his views candidly,

.. so in this dark season of my eclipse I took to business [printing]. I have sometimes been blamed for this by those who think that 'once a minister always a minister'. I do not remember the time when I believed that doctrine. When I went to college at sixteen years of age, I certainly dedicated myself solemnly to the service of what I thought good and right in the world, but I said then as I say now, that there are many ways of serving the holy and true beside that of the pulpit. And this business has proved to be a mighty lever for the propagation of the Tonic Sol-fa method. It has enabled me to produce some costly books great and small which must necessarily be unremunerative for many years. It has enabled me to keep a staff of helpers, whose daily correspondence has kept alive the Tonic Sol-fa spirit in all parts of the kingdom and in many parts of the world.

It is the insistence of trying to do what is 'good and right in the world' that makes John Curwen's life and personality so admirable and commendable.

The time and thought that had to be given to routine production planning and, not least, the pleasant, regular rhythm of printing machinery soon restored his health. He wrote to his friend, Colin Brown, in Glasgow that he had taken up printing: 'my printing office, which partly sharp competition and partly the peculiarity of our instrumental books has compelled me to burden myself with; my boys, am I obliged to make them Sol-faists and printers?' The burden of becoming a printer was in fact an enjoyable one; good for his health and good for the cause. As for the boys, then aged sixteen and fourteen, future careers were assured them. They were both faithful followers of Tonic Sol-fa and needed no prodding to work enthusiastically for the movement.

When the Press was first established, Curwen was still living at Richmond House only a minute's walk away. Like so many who 'lived over the shop' he found that he was depriving himself of daily exercise. So he did the sensible thing and moved to Upton Place, in the village immediately north of Plaistow and about a mile from the 'works'. And as he decided to do all his literary work in North Street and take an active part in supervising the printing, he was in for a daily two-mile walk which would do him good and only be interrupted by lecturing engagements. Publishing and trade distribution continued to be done from Paternoster Row.

The business acumen of Henry Donkin and the success of the Tonic Sol-fa Agency gave John Curwen considerable confidence. There was no lack of potential demand for Mr Curwen's books and as author and editor, after he recovered from his temporary breakdown in health, he was tireless. Teachers and Tonic Sol-fa pupils were increasing rapidly and continued to do so for the rest of the century. It was still, in the 1860s, a movement appealing to the less well off; therefore printing efficiency and consequent cheapness were of prime importance. He found he could be a cheap producer and, backed by the wholesaling skill of Henry Donkin, the growing requirements of the Tonic Sol-fa groups and societies were served. The first notable landmark of expansion was the transfer of the printing of *The Reporter* of January 1864 from John Childs & Son of Bungay to the Tonic Sol-fa Press at Plaistow.

The Reporter had by then become a regular monthly publication due out on the first day of each month; it required a substantial volume of type-setting and probably needed the services of three or four compositors. In those days, all type was hand-set and after printing had been completed, every letter and every space had to be carefully put back or 'distributed' into the correct compartment of the correct case so that the type could be used again when required. Printing *The Reporter* on a small platen machine would be uneconomic and, as it sold at the low price of one penny, keeping down production costs was of prime importance. Much favoured by general printers in the latter part of the nineteenth century was the Wharfedale cylinder machine; it acquired its name by being manufactured at Ottley in Wharfedale in the West Riding of Yorkshire. It was a popular machine and was the type of printing press used almost exclusively in the 'letterpress department' at North Street for sixty years. It did not have to be driven at great speed, as it could not run faster than the 'layer-on' could feed in the paper. The cylinder was accessible, thereby helping preparatory work, and the impression was firm and even. After 1925 the 'Wharfedale' was gradually superseded by the superior mechanical design and faster running 'Miehle' two-revolution press, which could take more advantage of the new developments in automatic feeding-in of paper.

The fact that the Tonic Sol-fa Press could undertake the production of *The Reporter* with confidence by the end of 1864 showed that printing in North Street was quite definitely no longer a cottage industry; it signalled that the Press had graduated into the real printing world.

The monthly journal was the steady rock, the regular printing order on which the foundation of the firm rested. For its production and sale at the price of one penny everything had to be at hand to assist its progress through the works. An ample supply of type for text and display, special 'sorts' for Tonic Sol-fa notation were essential, as was a foundry for casting printing plates from pages of type; adequate printing machinery was installed of a size so that eight pages of *The Reporter* could be printed at a time and there had to be provision of sufficient bench space for folding, thread stitching and the heavily constructed machines for trimming away surplus paper. These powerful, dangerous looking cutting-machines are known in the trade as 'guillotines'. All this equipment took capital outlay and needed a lot of floor space. It was a stroke of good fortune that the old North Street school became vacant in 1866, enabling the printing works to spread out still further. The equipment that was essential for *The Reporter* was also the right equipment for hymn books, Tonic Sol-fa songs and anything from a text-book running to many pages to a single leaf required by a group of choral singers.

Some of the early productions at Plaistow were printed in large editions and were remarkably inexpensive. There is, for example, *The Child's Own Hymn Book*, edited by John Curwen and sold through the Tonic Sol-fa Agency at 43 Paternoster Row, E.C.

[38]

Tonic Sol-fa Reporter;

AND MAGAZINE OF VOCAL MUSIC FOR THE PEOPLE.

No. 143.   October,   THE TONIC SOL-FA METHOD OF TEACHING TO SING.   1864.   Price 1d.

ADVERTISEMENTS are received by Mr. Donkin, 43, Paternoster Row, E.C., to the 20th of each month. The charge for advertising Tonic Sol-fa Classes, Concerts, and Meetings, and the Addresses of APPROVED Tonic Sol-fa Teachers, is as follows:— One Shilling for the first two lines, and Threepence for each line following. The charge for other advertisements is,—Eighteen-pence for the first two lines, and Fourpence for each following line. Seven or eight words are contained in a line. No advertisement will receive attention unless PRE-PAID.

CORRESPONDENCE should be addressed to the Editor of the TONIC SOL-FA REPORTER, T. S. Agency, 43, Paternoster Row, E.C., by the 20th of each month at latest.

PRICE OF THE REPORTER post-free to any address in the United Kingdom;—A parcel of thirty copies for 2s. 5d.; a parcel of twenty-five for 2s.; parcels of twenty, sixteen, twelve, eight, and four at the rate of 1d. each. One, two, or three copies at 2d. each. Send post-office order or stamps to Mr. Donkin, 43, Paternoster Row, E.C., with your order. 4s. sent to Mr. Donkin will supply you, for the year, with a copy for yourself and three for your friends. What social singing parties, what constant influence for our great movement would be gained, if such monthly distribution became general!

*** All Booksellers will obtain this publication when ordered.

RESOLUTIONS PASSED AT THE RECENT MANCHESTER CONFERENCE.

That this meeting rejoices to hear of the number of Tune Books published in the Tonic Sol-fa Notation, and would urge upon each other the desirableness of making special efforts in Psalmody during the coming winter.

Moved by Mr. Sykes of Ashton. Seconded by Mr. Ryder of Manchester.

The Conference of Tonic Sol-fa Teachers of Manchester and neighbourhood desires to express its cordial approval of the course adopted by Mr. Curwen in respect to the Certificate, viz., his determination not to attend any Concert, nor to allow the same to be noticed in the *Reporter*, in which uncertificated persons are allowed to take part.

Moved by Mr. R. E. Jones. Seconded by Mr. Powell.

That the Teachers here present, anxious for self-culture, would express their desire that the Tonic Sol-fa School should hold its next Summer Session in Manchester.

Moved by Mr. R. Griffiths. Seconded by Mr. C. A. Bradbury. [262

TO METROPOLITAN TEACHERS.—

MR. CURWEN will feel much gratified if all the Metropolitan Friends who have taught the Tonic Sol-fa Method during the past year, *and have used the Certificates*, will kindly take tea with him in the School-room, Plaistow, E., on Saturday, Oct. 8th, at half-past 5 o'clock. Trains from Fenchurch Street at 4.40, 5.40, and 6.40. Mr. Curwen's object in this meeting is to consult with his friends on the promotion of Psalmody, and to ask their help in promoting the use of the Certificates. [263

IMPORTANT NOTICE.—A new and

greatly improved edition of the "Account of the Tonic Sol-fa Method" will be on sale at the Tonic Sol-fa Agency, on November 1st. It will be printed on *Reporter* paper, and will occupy 16 pages. Its contents will be as follows:—

1. A Description of the Method, with illustrations in both notations.

2. The History of the Method, and statistical information.

3. Advice to young teachers and others—How to start a Class, and how to sustain it.

4. A List of Courses of Tonic Sol-fa Lessons, carefully prepared.

5. A large number of Testimonies, first, to the moral usefulness of the Method, and, secondly, to its truthfulness and simplicity.

6. Lecture Slip C will be printed on the last page.

It is offered at a price which will not even pay for the paper on which it is printed, namely, *eighteen pence* per 100 (*without* discount and carriage), in order to promote its general adoption by all our teachers and pupils, and other friends. It is the *best* book to place in an inquirer's hands. It gives him a clear view of our Method and of the state of our Movement. The outline of a Lecture and the illustrative pieces at the end, also makes this pamphlet well suited to place in the hands of an audience. [264

The Reporter issued monthly and printed at Plaistow, 1864

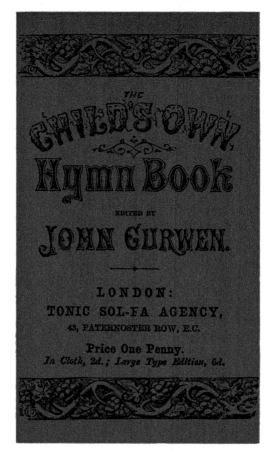

Cover of *The Child's Own Hymn Book*

for the price of one penny in paper covers and two pence in cloth covers; also a large type edition for sixpence. The penny edition measures $4\frac{1}{2}$ inches deep by $2\frac{1}{2}$ inches wide, has ninety-six pages of text and a red coloured paper cover printed on both leaves. In the preface, printed on the inside of the front cover, John Curwen notes that by the aid of cheaper paper and greater facilities for printing, the editor is able to add to this new edition twenty-three new hymns, and to improve the appearance of the page. He ends by stating, 'The Editor once more commends his little work, the first of the Penny Hymn Books, now twenty-five years old, to the loving favour of Sunday Schools, Cottage Meetings and Family Firesides.' The preface is dated 11 May 1865 and the imprint at the foot of the last page of text tells one that the hymn book was printed at the Tonic Sol-fa Press, Plaistow, London, E. *The Child's Own Hymn Book* was still selling at one penny in the late 1880s and hundreds of thousands of copies were produced at the Plaistow printing works.

John Curwen was a skilful exploiter of publishing opportunities. *The Child's Own Hymn Book* was issued as we have seen for a penny and in a large type edition for sixpence. There was also *The Plaistow Hymn and Tune Book* containing the same hymns as the *Child's Own* but with the tunes in Tonic Sol-fa notation costing sixpence in paper covers; one shilling in cloth. Additionally there was *The Child's Own Tune Book* with the same collection of hymns but the tunes in Staff Notation arranged for piano and voices, sold in cloth covers for a shilling. There is no explanation why customers of this edition were not offered as an alternative the cheaper paper covers. All these books were printed at the Tonic Sol-fa Press and sold through the Tonic Sol-fa Agency which was in effect Curwen's wholesale selling organization and 'trade counter'.

Religious and secular publications helped to build up a continuous output which took up any slack between the monthly issues of *The Reporter*. And there were other works from the pen of John Curwen to increase output, *How to Observe Harmony* and *Musical Statics* both with examples of staff notation as well as Tonic Sol-fa. Also *The Standard Course*, being lessons and exercises in the Tonic Sol-fa method of teaching and finally the great masterpiece, published in 1875, John Curwen's *Teacher's Manual* so highly commended by one of Her Majesty's Inspectors of Schools. All these works provided valuable material for students and teachers of music and also excellent printing orders for the Tonic Sol-fa Press.

It will be understood that for many of the books the printing of music in staff notation was required. This raised technical problems of far greater complexity than those required for the composition of Tonic Sol-fa. It was essential to employ a system of setting music from movable type. Music type for setting the most elaborate compositions had been devised as early as 1755 by Breitkopf, the famous printer and type-founder of Leipzig. Provision had to be made for the five stave lines and for any position and combination of semi-breve, minim, crotchet, quaver, semi-quaver and demi-semi-quaver. There was need for accom-

[41]

D

modating dots and ties and the various positions and kinds of
rests. The most complicated chords had to be free of wavering.
The type designed by Breitkopf was all cast on a standard body,
each bearing some fragment to make the complete note. There
were 257 different pieces in the Breitkopf fount and as the music
compositor had to identify fragments of notes, crooks and stems
the task was rather like setting Chinese: it required great experience and an ability to memorize a complicated 'lay' of very
large type cases. Music type, unlike type of the alphabet, had to
have its raised printing surface absolutely flush with the body or
shank on all four sides. As a note, stem, crook or rest might be in
fragments on two or more pieces of type, it was imperative that
they could be placed side by side or in vertical arrangement
without any visible unevenness in the shape of a note, without
any wavering of the stem or imperfect alignment of crochet or
rest. And clearly the stave lines must join closely so that continuous horizontal lines are presented. In founding music type,
after casting it had to be planed flush on all four sides with the
utmost accuracy.

John Curwen saw that progress of his printing works would be
impeded unless the Tonic Sol-fa Press had the ability to set both
the old and new notation. Tonic Sol-fa music type had already
been purchased from the Patent Type Founding Company. The
same firm was able to supply Curwen with type for staff notation.
The Patent Type Founding Company had their foundry in Red
Lion Square just off Southampton Row; eventually they became
well known as P. M. Shanks & Sons. Starting with Mr Phair, a
small group of compositors were trained to set staff notation from
music type. Mr Phair whose service with the firm began in 1866
worked at Plaistow for over fifty years and was as much respected
for his modesty and kindly nature as he was for his skill in
setting music. One of his younger colleagues was H. J. Ginbey
who was indentured as an apprentice to Joseph Spedding Curwen
in July 1891. Mr Ginbey* learned his music setting from Mr
Phair and thus skill and technique was passed on to survive until
the middle of the twentieth century. Music setting which began

---

*One of the last music setters at Plaistow was H. J. Ginbey, junior, still happily, in
1970, working with the firm. His son was apprenticed at Plaistow and the son's son
is now learning the skilled work of retouching colour separated film. It is probable
that four generations of the Ginbey family will span a hundred years of printing in
North Street.

with the *Plaistow Hymn and Tune Book* continued until it was decided to dispose of the last remnants of movable music type shortly after the end of the war in 1945.

Music type was expensive and there was a strict rule that no printing was to be done direct from the type. All music, after it had been passed as correct by the proof-reader was sent to the foundry where a plaster of Paris cast was made and from the mould a metal plate was cast. Printing was done from the metal plate, thus saving music type from premature wear and allowing it to be released for 'distribution' and use on the next job.

Music compositors were paid differently from the others. They were on a system known as 'stab-piece'. The 'stab' was the standard rate of pay earned for what was then a fifty-hour week; for music there was added to this a 'piece' or bonus if the standard agreed for a normal day's work was exceeded. It was usual for 'piece' to be earned and the small group of music compositors were held in great respect. Close study of music in staff notation set from movable type brings admiration for a highly disciplined skill and the feeling that the craftsmen deserved every extra shilling they were paid. Not only skill and experience was needed but also an unusual amount of judgement. Lines of music had to be spaced so that the bar at the end of a line was complete. Unlike the divided syllable of a word at the end of the line of ordinary reading matter, divided bars in music were not permissible.

The compositors who set Tonic Sol-fa or staff notation were an elite. Besides serving the usual seven-year apprenticeship they went through another four years of special training before qualifying for payment on the 'stab-piece' system. They were the exceptionally skilled in a trade of skilled journeymen. Curwen music compositors were able to transpose, direct from a manuscript, staff notation to Sol-fa and vice versa. As printing direct from type was not permitted, the foundry was fully occupied. At one time it was staffed entirely by the Wyllie family—father, two sons and a grandson.

[43]

VI

TEACHER AND PRINTER

RICHMOND HOUSE, since John Curwen and his family lived there, had served as the 'head office' of the Tonic Sol-fa movement. Mr Thodey was general amanuensis and dealt in detail with the business of the Tonic Sol-fa School, the issue of certificates, the arrangements for teachers wishing to enter the ever popular competitions and answering a huge daily correspondence. It was also Mr Thodey who bore the brunt of marking papers for the 'Crimson Prizes'. He announced, for example, on Tuesday afternoon at 3.30 p.m. 10 November 1863 Mr Curwen hopes to distribute Crimson Prizes. The 'hopes' sounds like the language of an over-busy man. There was also constant work with *The Reporter*. A monthly since January 1855, the inexorable routine of getting 'copy' off to the printer at Bungay, the checking of proofs and seeing that copies were available at Mr Donkin's Tonic Sol-fa Agency on the first of every month was a task to keep Mr Thodey and everyone else at Richmond House on their toes.

Although *The Reporter* became a monthly in 1855, it did not begin to pay its way until six years later. Writing in the first issue of 1861, Mr Curwen allows himself a little quiet jubilation,

It is a good new year for us which finds us able for the first time, to issue our monthly number without pecuniary loss. We can assure our friends that this fact gives us a peculiar lightsomeness of spirit. They must surely notice that everything we write is in a cheerful strain. We feel ourselves well rewarded for our six years' toil by such a triumphant result. Any magazine more costly than a penny could only be of surface power in our popular movement; this, we hope, goes down to the roots.

All the family were willing helpers and as they grew up they began to be so useful that it was soon evident that a younger generation of Curwens was going to carry on, with success and distinction, their father's pioneer work. Miss Mary Curwen, to whom one sent stamps or otherwise for a *carte de visite* to help the funds for building the Balaam Street School, was the precursor of new blood at the movement's headquarters. Just after the move to Upton and the concentration of all the work at North Street, John Spencer Curwen, the elder son of John Curwen, began his distinguished career as a part-time and probably unpaid assistant. Spencer went to the City of London School at the age of fourteen and left when he was seventeen in 1864; his father never professed to be a born musician and during his fruitful and active life in teaching he never considered himself more than a student; he was not in the accepted sense 'musical'. His sons were both excellent musicians and Spencer could claim to be a professional. After leaving the City of London School he studied at the Royal Academy of Music, specializing in harmony, and was a favoured pupil of Professors Macfarren, Prout and Sullivan. In 1879, when he was thirty-two, he was made an Associate and later became a Fellow of the Royal Academy of Music. Spencer Curwen, after his studies at the Royal Academy were over, could give up being a 'half-timer' at Plaistow and give his father valuable full-time help which was a new driving force needed by John Curwen and by the Tonic Sol-fa movement as a whole.

In a short time Spencer appears to be taking a leading part. He became assistant editor of *The Reporter* and was taking over more and more of the strenuous lecturing engagements which before would have been undertaken by his father. His enthusiasm for the Tonic Sol-fa method was profound and, in a single year, to give eighty lectures and travel nearly 7,000 miles seemed to him in no way remarkable. His younger brother, Joseph Spedding, was a model partner. 'In business,' according to John Graham's *Memoir of Mr John Spencer Curwen*, 'he [Spencer] knew little of the counting-house or parcel post which were so important for his financial welfare, but he had a grasp of large affairs and the direction of business policy, while any new scheme of his was thought out to the smallest detail. His fellow-director looked well after branches of the firm's activities for which he had no time.'

One of the activities for which he had no time to spare was the development of the Tonic Sol-fa Press. This is where the partnership of the two brothers proved so well founded, with a fortunate division of labour and responsibility. The printing business was prospering, having to service the printed material for a rapidly growing movement; by 1860 serious Tonic Sol-fa pupils were estimated to be about 100,000. Spencer Curwen looked after the publishing and Tonic Sol-fa teaching while the younger brother, Spedding Curwen, was responsible for the printing. It is true that most of the limelight seemed to fall on Spencer, but this in an age when primogeniture was still a sacred principle caused no resentment. In any case, Spencer Curwen was a musician of considerable attainment and his talents would naturally fit him for fostering a publishing business. The quieter and more reflective Spedding was an able developer of what was to become, before the end of the century, a fair sized music printing press.

On 1 January 1869 John Curwen arranged one of his more important breakfast meetings: he propounded to the small group who sat round the breakfast table his scheme for founding a Tonic Sol-fa College. The general idea was to up-grade the Tonic Sol-fa School and take over the issue of the various kinds of certificates and make sure that by intensive training courses the supply of qualified teachers matched up to the swiftly growing number of pupils. It was a visionary scheme but, like all John Curwen's ideas, it was soundly based; he envisaged with fair accuracy the course of future development. The Tonic Sol-fa College would have its own building and the courses would be residential. There would, in fact, be no hostels but undergraduates would be found moderately priced lodgings within easy reach of the college.

The scheme propounded was well timed: it was the eve of the Forster Education Act of 1870 which provided power for establishing free elementary education for the children of parents who could not afford fees. Local school boards were to be set up to see that proper provision was made so that the Act would become not only universal, but a universal reality.

School boards had a duty to erect 'Board Schools' where needed; education was to be free and controlled by Her Majesty's Inspectors appointed by the minister.

John Curwen and his eldest son realized the importance of getting the Hon. W. E. Forster, M.P. to recognize the Tonic Sol-fa system of teaching singing in all the new schools. At first all seemed well and, in August 1869, a letter was received from

[46]

the Education Committee stating that Tonic Sol-fa would be treated on the same footing as ordinary notation. In 1871, however, a decision was made which came as a shock to Tonic Sol-fa teachers. The system was not, after all, to be accepted on the same footing as ordinary notation: the reason for the volte-face, it was explained, lay in the fact that there were so few inspectors who could examine in the Tonic Sol-fa method. To meet this shortage, it appeared that the easiest way out would be to drop Tonic Sol-fa.

John Curwen, helped by his son and many others, immediately organized a deputation to express their dismay to Mr Forster and press for reinstatement of their new and simple system. It was claimed that it was music itself, the civilizer and educator, that was threatened, and not a mere notation. Many friends came forward to support Mr Curwen. In less than a month the issue was settled in favour of Tonic Sol-fa. The crisis was over and *Choir* wrote,

We are bound in honour to admit that the main credit for the successful issue of the contest is due to the Tonic Sol-faists, and their energetic leader in particular, and although they wisely eschewed the slightest appearance of making it a movement from the advocates of any one system, we believe we are not far from the truth when we assert that if Mr Curwen and his friends had been non-existent or inactive the result would have been very different.

Meanwhile, John Curwen, even when the attitude of the Education Committee was still in doubt, pursued his activities on behalf of the Tonic Sol-fa movement with undiminished zeal. His health continued to be unreliable but, being relieved of pastoral duties and having the blessing of the practical assistance of his two sons, the decade beginning in 1870 was one of further advance and achievement.

In 1870 John Curwen produced his 'hand signs'. These are illustrated on page 48; by manual signs mental effects can be indicated to a class. The descriptions of the various mental effects are clearly the authorship of John Curwen. SOH, the grand or bright tone; ME, the steady and calm; DOH, the strong or firm; TE, the piercing or sensitive; RAY, the rousing or hopeful and FAH, the desolate or awe-inspiring tone. Whether they were as inspiring or awe-producing as John Curwen hoped, they nevertheless were a help to teachers and became a recognized aid in

[47]

MENTAL EFFECTS AND MANUAL SIGNS OF TONES IN KEY.

FIRST STEP.	SECOND STEP.	THIRD STEP.

SOH.
The GRAND or *bright* tone—the Major DOMINANT, making, with *Te* and *Ray*, the Dominant Chord—the Chord S, and with *Fah* also the Chord ⁷S.

TE.
The PIERCING or *sensitive* tone — the Major LEADING-TONE, making, with *Ray* and *Fah*, the weak Chord T.

LAH.
The SAD or *weeping* tone — the Major SUBMEDIANT, making, with *Doh* and *Me*, the Chord L.

ME.
The STEADY or *calm* tone — the Major MEDIANT, making, with *Soh* and *Te*, the rarely used Chord M.

RAY.
The ROUSING or *hopeful* tone—the Major SUPERTONIC, making, with *Fah* and *Lah*, the Chord R, in which case it is naturally sung a komma flatter, and may be distinguished as *Rah*.

DOH.
The STRONG or *firm* tone — the Major TONIC, making, with *Me* and *Soh*, the Tonic Chord—the Chord D.

FAH.
The DESOLATE or *awe-inspiring* tone — the Major SUBDOMINANT, making, with *Lah* and *Doh*, the Subdominant Chord—the Chord F.

John Curwen's hand signs

conducting large classes of Tonic Sol-fa pupils. The hand signs were only a part of Mr Curwen's work in 1870. He also issued new editions of the *Standard Course* and *How to Observe Harmony*.

The Education Act of 1870, after local consultation, made it possible for West Ham to establish a School Board. One of the original members of the Board was John Curwen; he did not make 'rubber stamp' decisions and his individual outlook did not make him popular. As a nonconformist he was against public money being spent on church schools; what he was fighting for was compulsory, rate-supported, non-denominational elementary schooling.

He was, as a man with a deep social conscience, desirous that no distinctive religious formula should be foisted on the new elementary schools. Besides the numerous independents and dissenters of all kinds, he respected the views and feelings of large groups of Catholics and Jews; he never ceased to press for religious instruction which should not offend any individual's belief. This, at that time, seemed outrageous to most of his contemporaries. There was strong opposition and as he was busily engaged fighting for Tonic Sol-fa which was again in danger of attack from the Education Committee, he decided to conserve his strength and resigned from the School Board in 1873. What he was proposing for elementary education was too liberal in conception and perhaps too benevolent for most middle-class people at that time. What was anathema then was to become commonly accepted policy in the lifetime of his grandchildren.

In 1875 the Tonic Sol-fa College was incorporated and brought under the control of a properly constituted governing council. The council was elected but this did not lead to any curtailment of the founder's dictatorial powers. He calmly reserved for himself, for life, the right to veto any resolution he chose. And as was only just, he insisted on being elected life President of the College. The Incorporation of the College and its lessened 'family' administration was a wise move and led to an immediate and rapid increase of applicants for certificates.

Another important milestone in 1875 was the publication of John Curwen's *Teacher's Manual*. This book was essential reading for Tonic Sol-fa teachers: it is a large work and as it says on the title-page, it deals with the art of teaching and the teaching of music. The frontispiece shows Sarah Glover with her Norwich Sol-fa ladder and in his preface John Curwen declares that 'the main object of the book is to do as much as a mere book can do towards increasing the number of teachers of the Tonic Sol-fa Method, and improving the quality of their teaching'. J. R. Jolly, one of Her Majesty's Inspectors of Schools is enthusiastic, 'as giving excellent material for the right teaching of music, I cannot speak too highly of *The Teacher's Manual of the Tonic Sol-fa Method* by John Curwen'. It is a large book of 400 pages in his favoured size of foolscap quarto: many of the pages are in small type with three columns accommodating about 1,400 words to a page and it presented a formidable task for the hand compositors. The book was almost certainly set in stages: thirty-two pages would be passed by the author, then stereotyped so that the type could be distributed and another thirty-two pages set. It was a marvel of cheapness, retailing at five shillings; dark green cloth binding with the title gold blocked on the spine. It is competently set and well printed by J. Curwen & Sons, Music Printers, Plaistow, London, E. There is evidence that the book had a steady and even ready sale. Published in 1875, seven years later it was in its fifth edition.

Mr Curwen again shows his concern for a practical curriculum in Ragged, reformatory and industrial schools and refuges:

> In institutions of this kind, especially where pupils are frequently changing, it is difficult to maintain anything like systematic teaching. In such cases I recommend the teacher, whatever parts of our method he is obliged to drop, not to drop these three—the Pattern, the Modulator, and the working for certificates. It would be sad even in the lowest classes if there were not some whose ambition might be stirred to take the certificates, and the working for them gives aim and directness to the teaching. The worse the class, the better must the teaching be.

John Curwen was recommending a shortened course for young delinquents but he was specific in urging that these unfortunates were to have the best possible teaching. Singing and participation was seen to have a powerful therapeutic value: this view would be unchallenged today by those who work in approved schools. The great *Teacher's Manual* ends by giving a few statistics of the Movement. In 1872 it was calculated, by the sale of large modulators, that during the year persons using the method including children and adults had been 315,000.

The system is employed by missionaries in all parts of the globe. It has been introduced into Madagascar, Cape Colony (for the Kaffirs and Dutch), Hong Kong, Beirut, Mount Lebanon, Fiji, South Africa, Bombay, Calcutta, Barbados, St Helena, Norfolk Island, Spain, Japan, Burma, Chile, etc.

The music instructor to the London School Board, on visiting the 120 schools under his direction, told the teachers they were free to use what system they liked. He reports that all 'preferred the Tonic Sol-fa system'.

Of 11,000 singers at a recent Band of Hope Festival at the Crystal Palace—at which either notation can be used—9,000 sang from Sol-fa copies.

The last paragraph of the manual tells teachers that Mr Curwen has now on permanent sale upwards of 13,000 pages of part-songs, hymn tunes, anthems, school songs etc. At least twenty other publishers have issued work in the notation, being actuated by no enthusiasm for the method, but having merely obeyed popular demand. Thirty or forty hymn tune books have been issued in the Tonic Sol-fa notation by the various religious bodies or publishers to which they belong.

These statistics are not indications of self-satisfaction; they merely record in a vivid way the enormous following that the new

𝕳𝖞𝖒𝖓 336.

AUSTRIA (8787 8787).
KEY **F**. M. 88.

FRANZ JOSEPH HAYDN.

```
{ d :-.r |m  :r  | f  :m  |r.t₁:d ‖ l  :s  |f  :m  | r  :m.d|s  :— ‖
  s₁ :-.t₁|d  :t₁ | r  :d  |s₁ :s₁ ‖ l₁.t₁:d |r  :d  | r  :d  |t₁ :— ‖
  m :-.s |s  :s  | t₁ :d  |f  :m  ‖ f  :s  |s  :s  | l  :l  |r  :— ‖
  d :-.d |d  :s₁ | s₁ :s₁ |s₁ :d  ‖ f  :m  |t₁ :d  | f₁ :fe₁|s₁ :— ‖ }

{ d :-.r |m  :r  | f  :m  |r.t₁:d ‖ l  :s  |f  :m  | r  :m.d|s  :— ‖
  s₁ :-.t₁|d  :t₁ | r  :d  |s₁ :s₁ ‖ l₁.t₁:d |r  :d  | r  :d  |t₁ :— ‖
  m :-.s |s  :s  | t₁ :d  |f  :m  ‖ f  :s  |s  :s  | l  :l  |r  :— ‖
  d :-.d |d  :s₁ | s₁ :s₁ |s₁ :d  ‖ f  :m  |t₁ :d  | f₁ :fe₁|s₁ :— ‖ }

{ r :m  |r.t₁:s₁| f  :m  |r.t₁:s₁ ‖ s  :f  |m  :-.m|fe :-.fe|s  :— ‖
  s₁ :s₁ |s₁ :s₁| t₁ :d  |s₁ :s₁ ‖ s₁ :l₁.t₁:d |:-.d|d  :-.d|t₁ :— ‖
  t₁ :d  |t₁ :t₁| r  :d  |t₁ :t₁ ‖ m  :r  |d  :-.d|l  :-.l|s  :— ‖
  s₁ :s₁ |s₁ :s₁| s₁ :s₁ |s₁ :s₁ ‖ m₁ :f₁.s₁|l₁ :-.l₁|r₁ :-.r₁|s₁ :— ‖ }

{ d' :-.t|l  :s  | l  :-.s|s.f:m ‖ r  :m.f |s.l:f.r|d  :m.r|d  :— ‖ l  s ‖
  d :-.d|d  :d  | d  :-.d|t₁ :d  ‖ t₁ :-.t₁|d  :l₁| s₁ :t₁ |d  :— ‖ d  d ‖
  s :-.s|f  :m  | f  :-.s|s  :s  ‖ s  :-.s|s  :l.f|m  :f  |m  :— ‖ f  m ‖
  m :-.m|f  :d  | f  :-.m|r  :d  ‖ s₁ :-.s₁|m₁ :f₁| s₁ :s₁ |d  :— ‖ f₁ d ‖ }
```
Amen.

" Very excellent things are spoken of thee, thou city of God."

1.
GLORIOUS things of thee are spoken,
   Zion, city of our God!
He, Whose word can ne'er be broken,
   Formed Thee for His own abode;
On the Rock of Ages founded,
   What can shake thy sure repose?
f With salvation's walls surrounded,
   Thou may'st smile at all thy foes.

2.
See! the streams of living waters,
   Springing from eternal love,
Well supply Thy sons and daughters,
   And all fear of want remove;
Who can faint, while such a river
   Ever flows their thirst to assuage?
Grace, which, like the Lord, the giver,
   Never fails from age to age.

3.
Blest inhabitants of Zion,
   Washed in the Redeemer's blood!
Jesus, Whom their souls rely on,
   Makes them kings and priests to God.
Jesus' love His people raises,
   Over self to reign as kings!
f And, as priests, His solemn praises
   Each for a thank-offering brings. Amen.

(340)

'Glorious Things of Thee are Spoken' in Sol-fa notation for soprano, contralto, tenor and bass (A & M 545). *Church Hymnal* published Dublin 1880

[51]

method had attracted in just over thirty years of John Curwen's musical mission. He was too generous to consider keeping all the publishing in his own hands; but if commerce was the actuating lever for others, his own publishing ventures, which were on a large scale, were actuated more by his enthusiasm and desire to bring happiness to those whose lives were often made almost intolerable by poverty.

VII

TONIC SOL-FA COLLEGE

IN 1869, just before the struggle to get his new method of teaching accepted by the Education Committee, Mr Curwen moved from Upton Place to a larger house in the same road, more convenient to Forest Gate railway station. The new house was four storied and solid looking with the front door and the main windows on either side flanked with attractive Corinthian columns. Today the house still maintains its dignified looks and, although a little shabby, has grown old gracefully. The house was occupied by John Curwen until his death. Subsequently it has been a gentleman's club, a branch of a commercial college and is now the headquarters of a firm of transport contractors.

John Curwen named his new home Workington House after the hall in Cumberland where his family had its origin. Workington House was ideal for meetings and small gatherings of teachers and was conveniently near the site which had been purchased for building, when funds permitted, the Tonic Sol-fa College. The house, like Upton Place, was in the village of Upton and there was still the half-hour walk to his office at the printing works and about ten minutes to Forest Gate station and Earlham Grove where the college was to be erected.

After the publication of his monumental *Teacher's Manual* in 1875 his energy was again losing some of its resilience and his wife's health was causing grave anxiety.

In the summer of 1877 he took his wife to Karlsbad for medical attention. He was shocked by outward signs of luxurious living. He writes from Karlsbad in September 1877, 'We should not like our children to spend luxurious idle lives like those of many of the rich folk who come here. Some of them must be very rich. They have no work in the world—nothing to live for. Their

[53]

character grows flabby. They are always looking out for sensation, and when it comes it goes. Poor things!' It is understandable that a clergyman and a hard worker for the good of others should be shocked by displays of luxury. To do nothing useful in life, to be of no service, to have no civilized interests was, in John Curwen's view, morally reprehensible. The behaviour of the very rich was a subject of constant comment in middle-class circles. Duty came first and John Curwen shared with Richard Cobden a horror of the wasted talents of the idle rich. What he was expressing was the sensible and humane view that people fortunate enough to have health, wealth and good education should strive to 'give' more to their generation than they 'take'. Worldly success was not something sinful but its responsibilities had to be recognized.

The anxiety caused by the ill health of Mary Curwen was mitigated to some extent by the marriage of the eldest son, John Spencer, to Annie Gregg, an Irish woman born in Dublin. The marriage gave great satisfaction to the Revd and Mrs John Curwen and invested 1877 with a significance which Annie Gregg's father-in-law was quick to realize. There was, of course, the usual pleasure that marriage brings to a family; in this case it was heightened by the fact that the bride was herself a distinguished musician and had been trained at the Royal Irish Academy of Music.

In the following year an unusual performance took place which involved Joseph Spedding. The telephone had just been invented and it was, as could be well understood, acclaimed a wonderful advance in the field of communication. To prove that it was a practical invention, arrangements had been made for a quartet of Tonic Sol-fa singers to sing part songs over the telephone from Cowes to Queen Victoria in Osborne House. Queen Victoria had been presented with a telephone fashioned out of ivory by the inventor, Alexander Graham Bell. Spedding had a good voice and being the son of the famous leader of the Tonic Sol-fa movement was chosen to be one of the singers. So in 1878 he and three other Sol-faists had the honour of giving this unusual concert. The performance went off well and the Queen expressed herself delighted with the loyal singers and amazed at the wonders of the telephone. Clearly it was also excellent publicity for the Tonic Sol-fa method.

The plans for a permanent home of the Tonic Sol-fa College reflected the growing importance attached by the educational world to the Glover-Curwen method of teaching singing and to the growing need to train more teachers. John Curwen had asked Lewis Banks, his son-in-law, to draw up plans for a building which was to be erected on the site already secured in Earlham Grove near Forest Gate station. Lewis Banks was a trained architect and had married Margaret, the eldest child and only daughter of the Revd and Mrs John Curwen. A suburban site was preferred, partly owing to the high cost of land in central London and partly because students could find cheap lodgings more easily in Forest Gate. Raising funds for the new and spacious building put John Curwen's organizing abilities once again to severe test. A sum of at least £6,000 was required and even if the target seemed dauntingly large, John Curwen was never anything but optimistic. With his usual generosity he offered to contribute £1,000 from his own pocket if £3,000 more could be raised by November 1878. His £1,000 was gratefully matched and by 1879 sufficient funds were in hand to start building. Special demonstrations and bazaars played their part too. A mammoth bazaar was held in April 1879 and it is worthwhile following its fortunes in some detail as it shows the unusual organizing powers of John Curwen and the way a bazaar was publicized and made an 'event' in the latter part of the nineteenth century.

In the April 1879 issue of *The Reporter*, which was always published on the first of the month, there appears a displayed announcement on the front page:

A Bazaar in Aid of the Building Fund, April 23rd, 24th and 25th 1879 at the Oriental Buildings, Blackfriars Bridge (over the Metropolitan Railway Station). The Earl of Shaftesbury, K.G. will open The Bazaar at 12 o'clock, April 23rd. The Bazaar will be open each day at 12 o'clock and close at 9.30 p.m. Admission to the opening 2s 6d; after four o'clock 1s. Second and third days 6d. Children half price on all occasions.

This was the announcement prominently presented in the form of an advertisement. In the same issue of *The Reporter* there is an editorial follow-up headed 'How it will look'.

Of course we mean the Bazaar. That is the one subject of interest for Tonic Sol-faists this month. The Ladies' Committee is holding long and earnest and frequent meetings which it is difficult to break up and many gentlemen are offering their services as well.

Over the station—extending the whole length of the building—there are

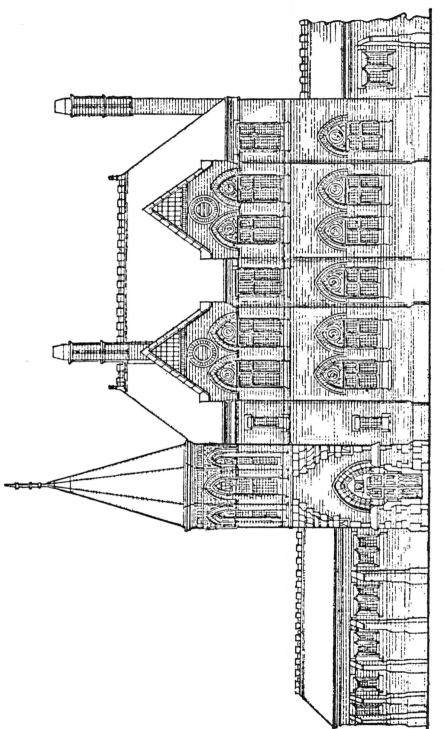

Elevation for Tonic Sol-fa College, Earlham Grove, Forest Gate

several floors of rooms and the Bazaar will occupy two of these. The building may be recognized by its cupolas and other tokens of the Oriental style.

As the door of the large room opens, the visitor will see a semi-circular stall filled with flowers and beyond (looking the other way) a second semi-circle furnished with pretty things. Beyond that again is the door to the 'Art Gallery'. If the visitor looks round by the walls and windows he will see nine brightly coloured and prettily tented stalls—the 'Sheffield', the 'Temperance', the 'South London', the 'Bow and Bromley', Mrs J. Curwen's, the staff of Mr Proudman's Choirs, that of the Working Men's College and the Refreshment and the Children's Stall, all served by ladies, bright and ready to help in the spending of money. An Organophone and one of Debain's Piano Mecaniques will enliven proceedings.

John Curwen's preparations are thorough and leave little to chance. The trump card of the arrangements was for the opening ceremony to be performed by the Earl of Shaftesbury. The Earl of Shaftesbury was well known for the legislation he had introduced to prevent the exploitation of children and young people in industry—especially in the coal mines and textile mills—he was a supporter of Ragged schools and for forty years had been president of the Ragged School Union. He also took a very active part in founding reformatories, refuges and working men's institutes. He did, in fact, support all those institutions for amelioration of distress which formed the foundation of John Curwen's own social work.

The Reporter dated 1 May 1879 confirms that John Curwen's fund raising plans were as effective as ever: 'a dull heavy day with rain at intervals did not favour the opening of the Bazaar for the Building Fund for the Tonic Sol-fa College. But the weather had apparently no effect on the audience. What the attendance would have been had the day been fine, it is fearful to contemplate. As it was, the rooms were packed from morning till night.' The June issue of *The Reporter* was able to tell its readers that the net proceeds, after deducting expenses, were estimated to be over £450. A noble contribution to the £6,000 which was being aimed at. It is of interest to find that the refreshment stall was looked after by Joseph Spedding Curwen and Miss Rowell. Spedding's participation in the great Bazaar may sound modest enough but having Miss Rowell as his assistant was delightful.

Hardly had the doors of the bazaar been closed than the ceremonial laying of the foundation stone of the Tonic Sol-fa College was performed on 14 May 1879 by the Earl of Kintore. Later on

[57]

E

the same day there was the ceremony, performed by John Curwen in the presence of thirty or forty friends, of laying a memorial stone inscribed with the name of Sarah Glover. The stone was positioned on the left of the main entrance and bears the following inscription: 'This stone was laid by John Curwen May 14th 1879, in memory of MISS SARAH GLOVER, on whose scheme of rendering psalmody congregational the Tonic Sol-fa Method was founded.' After an address by his father-in-law, Lewis Banks the architect of the building gave a detailed account of the plans.

The elevation of the building is shown on page 56. It includes a roofed-in central quadrangle large enough to accommodate a concert audience of 3,000. Surrounding are a board room, president's room, four piano or harmonium rooms, eight class rooms, a student's common room and necessary lavatories. The rooms are sound proofed so that one student does not inconvenience another. But if a teacher wishes it, all the doors can be opened and all instruments play the same tune to listeners in the great hall. A considerable outlay had to be made for the 'furnishing account,' a sum which it was confidently expected would be made good by a bazaar coinciding with the opening ceremonies on 4 and 5 July.

The opening ceremony was performed on 5 July 1879 by the Earl of Kintore. They were not favoured by fine weather: a squall of wind and rain beat down on the tent as the opening speeches were being delivered. But enthusiasm remained undampened and a crowd of between 300 and 400 took tea in the tent, which was described as being 'packed with people'. More speeches followed and John Curwen declared that 'they were going to fill the place with students, and to teach them well, so that our College might have a good name in the Educational World'. Professor Proudman said he looked at the new rooms with much pleasure and congratulated the architect on the promise of the building, and congratulated the College on the rapidly rising value of the land, so that if it ever were desirable to sell it, it would probably fetch several times what was given for it. On this happy thought the evening of the opening day came to an end; it was announced £102 had been contributed to the 'furnishing account' by the sale, and that even this substantial sum did not include all the goods as some were being reserved for an autumn sale.

The building which for long was the headquarters for teacher-training and subsequently became the Metropolitan School of

Music can still be seen towering above the surrounding houses. A good view may be had from the corner of Forest Gate station and Forest Lane, the road leading to Stratford Broadway. In 1939 the building was purchased by the London Co-operative Society and used as a testing laboratory by their food-stuffs division.

The seed for the Tonic Sol-fa College was sown by John Curwen and Alfred Brown in their modest experimental school which they conducted next to the chapel in North Street. Despite all the personal distress for John Curwen which was caused by Mary Curwen's declining health, 1879 was a year which set the seal of unimpeded progress for Tonic Sol-fa for the rest of the century. At last the movement was to have a proper training centre able to meet the growing need for more and more teachers.

The hard work of organizing bazaars and all the excitement of seeing his dream of a Tonic Sol-fa College taking solid shape did not prevent John Curwen continuing to be the movement's leading evangelist. Early in December 1879 he is delivering a lecture in Sheffield in the old banqueting room of the Cutler's Hall. The lecture was held under the auspices of the Sheffield Tonic Sol-fa Association: members of the choir under their famous conductor (Henry Coward) were arranged on the platform at the end of the room. The Master Cutler presided. John Curwen rejoiced that Sol-faists were gathered together in such large numbers. It had been said of the Tonic Sol-fa method, 'It is very good for children, and when they grow up it does them no harm.' 'They are thankful', said the lecturer, 'for that criticism. If Tonic Sol-fa did nothing else it would be of immense service to the world, but he stood before them that night to tell them that it could do more. While it was helpful to children in schools, it was helpful also to the student of the college, to the young composer, and to the player. It was quite true it did not attempt to set aside the established notation, but it was there to assist.'

To the last he never claimed that his method replaced staff notation: what he justly claimed was that it was a new method which brought the joy of music to countless people who would otherwise have no opportunity of learning.

Besides lecture tours and, as life president, taking the main responsibility of directing the work of the newly opened Tonic Sol-fa College, he still had the formidable task, assisted by his eldest son Spencer, of bringing out on the first day of each

[59]

month *The Reporter*. It was a task without end: as soon as one issue had been sent to the Press, work started on the next. To gather news from all over the United Kingdom, to write a monthly leader and report on events in the Tonic Sol-fa world was hard work; in addition there were advertisement pages to be arranged and the lists published of successful candidates for the different grades of certificates, and finally the cares of proof-reading and passing the pages for printing. *The Reporter* was never less than twenty-four pages and occasionally ran to thirty-two pages; all in double column providing steady work for the compositors of the Tonic Sol-fa Press in North Street. It was good value for a penny and a valuable news bulletin for Tonic Sol-fa supporters. John Curwen continued to take partial editorial responsibility until his death.

The Tonic Sol-fa College had been in existence for less than six months when on 17 January 1880 Mary Curwen died. John Curwen's spirit was utterly broken by the loss, as he put it, of 'half his life'. But deeply moved as he was, he had the good sense to carry on his work and even more actively seek the companionship of the family and friends. Mrs Curwen mirrored all the excellent qualities of a Victorian housewife. Servants never left her except to get married; on a few occasions when servants were married from Workington House Mrs Curwen would superintend the wedding breakfast and give the newly married couple the run of her dining room for the rest of the day. She was not musical and her interest in Tonic Sol-fa did not go beyond a general interest in her husband's work. Like her husband, she revelled in doing good works and felt they were a way of giving thanks for all the happiness which had come to her. Scoffers of 'good works' would have made no impression on Mary Curwen; sensible and sensitive, she preferred good to bad; she was ready to fight for welfare. She was a determined person well able to look after herself and also prevent her kindly husband from being exploited. Her father-in-law, the Revd Spedding Curwen, said,

I thought at one time John was spending too much money in his psalmody ventures, and I took it for granted that I should find his wife somewhat in sympathy with me on the question of expenditure; so I was bold enough to ask whether she did not think he was laying out too much money in that direction. Did not I find that I had put my foot in it? For she exclaimed, 'Let John do what he likes with his money. Nobody shall interfere with him!'

A broadside which old Revd Spedding did not forget and a splendid example of Mancunian independence.

John Curwen never gave up his evangelizing tours and Scotland and the north of England were visited regularly. There were so many eager school and Sunday school teachers waiting to hear from the leader of the Tonic Sol-fa method that his life, from a travel point of view, must have seemed like a politician being perpetually engaged in 'Midlothian' campaigns. The burden of all this travel was often made less strenuous by the company of one of his sons. In the itinerary of 1877, the Revd and Mrs Curwen visited Newcastle-upon-Tyne; it was usual for hospitality to be offered by leading members of the Congregational church. Joseph Spedding accompanied his parents on this visit to Newcastle and they stayed with Mr and Mrs Rowell. The Rowells lived at Jesmond Gardens and Mr Rowell was a partner in the famous shipbuilding firm of Hawthorn Leslie, whose shipyard was, and still is, situated on the south bank of the Tyne at Hebburn. There he met again Mary Rowell, who had assisted him at the grand bazaar at Blackfriars, and Spedding fell in love. The wedding took place in April 1880. Spedding Curwen was thirty-one and in charge of the printing works in North Street. The wedding was an occasion of joy for John Curwen but it was also an emotional strain coming so soon after the death of his beloved wife. It was with some difficulty he managed to restrain his emotion as he conducted the marriage ceremony.

The bridegroom made a speech which was 'full of good humour and good fellowship' and made reference to the memory of his mother in a touching way which was some consolation to his grief-stricken father. When the bride came down dressed for her honeymoon, it was seen she wore a jet necklace with a pendant bearing a photograph of her husband's mother. John Curwen was overwhelmed that neither of them on their great day had forgotten the precious memory.

Mr and Mrs Joseph Spedding Curwen on their return lived at Upton House, the birthplace of the famous surgeon, Joseph Lister. It stood opposite what is now West Ham park in Upton Lane, about halfway between Workington House and the Tonic Sol-fa Printing Press.

The continual travelling, the long fought battle to get Tonic Sol-fa teaching recognized by the Education Committee and, finally, the serious illness and death of his wife in January

[61]

were a strain on John Curwen which undermined further his physical powers. He never spared himself and had already suffered two distressing breakdowns caused by overwork. In May, just a month after his son Spedding's wedding in Newcastle-upon-Tyne, he set out for Manchester to see if he could help the only surviving brother of his late wife who was seriously ill. He was able to comfort his brother-in-law but the journey was too much for him. He died at Heaton House, Heaton Mersey, near Stockport on 26 May 1880 in his sixty-fourth year. There is little doubt that his life was shortened by his work for others, his heavy lecturing programme and the increasing responsibilities, which he gladly accepted, of leading a rapidly expanding Tonic Sol-fa movement. The Sunday School Conference at Hull in 1841 gave John Curwen the special mission of finding the simplest way of teaching music and getting it generally accepted. His mission was successfully accomplished.

An obituary of John Curwen printed in *The Congregational Year Book* of 1881 shows how deeply he valued the right of people to be free to dissent from established views; a free thinker was never an outcast in his estimation. The obituary states

Mr Curwen took an earnest interest in all political, educational, social and religious movements. He bravely fought the battle of right and liberty in the parish where he lived. He was not ashamed of being a political Dissenter, while, at the same time, the most bigoted opponents were constrained to acknowledge that he was a religious Dissenter. He never shrank from avowing his principles, but this he always did with courtesy, gentleness and kindness. This characteristic came out most markedly in the struggle for the formation of a school board in the parish, which was successful mainly through his efforts. Whatever aided the social and religious improvement of the people, he was ever ready to help to the utmost of his power by purse, pen and personal effort.

His daughter, Margaret Banks, contributed the concluding chapter of the *Memorials of John Curwen*. It is the picture of a thoroughly good man and a staunch fighter for the poor and oppressed. 'I never knew a mind', she wrote, 'so thoroughly without prejudice. Were it a new doctrine, a fresh cure of disease, a new system of medicine, a scientific truth, a fresh aspect of politics, or a new acquaintance, his mind was ever ready to investigate and then accept all that was good.'

Like many Victorians he was interested in public health and

new advances in medicine. He became a firm believer in the virtues of homoeopathy and when each of his children got married, they were presented with a case of homoeopathic medicines and a Ruddock's Manual.

His belief in the power of Tonic Sol-fa never wavered; it was the 'good, cheap and true' method of teaching singing and thereby bringing joy and moral strength to millions. Eleven years after his death the returns from the Board of Education show that two and a half million children were studying Tonic Sol-fa in elementary schools. This astonishing support for Tonic Sol-fa is some measure of the success of John Curwen's life work.

VIII

TRIUMPHS

OF SPENCER CURWEN

THE DEATH of John Curwen in May 1880 left the presidency
of the Tonic Sol-fa College vacant; it was promptly filled by his
eldest son, John Spencer Curwen. The college was lucky to have
a young president able and ready to do battle on its behalf.
There was conflict again with the Education Committee. In the
very month of the founder's death, Mr Mundella, who had
fought hard for the Education Act associated with Mr Forster's
name, announced in the House of Commons that it was intended
to pay only half the usual grant to Tonic Sol-fa pupils. The Tonic
Sol-fa movement was outraged; the old battle which had been
fought so successfully with Mr Forster on the eve of the Education Act of 1870 had, ten years later, to be waged all over again.
This time the opposition to down-grading Tonic Sol-fa was led
by John Spencer Curwen and again unqualified success was the
outcome. In 1881 a new code was published by the Education
Committee granting Tonic Sol-fa complete equality with staff
notation. Spencer Curwen's appointment as president of the
college was amply justified. As an Associate Member of the
Royal Academy of Music, editor of *The Reporter*, the eldest son
of the founder, President of both the Tonic Sol-fa College and
the Tonic Sol-fa Association and supported by many friends in
the world of music he had great influence. Everyone who could
speak up in his support was valued and none more than Dr
(later Sir John) Stainer, the organist of St Paul's and composer of
many admired hymns. Stainer commanded universal respect and
set down his views on the comparative merits of Tonic Sol-fa
and old notation in a letter published in 1881. What he says

seems a fair and balanced assessment and proved most opportune support for the Tonic Sol-fa method of teaching. Dr Stainer held the view that Tonic Sol-fa had great educational value but not at the expense of dispensing with staff notation. He sets out his creed on the whole subject with the following affirmations:

1. I believe in the staff system, as a pictorial representation of the locality of sounds, to be best for chromatic instruments of large compass.
2. I believe the Tonic Sol-fa system, as an exposition of the relation of scale-sounds, to be the true notation for voices.
3. An instrumentalist wants to know where to put his fingers; the singer wants to know his bearings with regard to the key-note; these being known, the difficulty of singing any intervals disappears.
4. The Tonic Sol-fa system is therefore invaluable as a logical and philosophical method of teaching singing.
5. I do not for one moment think that the Tonic Sol-fa is a bar to the appreciation of the staff; quite the contrary. All gifted persons who begin with Tonic Sol-fa will assuredly add to it a knowledge of the staff. Should any prejudice against the staff rise up, a serious responsibility will rest on the head of Tonic Sol-fa teachers.
6. I believe that the staff presents special difficulties to would-be singers who cannot play on any instrument, and that the Tonic Sol-fa removes these difficulties.
7. And lastly, for elementary schools, rural choirs, and persons generally who have no time to devote to an instrument, I consider the Tonic Sol-fa the best possible system.

This creed of Dr Stainer's, literally ex-cathedra, was a well timed thrust in sustaining and winning the battle for official equal recognition. There were many other notable supporters: Dr McKendrick, Professor of Physiology at Glasgow University, gave support to the movement in a speech made in Glasgow in 1881,

No one had done more to make musical education popular and to bring it to the great masses of the people than Mr Curwen's father. They would all admit, even those who might not be prepared entirely to approve of the particular system of education which he advanced, that there could not be the slightest doubt that that method of teaching the art of singing and teaching music had done more than any other in the country, especially to educate large numbers in musical matters, and to give them an interest in music which otherwise they probably would not have had. . . . The man who had developed a system of musical education which had taught the

[65]

masses of his countrymen was a man worthy of the highest honour. They bid their friend Mr [Spencer] Curwen God-speed in the great work in which he was engaged carrying on a system of musical education which was founded and developed by his worthy father.

There were indeed many to testify to the worth of Tonic Sol-fa and no further attempts were made by educational authorities to introduce rules which would have relegated the system to inferior status. John Spencer Curwen took over the direction of the movement with all the energy displayed by his father, but with the added advantage of the professional training he had received at the Royal Academy of Music. The movement continued to be amazingly popular and when the tenth edition of Spencer Curwen's *The Story of Tonic Sol-fa* appeared in the jubilee year of 1891, he was able to state without, he claims, any exaggeration that there were at least six millions who were learning or had learnt singing by the Tonic Sol-fa method.

Spencer Curwen was a good organizer and possessed immense confidence. The Tonic Sol-fa Association which was concerned in the main with choral singing and choral societies made him their president. Choral societies affiliated to the Association were, as was to be expected, spread all over the country. He made it his duty to visit as many choral groups as possible and he was ever a ready speaker. In 1881, the year after his father died, he made his grand tour of the country giving no less than eighty lectures.

In 1881 Spencer Curwen was asked to act as one of the adjudicators at the Merthyr Tydfil National Eisteddfod. He found the competitive singing stimulating and exciting and wondered whether competitive choral singing could be introduced to English choirs. He was slightly worried by the fact that industrial discipline in England was more rigid than in Wales. He noted that Welsh miners, if they wanted a holiday, could get one by the simple expedient of staying away from work. In most commercial establishments in England, this sort of behaviour would probably mean instant dismissal.

However, after his experience at the Eisteddfod he decided to try a competitive festival. He started the Stratford Musical Festival in 1882; it was a huge success and became an important annual event. Stratford was the centre of East London, not far from the Tonic Sol-fa Press in Plaistow. The Press formed its own choral society under the direction of Spedding Curwen. In 1900

[66]

The Story of
Tonic Sol=fa.

BY

J. SPENCER CURWEN,

Fellow of the Royal Academy of Music, and President of the Tonic Sol-fa College.

TENTH EDITION.
REVISED TO JUNE, 1891.

London :

J. CURWEN & SONS, 8 & 9 WARWICK LANE, E.C.

PRICE TWOPENCE.

Title page, *The Story of Tonic Sol-fa*

[67]

the Choir of The Curwen Press won the Clarnico Shield at the Stratford Festival and distinguished itself still further by winning it in the next two successive years. Practice began at 7.30 a.m. and went on until interrupted by the works bell tolling at 7.55 a.m. reminding the singers that the printing day was about to begin.

Spencer Curwen visited the 'Mrs Sunderland' competitions at Huddersfield and was clearly impressed,

I am convinced of the value of these competitions. In the first place they educate the audiences. In the second place they discover talent. It seems to me that in all departments of life we should seek to help talent to rise. More than ever is this the case in music. Providence scatters talent both in regard to performances and composition with a total disregard of our social standards and conventions. If I may say a word to music-lovers of your district it would be to honour your own prophets, encourage real capacity to come to the front, let wealthy people keep in touch with music teachers like those who adjudicated so well, and ask them to let them know of cases of gifted young people hindered by poverty, and then lend them a helping hand.

This advice is typical of Spencer Curwen's deep interest in education and shows his real concern for people: he was always ready to find means of giving a chance to those who were worthy but often too poor to take a first step unaided. Huddersfield must have taken Mr Curwen's advice seriously for the Huddersfield Choral Society has for generations been one of the most famous in the world. For years no Christmas would be complete without a performance by the Huddersfield choir of 'The Messiah'. Mrs Sunderland would not allow poverty to keep young singers out of her competitions. If it was a question of a decent pair of shoes or even a dress or suit, she would provide what was necessary.

The idea of competition festivals, pioneered by Spencer Curwen with the establishment of the Stratford Musical Festival, spread rapidly. In Glasgow, Hugh (later Sir Hugh) Roberton formed out of a Co-operative Society background the Glasgow Orpheus Choir. Like Huddersfield, the Glasgow Orpheus Choir was to win fame throughout the world.

The elaborate arrangements made for the celebration of the Tonic Sol-fa jubilee in 1891 gives some idea of the massive support competitive festivals were attracting. Tonic Sol-fa associations were announcing demonstrations in Portsmouth, Runcorn, Hawick, Falkirk, Pontypridd, Upper Cwmtwrch,

Liverpool, Brighton and Swansea; and, of course, mammoth celebrations in Glasgow, Manchester and Huddersfield. The list is endless and records once again the universal acceptance of Tonic Sol-fa. Arrangements were being made in the Potteries and Birmingham, and Aberystwyth, Caernarvon and Anglesey were reported to be 'showing spirit'. As the joint editors of the *Tonic Sol-fa Jubilee Popular Record and Handbook* conclude, 'all these celebrations must inevitably command the attention and respect of the whole British people, and Sol-faists will increase in numbers, enthusiasm and importance as a result'. A memorial plaque to Sarah Glover was placed in the church of St Laurence, St Benedict's Street, Norwich during jubilee year. Celebration was world-wide. Dr Tanaka, a clever Japanese musician who had studied Tonic Sol-fa, had just invented an enharmonium which, it is claimed, fitted in well with the physical basis of the system; it was one of Japan's contributions to jubilee year.

John Curwen who never claimed to be a trained musician received, as a rule, nothing more than a lukewarm reception for Tonic Sol-fa from most professionals; many teachers in established schools of music were definitely hostile, fearing anything associated with radical change. The view that Tonic Sol-fa was a good system for elementary teaching and for giving a helping hand to the lower orders who would, in all probability, never have the opportunity of higher education, was never universally accepted. Spencer Curwen, with his orthodox musical education and an acknowledged authority on church music, was able to weld the staff and Tonic Sol-fa into effective partnership. He published works where the staff and Sol-fa notations were combined, so that sight-reading by either method was available to singers. The welding together of the two systems helped to develop a revival in English choral singing. This, and the introduction of the competitive festivals throughout the country, provided a new stimulus for British composers. Choral music, following the pioneer work of Spencer Curwen, became an attractive field for new composition; it is a field that has not been neglected by modern composers and has given to British music added fame. The choral works of Elgar, Granville Bantock, Walford Davies, Hugh Roberton, Vaughan Williams and Gustav Holst provide a group of compositions published in England giving delight to countless singers and their audiences. It is still a live movement and, to the list of composers should be added Peter Warlock, Sir

[69]

Arthur Bliss, Dame Ethel Smyth and others who were continuing the fine choral tradition. Choral competitions and numerous 'arrangements' by Maurice Jacobson kept the Curwen participation at concert pitch. Maurice Jacobson, who retired as Chairman of J. Curwen & Sons in 1971, and one of his colleagues Kenneth Roberton, the son of the founder of the Glasgow Orpheus Choir, are still much in demand as adjudicators at musical festivals. Their work takes them all over Britain and often to distant places such as British Columbia, Tokio and Hong Kong. It is gratifying to find the Curwen* name still associated with competitive festivals and sharing fully in the exacting work of adjudicating.

The *Tonic Sol-fa Reporter* continued to be edited by Spencer Curwen; in 1888 there was a change of name and it became *The Musical Herald*. Covering a much wider musical field than the old *Reporter*, *The Musical Herald* continued under the editorial control of Spencer Curwen until his death in 1916. In 1920 J. Curwen & Sons purchased *The Musical News* and the shades of *The Reporter* became a weekly publication called the *Musical News and Herald*. In 1927 the magazine was sold and what originated as *The Reporter* came to an end in the Curwen fold after a long and useful life extending over seventy-five years.

Mr and Mrs Spencer Curwen had two daughters and a son, but bringing up a family did not seem to lessen their work in the musical world and, in particular, their participation in musical education. They were responsible for much of the preparation for the celebration of the Tonic Sol-fa jubilee in 1891. The portrait gallery in the *Jubilee Handbook* pays tribute to the movement's leading figures. There is a portrait of a powerful looking Mrs Stapleton who had the distinction of being the first woman Sol-fa teacher. She became a teacher in about 1837 and was much sought after. She met John Curwen soon after his appointment to Plaistow, describing him as a 'young minister with black hair and a very bright and loving face'. His frankness disarmed her and the modulator captivated her. She jumped at it and into fame. Her skill as a pianist, playing and teaching either notation and a voice-trainer and popular Sol-fa teacher left an undying memory which has been preserved by an oil painting hanging at the Tonic Sol-fa College. She died in 1885.

---

*J. Curwen & Sons Ltd no longer trades under its own name: the firm was taken over in 1969 by Crowell, Collier & Macmillan Inc.

Another worthy in the portrait gallery is Henry (later Sir Henry) Coward. He started life in the Sheffield cutlery trade but decided later to become a school teacher. At one time music critic of the *Sheffield Independent*, a regular attender of festivals, he was well known for his skill in conducting large choirs of children. A member of the council of the Tonic Sol-fa College, he was chosen for the honour of conducting the mass choir at the Jubilee Celebration. Sir Henry Coward was immensely energetic in the cause of music throughout his long life. Born in 1849, he was still lecturing breezily seventy years later and was always faithful in his support of Tonic Sol-fa. He died at the age of ninety-five in 1944.

Mrs J. Spencer Curwen has her place in the jubilee portrait gallery. Mrs Curwen was famous as the author of *The Child Pianist*, a work in graded steps to help pianoforte pupils. First published about 1885, it has become known all over the world as *Mrs Curwen's Pianoforte Method*. It is still in print and sells steadily. There are altogether twelve parts in Mrs Curwen's method; also an indispensable teacher's guide and, recently added, supplementary duets to first steps by Maurice Jacobson; all in the former Curwen catalogue and all still in demand.

The mechanical connection between the keyboard and staff Mrs Curwen found helpful to young learners, therefore staff notation is employed, but pupils were put through a Tonic Sol-fa singing course before beginning their piano lessons.

Mrs Curwen's Pianoforte Method has been for generations a best seller in educational music. After the first war there were Mrs Curwen's method specialists. Examinations in Mrs Curwen's pianoforte method were held in February and July under the auspices of the Curwen Method Office at 55 Berners Street, London, when teacher's or pupil's examination papers were offered. At the Wigmore Hall Studios training classes in Mrs Curwen's Method for music teachers were held on Wednesdays and Saturdays by Miss Scott Gardner and Miss Margaret Knaggs. They were advertised as 'Mrs Curwen's Pianoforte Method: Ear Training and Sight Singing from Sol-fa and Staff'. Mrs Curwen's method continues to be helpful in teaching beginners and remains a favourite with large numbers of music teachers.

Spencer Curwen continued the work his father had fought for so valiantly, but clearly the scope of his work was bound to be far wider. Being just as concerned with staff notation as with Tonic Sol-fa, he was able to appeal to a broader field of musical interests. Spencer Curwen was certain that interest in the Tonic Sol-fa movement would not show any signs of flagging. Indeed, thanks largely to the expansion of popular education and the acceptance, if at times reluctant, of the Tonic Sol-fa method by the Education Committee, it was inevitable that Spencer Curwen's abilities would be fully stretched.

The spread of the competitive festival brought in the participation of still more singers and Spencer Curwen's pioneering and adjudicating at festivals all over the kingdom gave added impetus to musical performance. As a writer he contributed important work, and as a musician he was able to bring together effectively Sol-fa and staff notation. All this helped his publishing business which was growing in importance year by year. As a publisher, it was a source of pleasure and probably some profit to have a wife who was a distinguished musician in her own right, both as a writer and a teacher. It must have provided her husband with a glow of pride to offer in his 'list' *Mrs Curwen's Pianoforte Method*; a best seller then and by no means a slow seller seventy years later. Annie Curwen was also the author of *The Psychology of Music Teaching*, a book which is much esteemed and widely read in the world of musical education.

Spencer Curwen's contribution to the literature of music is considerable. *How to Read Music and Understand It* was published in 1881; largely inspired by his father, although written entirely by Spencer Curwen, it was a highly successful publication. His *Studies in Worship Music* reflect his special interest in church music and is considered an important standard work. *The Boy's Voice* was another success and by the time of the Tonic Sol-fa Jubilee it was already in its fourth edition.

Spencer Curwen was a total abstainer and a vigorous supporter of the Temperance Union; he was a great believer in the virtues of temperance music. He never favoured compulsion and was a staunch defender of personal freedom. In an address at a conference of the National Temperance Union he said,

In a country like this where there was a passionate love of freedom and a great dislike to be over-governed, they could not compel men to join temperance societies, and they must win them by making temperance attractive and magnetic. That was why they sought music to help them. All healthy

[72]

art was on the side of temperance—it stirred higher instincts, revived people and occupied their leisure. But music, he supposed, would always be the most popular and constant art that they would use in temperance work.

All this might have been said a decade earlier by Spencer Curwen's father: the views which may seem unusual to later generations had a good deal of practical sense at a time when 'drink' was a very serious social problem. It would be interesting to know more precisely how temperance could be relied upon to 'revive people and occupy their leisure'. But whatever may be said of the Temperance movement in the nineteenth century, it had great power and was immensely helpful in giving hope, strength and health to its numerous supporters.

Before looking at the printing and publishing work of Spencer Curwen and the long and fruitful partnership with his younger brother Joseph Spedding, something should be said of Spencer Curwen's social views. He was a real front line worker bent on helping those who were condemned to live in sordid surroundings. He was for ever agitating for better housing, better wages and better education for the poorer sections of the community. Like William Morris, he was prepared to take part in street corner meetings and speak up for a 'fairer share' for those who were obviously being denied it. If a label were to be attached to him, he could be described as a Christian Socialist. At one time it was hoped Spencer Curwen would stand as a Radical Liberal candidate for West Ham South. There was, as it turned out, some bitterness behind the scenes which caused Curwen to withdraw and he used all his influence to persuade a member of the Independent Labour Party to stand in his place. His persuasion won the day and in 1892 Keir Hardie was elected member of parliament for West Ham South, becoming the first Labour member to enter the House of Commons. Spencer Curwen had the satisfaction of being his local sponsor; if there had not been rows 'behind the scenes' John Spencer Curwen might have gone to Westminster instead of Keir Hardie.

Spencer Curwen was described as being the 'best kind of socialist'. This was not meant to be patronizing but a way of saying that he was a practical reformer rather than a Marxist. Considerable firmness of purpose was required of a middle-class person in those days to profess being a socialist; firmness of purpose was a Curwen family characteristic. They were truly

[73]

F

independent and free thinking, both in their religious and temporal life. Spencer Curwen and his brother Spedding had deep feeling and compassion for their fellow human beings and were free from the usual snobbish notions about a person's station in life which caused so much division in Victorian England. Spencer Curwen was never happier than when working in East London and was one of the founders of Mansfield House in Canning Town. To work among dockers and factory workers was quite natural for a man who was directing his energies, as his father did, towards bringing the blessings of music to millions and, with it, a fuller and often happier life.

IX

PUBLISHING

AT WARWICK LANE

AFTER THE DEATH of the Revd John Curwen in May 1880, the music business was carried on as a partnership between John Spencer Curwen and his younger brother Joseph Spedding. It was already a thriving firm with a publishing office known as the Tonic Sol-fa Agency established in Paternoster Row, then the centre of the London publishing trade.

The partnership of J. Curwen & Sons was divided into twelve equal parts, of which seven parts were allocated to Spencer and five to Spedding. This unequal sharing of the partnership was probably justified but it cannot have been wholly acceptable to the younger brother. There was some mild resentment, but it was an acceptable arrangement and did not interfere with the vigour with which the two brothers went about their business. Progress was satisfying. Spencer was undoubtedly more ambitious than Spedding and in claiming the larger share he must have recognized the creative aspect of his work. Book-keeping and parcel post were important but, in Spencer's estimation, pedestrian activities compared to publishing, authorship and building up a strong 'list'. Furthermore, Spencer Curwen's contribution as a compiler of musical anthologies and his successful editing of *The Tonic Sol-fa Reporter* were a source of profit and strength to J. Curwen & Sons. He was indeed the creative partner providing the bulk of the printing orders for the Tonic Sol-fa Press. It is reasonable to believe that without the creative energy and publishing ability of Spencer, Spedding's printing works would have had little to do. On the manufacturing side, the partnership had the advantage of producing for itself at the Tonic Sol-fa Press in

[75]

North Street, Plaistow, most of the text-books, educational manuals, song sheets and modulators required by the publishing business. The publishing office, in deciding what to publish, largely determined the business policy of the firm; Spencer Curwen always claimed he knew little about book-keeping or 'parcel post'; business detail, as well as actual manufacture, was under the care of Spedding.

There was the firmly held Victorian conviction that an elder son was in some way superior in ability to a younger. In the case of Spencer the claim could be put forward with a good deal of assurance. Spencer was an acknowledged expert on church music and the author of an important book on that subject; he was also a public figure in the world of music, being a Fellow of the Royal Academy of Music and President of the Tonic Sol-fa College and the Tonic Sol-fa Association. The brothers had so many common interests that it would be inconceivable if they had been unable to work in harmony. They were indeed well matched: Spencer had plenty to do building up the publishing while Spedding gradually expanded the printing works to meet the growing programme thrust upon it. They were both supporters of the Tonic Sol-fa method of teaching and offered every inducement for it to be taken up by the elementary schools and choral societies. They were convinced that the love and practice of music was bound to bring increased contentment and moral elevation to the great numbers of boys and girls in the elementary schools and to the grown-ups in numerous choral societies and glee clubs. In the matter of temperance, Spencer and Spedding were as strict as their father: both were life-long total abstainers and solid supporters of the Temperance movement. Again, like their father, they were free thinkers and independent of the established church and were untiring in their efforts to secure social justice for those who were struggling against poverty and suffering and having to endure the two-fold agonies of low-standard housing and low-paid work.

Spencer and Spedding sound full of goodness; to some extent this was true, for they possessed a social conscience which set them far above the luxury seekers that so shocked the Revd John Curwen at Karlsbad. However, the partners shared one serious deficiency: neither of them had any appreciation of the visual arts. They accepted and went along with the muddy stream of nineteenth-century industrial ugliness. That they should have visual blindness is surprising as they must have been

𝔑ational 𝔊emperance Choral 𝔘nion

President - - - - - Mr. C. CLEMENTS, J.P.
Musical Adviser - - - Mr. W. G. W. GOODWORTH,
Lic. Mus. Trin. Coll. Lond., Fell. Ton. Sol-fa Coll.

MUSIC AND WORDS

TO BE SUNG AT THE

𝔉IRST 𝔊ONCERT

BY JUVENILE SINGERS

AT THE

NATIONAL TEMPERANCE FÊTE

AT THE

Crystal Palace

ON

WEDNESDAY, JULY 5th, 1899.

ORGANISED BY THE

𝔑ational 𝔘nited 𝔗emperance 𝔊ouncil.

President: Mr. ARNOLD F. HILLS, D.L.

Conductor:
Mr. G. W. HARDWIDGE,
1, MARTINEAU ROAD, HIGHBURY HILL, N.

Organist - - - Mr. F. WILSON PARISH, F.R.C.O.

𝔓rice 𝔖ixpence.

Concert programme cover for National Temperance Choral Union

[77]

influenced and certainly aware of the political views of William Morris and have known something of his great work as a designer-craftsman. The social idealism of Morris had a strong appeal to the non-conforming, emotional Curwens. But they appear completely unmoved by William Morris, the practical designer and maker of beautiful things. It never occurred to the Curwen brothers that ugly towns and ugly lives needed beauty to transform them, and the production of beautiful goods was worth doing as a practical challenge to squalor; in Morris's view too participating in the making of beautiful things brought dignity and a sense of purpose to the lives of skilled men and women in the factories and workshops. As far as the Tonic Sol-fa Press was concerned design and the precepts of William Morris went unheeded for a very long time.

Spencer Curwen had, in fact, been taking the main responsibility for the publishing side of the business and for the editorial control of *The Reporter* for almost a decade before his father died. He was indefatigable as an anthologist and poured out a steady stream of work which, of course, added to the selling range of the Tonic Sol-fa Agency. The October 1879 issue of *The Reporter* advertises a typical Spencer Curwen collection of songs. *Ready this day* cheerfully heads the announcement of *Songs of Work and Duty for Schools* edited by J. Spencer Curwen. This new song book, the advertisement announces, contains thirty-eight pieces, the words of which teach thrift, earnestness, love of parents and warnings against debt, the mere military spirit and idleness. There were also songs for the iron-workers, the farmer, shoemaker, miner, blacksmith, miller and so on. The following are some of the titles to other pieces: 'Be a Man', 'Bright and Early,' 'The Carrier's Cart', 'Don't Forget the Old Folks', 'Friends Don't Run into Debt', 'Hold Your Head Up Like a Man', 'Of Debt Beware', 'Never Give Up', etc. Price in stout wrapper 3d; postage on two copies ½d. Very good value and titles of the kind which would have the support of Samuel Smiles. It is heartening to find Spencer Curwen sounding the alarm against 'mere military spirit'; the Franco-German war of 1870 may have turned his thoughts towards the danger of nations tearing themselves to pieces in cruel and costly warfare.

In the July 1880 number of *The Tonic Sol-fa Reporter*, Spencer Curwen writes an editorial recording the long association with his father,

[78]

A word is due to the reader, as I take upon myself the sole direction of *The Reporter*. Fifteen years of association with my father in the editorship—during seven of which my name has appeared in conjunction with his—have, I hope, taught me his habits of action and his policy as a public worker. Of late years the responsibility of filling *The Reporter* month by month has fallen entirely into my hands. It will now be my purpose not to change in any way the character of *The Reporter* but to follow along the lines my father laid down; to deal with the religious, social and educational uses of music; to promote the movement of which he was the founder; and to help the school of teachers which he originated to compare notes and to improve their work.

So far as *The Reporter* and kindred publications go, my father's death brings to me responsibility rather than a change of work. Subject to his general direction, the choice of music for *The Reporter*, as well as for the various collections of part-songs, anthems, school songs, elementary courses, etc. has been in my hands for many years; during which my father confined himself to the writing of those educational books which are his monument as a literary worker, and to duties connected with the Presidency of the Tonic Sol-fa College. Thus my apprenticeship has been fully served, and it will be my own fault if I do not now make a good journeyman.

It is interesting to find that for long there had been a sharing of labour between father and son. Filling a twenty-four or thirty-two page *Reporter* every month was clearly an exacting task and, as far as Spencer Curwen was concerned, it was only one among several equally important duties. He had his duties as President of the Tonic Sol-fa College and shared the 'Art of Teaching' class with Mr Proudman, Mr McNaught and Mr Venables; the lecture tours continued to take a great deal of his time. His creative skill was rapidly building up sales for the Tonic Sol-fa Agency and as a matter of policy he was gradually introducing the name of J. Curwen & Sons on the covers and title pages of the firm's publications.

Spencer Curwen was determined to put an end to any warfare between Tonic Sol-fa notation and staff notation. As President of the Tonic Sol-fa College he declared,

Some of our Council say that the only business of the Tonic Sol-fa College is to teach Tonic Sol-fa. I agree with this, but I put a fuller meaning on the phrase than they do. I say it is our business to carry the light of Tonic Sol-fa into all the branches of musical study and that when the elementary foundation has been laid in Tonic Sol-fa notation, we ought to leave it optional to the student of harmony, instrument, or voice in which notation he or she will proceed further.

What he was recommending was exactly the course Mrs Annie Curwen took in her method of teaching piano playing for beginners.

In 1892—the year after the celebration of the jubilee of Tonic Sol-fa, Spencer Curwen wrote *Old Plaistow*, a history of the village based on a paper he had read at the Balaam Street Schools on 15 October 1891. The first edition was published by H. Parker, 198 Balaam Street, Plaistow and was printed by J. Curwen & Sons in North Street. The cover of *Old Plaistow* is about as uninspired typographically as it was possible to be. What is interesting is the printer's device which appears on the verso of the title page. There are two hands clasping each other in friendship; one hand bears the legend 'old notation', the other 'tonic sol-fa'. The hands are placed in a commercial mock-heraldic setting with the initials J.C. & S. at the top and, beneath the hands, the firm's name J. Curwen & Sons. The device, a symbol of peace approved by Spencer Curwen, shows his desire to make the fullest possible

Device adopted by Spencer Curwen symbolizing peace between staff notation and Tonic Sol-fa

use of both Tonic Sol-fa and the old notation. His breadth of vision enabled him to extend the range of his publishing ventures. Music could be printed with staff notation or with the staff and Tonic Sol-fa combined; where sight-reading only was being taught Tonic Sol-fa and words were offered.

At the time of the Tonic Sol-fa Jubilee celebrations there were expressions of satisfaction at the tremendous growth in Tonic

Sol-fa literature. John Curwen & Sons participated fully in this growth and despite the fact that the partnership was publishing a great deal of music in old notation and some with combined staff and Tonic Sol-fa, its interest in Tonic Sol-fa remained dominant. The sales of the Tonic Sol-fa Agency were world wide: schools were the largest identifiable group of custom but there was strong demand wherever singing in church, chapel or choral society was deeply rooted in day to day life. Wales, especially industrialized South Wales, made heavy demands on the Tonic Sol-fa Agency. Hundreds of thousands of song sheets were sold in Wales to meet the requirements of singers at choral festivals and in local chapels. It was unusual in most of this work to print the music in the old notation; there was really no demand for staff as the singers were more than likely to read from Tonic Sol-fa. Song sheets for choral societies were produced at very reasonable prices. The quantities needed made low cost 'per copy' a possibility and it was not unusual for an eight page sheet containing both staff notation, Tonic Sol-fa and, of course, the words to be sold for a penny or twopence. This low price would have to cover cost of production, the cost of publishing and presumably some profit for the publisher. In the late nineteenth century the demand for song sheets—mostly in Tonic Sol-fa—was on such a satisfactory scale that J. Curwen & Sons were able to live up to the claims printed round the cartouche on the front page of the early issues of the *Tonic Sol-fa Reporter* that the method was 'easy, cheap and true'. There was no doubt whatever that it was cheap.

Another quite different kind of publication became popular towards the end of the nineteenth century. This was the 'action song' when singing and acting with the consequent fun of dressing up were combined. These publications were not cheap like the song sheets; they retailed as a rule for a shilling and were handsomely produced with engraved staff notation and Tonic Sol-fa printed between the staff and the words. John Curwen & Sons had a grand selection of action songs and an impressive number of titles were kept in stock. There were action songs specially for school concerts all selling at the standard rate and costumes for the relevant pieces could be hired from the publisher. The character sketches by J. Frise were extremely popular. *The Tramp* was performed, it was claimed, with great success by Mr Frise's Musical Mimics. *From Behind the Speaker's Chair* was described as humorous patter and *The Market* was a humorous

[81]

sketch, all acted and sung with great success by the Musical Mimics. Little was left to chance; there was, where it was thought necessary, guidance for performers. In *The Market* the hints conclude with the sound advice that 'the salesmen should gesticulate freely and not be afraid to let their voices be heard in the market place. The patter will need much practice to be well delivered.'

Patriotic choruses were popular: A. L. Cowley was responsible for *The United Kingdom*; Union Jacks, Prince of Wales' feathers at net school prices were offered by J. Curwen & Sons. Another A. L. Cowley success in the same genre was entitled *Up with the Flag*. For this song royal standards were available as well as Union Jacks and Prince of Wales' feathers. Although the action songs were directed primarily to schools, they must have done a lot to promote amateur acting and singing among adults. Spencer Curwen's list of action songs became very well known and justly so, for much of what he published was both charming, light hearted and encouraged participation by providing simple acting parts.

In June 1875 the Tonic Sol-fa College had been entirely separated from J. Curwen & Sons and was administered by a council. Spencer Curwen, as president, maintained a great influence but the publishing and printing firm was not involved financially. All supporters of Tonic Sol-fa recognized the need of teacher training and the college remained the chief centre for examinations and the issue of the different grades of certificates. The College had been built at Forest Gate where the cost of land was relatively cheap and accommodation for students was thought to be more easily available in what was then a fast growing suburb. It remained at Forest Gate for just over eleven years and in October 1890 the College moved to 27 Finsbury Square. A more central situation was considered desirable: Finsbury Square at that time was the southernmost terminus of a system of horse-drawn trams known as the North Metropolitan. This network of trams gave easy access to the college from most of the northern and north-eastern suburbs and the terminus in Finsbury Square had the convenience of being within walking distance of 8 Warwick Lane where Spencer Curwen presided over his growing publishing business. The Tonic Sol-fa College remained in Finsbury Square for nearly thirty years, removing in 1919, this time on a twenty-year lease, to 26 Bloomsbury Square.

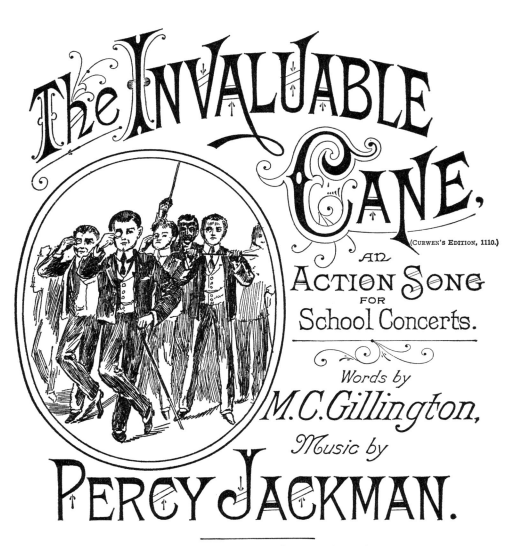

The Invaluable Cane,

(Curwen's Edition, 1110.)

An Action Song

FOR

School Concerts.

Words by

M. C. Gillington,

Music by

Percy Jackman.

Copyright in U.S.A. 1899 by J.Curwen & Sons Lᵗᵈ

London.

J. CURWEN & SONS Lᵀᴰ 24 BERNERS STREET, W.

RIGHT OF PERFORMANCE ETC

Curwen action song cover, 1902 (reduced)

[83]

In making this second move, the College was following the west-ward migration of the publishing trade. In 1900 most publishers were within a stone's throw of St Paul's. After the war of 1914–18 there was a steady move to the beautiful Georgian squares and terraces between Southampton Row and Upper Regent Street. The Tonic Sol-fa home on the north side of Bloomsbury Square had a simplicity and eighteenth-century elegance which was architecturally the opposite of Lewis Banks's ecclesiastical-looking building in Earlham Grove.

1891 was the year of the Tonic Sol-fa jubilee celebrated on a grand national scale. The popular record and handbook was pre-pared by Spencer Curwen and John Graham and published by J. Curwen & Sons, 8 and 9 Warwick Lane, E.C. at the reason-able price of sixpence. The jubilee president was Spencer Curwen and he had as his treasurer R. Griffiths who was the Tonic Sol-fa leader in Manchester; the secretary was W. H. Bonner, an indefatigable worker in the Temperance movement, a devoted advocate of the training system for Tonic Sol-fa certificates and principal of the Forest Gate School of Music. The Bonner family were long connected with teaching at Forest Gate; when the Tonic Sol-fa College removed to Finsbury Square, the build-ing in Earlham Grove became the headquarters of the Metro-politan Academy of Music under the direction of Frank Bonner. The Tonic Sol-fa College for years held a holiday course at Earlham Grove; interrupted by the 1914–18 war, they were resumed in 1919 with a course lasting four weeks directed by Frank Bonner.

The jubilee celebrations were carefully planned; the groups in the provinces were consulted early and played a large part in making the special programmes a popular success. And there was solid satisfaction for the Curwen partnership in the announce-ment that in 1891 the returns of the Education Department showed that two and a half million children were studying Tonic Sol-fa in the elementary schools. The Tonic Sol-fa method no longer needed statistics to underline its triumph; it was a world-wide movement and its very scale ensured that the Tonic Sol-fa printing works at Plaistow, along with others, would have bulging order books; for the music publishers the outlook was set fair. The Curwen partnership stood to benefit by being both producers of music and publishers. They were specially in debt to Spencer Curwen who, as a teacher, lecturer and encourager of competitive festivals, was looked upon as the leading Tonic Sol-fa advocate and a professional musician of some note.

Spencer Curwen continued with his lecturing engagements and was much in demand as an adjudicator at competitive festivals which were often held under the auspices of the Tonic Sol-fa Association. He was honoured in 1896 by being made a Welsh Bard (Derwent Pencerdd), an honour which must have given him intense pleasure coming, as it did, from the land of Tonic Sol-fa's most fervent supporters.

In 1901 the lease on 8 Warwick Lane came to an end and Spencer Curwen decided to move away from the old publishers' quarters. He took a sixty-year lease on 24 Berners Street: a beautiful Georgian house with fine panelled rooms and a setting which seemed perfect for a publisher of educational music. J. Curwen & Sons Ltd occupied this lovely house until 1961: since then, like so much that seemed worth preserving, the building has been demolished and all the beauty and workmanship of a fine town house lost for ever.

X

MUSIC PRINTING

WHEN HIS FATHER'S exhaustive *Teacher's Manual* was being prepared for printing, Spedding Curwen was still a young man. The administration of the printing works was then largely under his control and during the quarter of a century from 1875 to 1900 the printing side of J. Curwen & Sons was steadily and prudently developed.

The main work of the printing press was to produce orders sent down to Plaistow from the publishing office in Warwick Lane. The printed work was stored, on completion, in a vast stock-room in Plaistow and delivered to customers as directed by Warwick Lane, which was essentially the publishing office, showroom, trade counter and counting house. At first, Curwen's Tonic Sol-fa Agency handled all Curwen productions and also kept a stock of modulators, conductors' batons, metronomes and harmoniums. Gradually Spencer dropped from his title pages the Tonic Sol-fa Agency name and printed instead the name of the partnership, J. Curwen & Sons. The new style was generally adopted by 1881 when the publishing office moved from Paternoster Row to 8 Warwick Lane.

For many years the printing works in North Street was known as the Tonic Sol-fa Press; the issues of *The Reporter* from January 1865 bear this imprint and so does *The Child's Own Hymn Book*. There was, however, some inconsistency and variations in the wording of the imprint. *The Teacher's Manual* fifth edition published from 8 Warwick Lane has the imprint 'J. Curwen & Sons, Music Printers, Plaistow, E.', while the *Memorials of John Curwen* published in 1882 from the same address has the imprint 'Printed at The Tonic Sol-fa Press'.

Later the imprint varied from J. Curwen & Sons, Plaistow, E.

to J. Curwen & Sons, Lithographic and Letterpress Printers, Plaistow, E. and sometimes just J. Curwen & Sons, General Printers; its most fully descriptive imprint was J. Curwen & Sons Ltd, Lithographic and Letterpress Printers, Account Book Makers & Manufacturing Stationers. The 'Curwen Press' did not become the regular trading name of the firm's printing side until Harold Curwen, the youngest son of Spedding, took over the management at Plaistow just before the 1914 war. But the Tonic Sol-fa Press died hard; it appeared surprisingly as late as 1913 in Bacon's *Atlas of London and Suburbs*.

Spedding Curwen was in what might be considered the envious position of enjoying the advantage of practically all his printing orders being 'captive' orders. They came from the publishing office and automatically the Plaistow works received 'most favoured nation' treatment. But it is questionable if these captive orders were quite as advantageous as they seemed. There is evidence that they were not an unmixed blessing and Spedding was worried by production being too closely tied to a single source. There is a fatal temptation to be less watchful of costs if orders are going to flow in in any case and there is a tendency for the manufacturing processes to remain unchanged and become stuck in a groove if there is little incentive to go beyond what is necessary to cope with a comparatively narrow range of essentially repetitive work. Here was a dangerous problem facing the Tonic Sol-fa Press. Through the rapid growth of the Tonic Sol-fa movement and the demands made by new elementary schools established after the Education Act of 1870 and also through the greater volume arising from the publishing enterprises of Spencer, there was nearly always more work available than the Press could comfortably undertake.

This situation, satisfactory as it must have seemed in the short term, weakened a resolve to seek any kind of outside custom. When the works were already over busy, it would seem a waste of money to employ staff who were going to bring in even more work. Nevertheless, Spedding, appreciating the dangers of being completely dependent on the success of the publishing office, encouraged a general printing trade that helped to spread the risks and did not leave him entirely at the mercy of one source for his business; also, despite the temptation for a status quo created by captive orders, much energy was devoted to developing printing techniques which would keep costs down and improve quality; Spedding was anxious to keep the works abreast of modern methods.

It was found that by doing work for customers in a variety of different trades the Press was able to broaden its manufacturing experience; they had to learn how to produce well and economically both song sheets and shoe-polish labels. It was indeed essential to maintain the vitality of the printing side of the business; staff, whether working in the offices or on the factory floor, do not like to feel their ship getting rusty. Spedding avoided this happening. Although he was nothing like so prominent in musical and publishing circles as his brother Spencer, yet in an unobtrusive way he served the partnership well. The progress made by the printing side under his direction matched the progress of the more spectacular publishing.

When Spedding became effectively in charge of printing in the mid 1870s, the firm had special skills which were not usually found in general printing offices. The actual printing was ordinary letterpress; that means that each impression made on the paper came from the raised surface of previously inked type, blocks or stereo plates. The unusual skills were in the composing of music in Tonic Sol-fa notation and setting music from movable type, with or without words, in the more general staff notation.

Setting staff notation from movable type was never entirely satisfactory. It was expensive and slow, especially for elaborately scored compositions. Song books for choral singers where all that was wanted were the words and the tune in the treble clef, with or without the addition of Sol-fa, movable type for setting the 'tune' could be practical.

Spedding decided to follow German practice and go in for engraved music and lithography. The centre of German music printing was Leipzig where Breitkopf developed his founts of movable music type; here was a concentration of firms concerned with the production of complete musical scores for operas, oratorios and fully orchestrated works. The later Leipzig method for reproducing music which was at all complicated was to engrave it on pewter by tapping the relevant steel punches into a surface of the soft metal. Pewter plates with an area to accommodate a complete page were used. The plate, after it had been engraved, was inked, the surface wiped clean as in the normal practice of printing an etching, and then a print taken on transfer paper. The print, being based on an intaglio (below the surface) image was

[88]

THE CURWEN CAXTON CHOIR PRESENTED WITH TROPHY BY THE LORD CHIEF JUSTICE ON 26 MARCH 1904

remarkably clear and distinct. The transfer paper was then laid on the surface of a stone or zinc plate and the image transferred. When all the pages were transferred in the correct order and position, printing was carried out on a lithographic press. The result was far superior to type-assembled music printed letterpress and during the last quarter of the nineteenth-century lithography was, as far as music printing was concerned, driving letterpress off the field. Spedding Curwen saw the economy and quality which lithography offered and, by the last decade of the nineteenth century, had established the process in North Street.

In 1895 Spedding took his fourteen-year-old eldest son Kenneth on a visit to Leipzig during the Easter holidays. He reports,

We went carefully over Röders and Brandstetters music printing offices. We saw much that interested us and we were much impressed by the excellence of the work—the high style and fittings of the whole place. The Germans, especially in Leipzig, have first rate technical instruction; the workmen seem intelligent, they work sixty hours a week and earn 25s to 30s as journeymen. Thus, although in a large city like Leipzig wages are less than our lowest country rates. This is what we have to compete with in taking over our own litho work.

Some allowance must be made for the fact that other people's works always seem to impress the visiting printer, especially when the firms visited are on the continent. Nevertheless Spedding was likely to think well of Röders and Brandstetters; they were leading Leipzig printers with fine buildings and exceptionally good machinery and equipment.

Despite the natural alarm at the low wages paid in Germany Spedding decided to press on with his plans for establishing his own lithographic department.

In 1896, the year after the visit to Leipzig, Spencer and Spedding purchased the North Street freehold for £5,000. The old Temperance Hall was pulled down to make room for more printing machines. During the whole year they were busy building new workshops, altering the old and installing new machinery. It was a year of new construction and high capital expenditure.

The new plan about doubled the available floor space and in September the new litho machinery began producing. For the first time zinc plates were used and Spedding reports cheerfully that 'Herbert, our first press man, seems very capable and

[89]

G

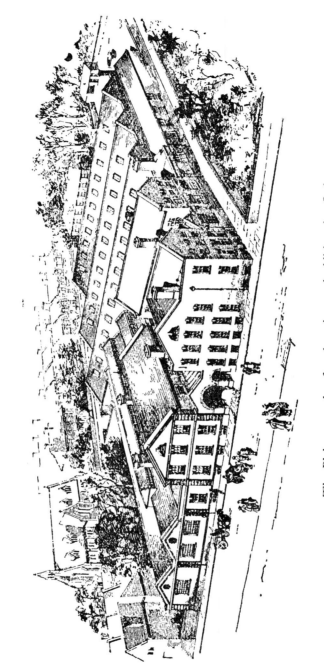

The Plaistow works after alterations and additions in 1896

relyable' [*sic*]. Herbert would be responsible for the preparation of the plates or stones for the litho printers. But Spedding like everyone else experienced teething troubles. He records in December that he 'sent away Pearse our first litho machine man as no good. Work not well printed.'

1896 was a year when the purse strings were loosened. Besides all the building and the establishment of lithography, a new Wharfedale letterpress machine was installed, a new cutting machine for the warehouse, a new Smythe (American) sewing machine for the bookbinders and a second-hand stitcher from Longman's bindery was bought for the girls' room.

The bird's eye view of the works (opposite) shows how the Tonic Sol-fa Press looked after the changes made in 1896. Very little further building was undertaken before the outbreak of the second great war in 1939. The building facing North Street behind the horse and cart which is crossing to the right hand side of the road is the original Independent Chapel with some additions incorporating a pedimented frontage. The old 'Public' School is behind and at right angles to the chapel with windows facing North Street Passage. To the left of the chapel can be seen the clerestory roof tops of the lithographic and letterpress printing machine rooms. The large building at the back with the three rows of roof lights is the store for the printed stock. This room was by far the largest of the buildings and is eloquent of the scale of the publishing business at the beginning of the present century. It was not until 1933 that the huge stock room was turned into a manufacturing department and the cottage garden seen on the extreme left built over for an addition to the letterpress machine room; the added floor space made it possible to instal some large presses capable of book printing at reasonably low cost. There is a record of the number employed in different capacities in 1902. Allowing for apprentices, the number employed was about 120 which shows that the Press had grown to a fair size since the cottage beginnings in 1863. The departmental divisions show the numbers employed in the different sections.

The hierarchical structure which persisted, and still persists, in industry is underlined by the provision of separate lavatories for office staff and works staff. A caretaker was employed to attend to the heating plant, cleaning and general maintenance.

The women in the machine room were the 'layers on', which means they had the job of feeding the paper into the machines.

Ground Floor		First Floor	
Machine room	40 men and women	Office	2 clerks
Foundry	3 men and a boy	Mounting and varnishing room	3 men and boys
Compositors	20 men and boys	Foundry and stone handling	3 men
Cutting and bundling	4 men	Reading room	1 man and a girl
Packing	2 lads		
Binders' room	7 men and boys		
Girls' room (folders)	25 women	Basement	
Plate room and parcelling	4 women	Heating apparatus and coals	
General office	4 clerks	Girls' lavatory and hats and cloaks	
Private office	1 occupant	Men's lavatory	
		Office lavatory	

Departmental structure

When the faster two-revolution printing presses appeared, laying on became men's work and later the task became, on certain machines, wholly mechanized with the development of automatic feeders. The binders' room was devoted to making account books and ledgers and forwarding the steady flow of cloth-bound books. When binding became highly mechanized, cloth binding was sent out to the specialist firms. The girls' room did all the folding and gathering. If a pamphlet, as opposed to a full bound book, was being produced, the girls' room would be responsible for thread stitching and, later, work the speedier wire stitching machine. The numerous kinds and sizes of Tonic Sol-fa modulators provided steady work for the mounting and varnishing group. This section also undertook varnishing labels which were printed on the lithographic presses.

It will be noticed that no provision was made for music engravers. The reason for this is that the organization of engravers was not always on a factory basis. Some of these highly skilled craftsmen preferred to work on their own and be their own masters. Until 1914 there were a number of German music engravers working in England; as the demand for engraving varied greatly from month to month, it was often more convenient and economical to send work out to one or more of the small workshops. There remains a faint echo of the old engravers' invasion in that music punches are still a German speciality.

[92]

Establishing lithographic printing at Plaistow showed enterprise on Spedding's part. The flood of work with Tonic Sol-fa
notation was being matched by an increase in music with staff
notation or with a combination of staff and Sol-fa. The resources
of the composing room in setting music from movable type were
limited: furthermore, music typesetting was slow and could not
keep up with demand and the final quality of the printing was
often below desired standards. Spencer Curwen was committed
to publishing more in staff notation and he was also carrying out,
in practice, his constantly repeated desire to see staff notation and
Tonic Sol-fa go hand in hand.

Additional floor space in the machine room allowed for the
installation of three or four flatbed lithographic presses. Spedding
had to employ men with different skills from compositors and
letterpress machine managers; he now needed men who could
prepare the surface of the large lithographic stones and who could
take perfect proofs from engraved pewter plates and transfer the
music on to stone. The mere task of lifting the heavy stones on
and off the bed of the printing machine was something requiring
care and a specially developed drill.

The development of lithography made it possible for the
Plaistow works themselves to undertake the printing of the
action songs, the publishing venture referred to in chapter IX,
which had become firmly established towards the end of the
nineteenth century. The publishing of these songs continued for
many years. The Boer War was the occasion for patriotic action
songs and there was a crop of similar songs during the war of
1914–18. Action songs having survived two wars were eventually
brought to a halt by the entertainment offered by broadcasting.
These songs were always subtitled 'An Action Song for School
Concerts'. Until Plaistow was able to produce them, they were
printed in Germany by Leipzig firms. The number of titles grew
to hundreds and the work, although spread over many years,
represented a considerable output for the lithographic department,
especially when reprint orders are taken into account. They consisted of either eight or twelve pages with the front page occupied
by a drawn title and the last page devoted to a list of other songs
in the series. There was an astonishing variety of themes: sex
segregation was the order of the day there being character and
costume songs for boys and a similar series thought suitable for
girls. Humorous, domestic, patriotic and opening and closing

[93]

The BEES' SONG

Curwen Edition 1465.

Words by
WALTER DE LA MARE
Music by C. ARMSTRONG GIBBS

LONDON
J. CURWEN & SONS LTD., 24, BERNERS STREET, W.1
PRICE TWO SHILLINGS
The right of performance of this song
in theatres & music halls
is reserved

Restyled cover for action songs (reduced). Calligraphy
by Henry Ball, decoration by Aldo Cosomati, 1920

songs are some of the main groupings. In the domestic character
songs for girls there are 'Busy Little Housemaids', 'Dainty
Domestics', 'Little Laundresses' and the 'Sweeping Brush
Brigade'. In the opening and closing section we have 'At Our
Bazaar', 'Song of Welcome', 'Good Night', 'March' and 'O
Merry it is at Close of Day'.

Most action songs combine words, tune and Tonic Sol-fa with
treble and bass staff notation. The engraving is good and so is
the printing. What are not good are the designs for the front page
titles. An example of one is shown on page 83 and they were all
deplorable until a new style initiated by Harold Curwen came
into use about 1910; an example of the improved style is shown
opposite. The lack of style or interest in typographic design persisted at Plaistow until Harold Curwen started his typographic
revolution.

Spedding Curwen was greatly liked by all who worked at
North Street. He was a father figure and inspired so much
confidence that nobody had any hesitation in asking his advice,
especially on difficult personal problems. The office staff at
Plaistow in the nineteenth century was very small indeed:
besides Spedding, there was the manager, Mr Sidney Barras and
two clerks and a boy. The costing system was rudimentary and
required very much less staff than it does now and it appears that
the invoicing and keeping accounts of debtors and creditors was
done by the counting house staff in Warwick Lane and subsequently from 24 Berners Street. The two clerks were in all
probability fully occupied in seeing that the right kind and
quality of material was issued for each order, the correct instructions given for the dispatch or stocking of finished work and the
weekly computation of wages.

Fortunately it has been possible to get some idea of the atmosphere at the works in the late nineteenth century from Edwin
Truscott who was born in 1876 and remained in good health and
possessed of an excellent memory until his death in 1971.
Truscott was Curwen's oldest pensioner and worked at Plaistow
for over fifty years: his craftsmanship in bookbinding can rarely
have been excelled and his even temperament and insistence on
all work measuring up to his exacting standards made him in
due time a very able head of the bindery.

Truscott, whose first job was 'boy' in a shop in the nearby
Barking Road, selling pianos, harmoniums, banjos and all kinds

of musical instruments, had his half-day on Thursdays. Walking down North Street one Thursday, he saw a notice saying 'boy wanted'. Very enterprisingly he went in and was seen by Mr Sidney Barras who asked him what he could do. Truscott, after a moment's hesitation, replied, 'I can do what I'm told.' This impressed Mr Barras who went to report to Spedding Curwen who, coming out of his private office all smiles, said 'Fancy finding a boy nowadays who can do what he is told'. After a few days a letter was sent to young Truscott offering him an apprenticeship in the bindery. Truscott learned his trade from Clement George, the head of the department. This 'in-works' training was supplemented by attending evening classes for two terms at the People's Palace in Mile End Road. Here he was taught gold tooling and finishing and leather binding. Truscott joined The Curwen Press in 1892 becoming one of its many devoted servants and, after a career of great distinction, retired in 1947.

In 1890 the highly mechanized binding specialists had not come into existence. Binding work at Plaistow was mostly done by hand. There was a German-built sewing machine for sewing together sections of books and there were two treadle-operated wire stitching machines in the girls' room for stapling booklets and *The Musical Herald*. There was never any shortage of work. Enormous numbers of cloth-bound copies of the popular oratorios formed a large part of production. In octavo and small quarto, in staff or Tonic Sol-fa, there was the stream of Haydn's *Creation*, Mendelssohn's *Elijah* and Handel's *Messiah*, *Judas Maccabeus* and many other works in popular demand by choral societies and schools. The oratorio scores were astonishingly reasonable in price. *Judas Maccabeus* in the Tonic Sol-fa edition was a crown octavo of 192 pages, Tonic Sol-fa and words, and bound in cloth blind stamped and gold blocked. Cloth bound it sold at 1s 6d and paper covered at 1s. This was before 1914; after the war the cost was 2s and 1s 6d respectively. Modulators were produced by the thousand. They were printed on paper and then backed with calico and fitted top and bottom with a wooden bar. Backing with calico was a binder's task and it made the men very efficient in using the paste brush. This skill, in turn, developed a trade in showcard mounting.

Some unusual tasks were, Truscott recollects, assigned to the bookbinders. The provision of actors' material for the action songs caused the binders to manufacture four dozen swords made in cardboard, covered with silver paper and two or three gross of diaphanous fairy wings, made out of waxed paper and edged with coloured stripping.

In 1890 the works were gaslit with flat flame burners: incandescent mantles came later. Until the heating system was installed in the early twentieth century, each workshop possessed a large centrally placed iron stove. It was part of the apprentice's task to see that the stove was shining black with liberal applications of 'Zebo'. The girls' room was looked after by Miss Craddock who was very strict and very sedate. She, and her deputy Miss Gretton, were true Victorians and were determined that no work should go out which could possibly bring discredit on The Curwen Press. Both served the firm for over fifty years and the picture of Miss Craddock with her black laced high boots and neat black serge dress with a white lace collar evokes the atmosphere of an era long vanished. Both Miss Craddock and Miss Gretton were keen church-women and would not allow a word to be said against any member of the Curwen family. They were staunch supporters of temperance and were appalled at the thought of anyone showing the slightest interest in alcoholic beverages.

The service of the foreladies of the girls' room is impressive. Miss Craddock started at Plaistow in 1880 and retired in 1934. She was succeeded by Miss Gretton who started in 1889 and retired in 1938. Her successor was Mary Reece, another strong upholder of temperance, who began work in 1902 and retired in 1955 when she was succeeded by the present forelady Ethel Lambert, the daughter of Charles Dilley who joined the firm in 1913 and worked in it for more than fifty years.

In an era when there were no holidays for factory workers apart from the Bank holidays, the annual outing, when everyone was the guest of the firm, was an event looked forward to with some excitement. The twenty-second annual excursion took place on Monday, 10 July 1893: the meeting place was The New Inn, Park Street, Windsor. Tea was to be provided for the party and there is a reminder in the printed programme of 'Tea on Table at four o'clock'. The annual excursion or beanfeast on Monday, 3 July 1905, was a more enterprising affair. Train to Tilbury and by paddle-steamer to Margate. Dinner on table at one o'clock in a special dining room at the Terrace Hotel. The menu offered an amazing choice: joints—veal and ham pie, roast

[97]

beef, lamb and mint sauce or boiled leg of mutton and caper sauce. For sweets a choice of Christmas plum pudding, fruit tarts, custards or cabinet pudding. After the loyal toast and one verse of the national anthem, there followed a toast to the success of J. Curwen & Sons Ltd, proposed by A. W. Dixon, overseer of the letterpress machine room and replied to by John Spencer and Spedding Curwen. The 'Third Generation' was proposed by Sidney Barras and replied to by Kenneth Curwen, and the visitors proposed by A. Anderson and replied to by Alfred Sears, the conductor of the Curwen Caxton choir. Everything was supplied by the firm except, of course, alcoholic drinks. It was unthinkable that total abstinence could be disregarded even on an annual beanfeast.

An important social side of life at Curwen's was the existence of the Caxton Choral Society. The choirmaster was Alfred Sears who conducted at the Congregational Chapel in Balaam Street. There were more than fifty active singing members and they were so keen that they met for practice before starting work. Practice also took place in the garden of Mr Warne who was for many years responsible for maintenance at the works. Early morning meetings were very helpful when the choir was competing at the Stratford Musical Festival for they were able to devote adequate time to practising the 'test' pieces. As has been said the Caxton Choir was the star of the Stratford Festival at the beginning of the twentieth century. Three years in succession they won the Clarnico Challenge Shield which was competed for by commercial choirs. Spedding Curwen was president of the Caxton Choral Society and after the third successive victory he had the great happiness of seeing the shield presented to the Curwen singers by the Lord Chief Justice at Stratford Town Hall on 26 March 1904.

A rule book was given to every employee who was urged to 'study, remember and obey the Rules and Regulations which are drawn up for our mutual benefit'. The 1911 edition starts with a prayer 'At Morning'. This was to be read before starting a day's work; there is no evidence to show that the prayer was actually recited at any gathering of departmental groups. The prayer is by Robert Louis Stevenson* and provided, one supposes, some crumbs of comfort: 'The day returns and brings us the petty round of irritating concerns and duties. Help us to play the man, help us

*From a collection of prayers entitled '*Prayers written at Vailima*', 1904.

FIFTIETH
BEANFEAST
of
THE CURWEN PRESS
J. Curwen & Sons Ltd.

RYE HOUSE   **JUNE 29, 1925**

Contrast in styles. Programme for outing to Margate 1905 printed in
red, yellow, purple and brown. 1925 programme of simple design by
Harold Curwen

to perform them with laughter and kind faces, let cheerfulness abound with industry. Give us to go blithely on our business all this day, bring us to our resting beds weary and content and undishonoured and grant us in the end the gift of sleep.' After this followed a Samuel Smiles kind of introduction: 'If one of us wastes time or does work which is not his or her best, the prosperity not only of the firm but of all in its employ is injured. Further, in order that the pulse of the business may be felt effectively, a careful cost system, comprising accounts of all work done and time occupied, must be kept.' This note about cost accounting is evidence that the costing system devised by Harold Curwen, Spedding's youngest son, was being given the importance it merited. The Curwen system and the Hazell, Watson & Viney system formed the basis of the modern method of costing. The system used at Plaistow required much modification and it was not until June 1913 that Harold Curwen was able to announce that the firm was operating a costing system approved by the Master Printers Federation. The rest of the rule book follows the usual pattern of the times. Bad language, loitering, smoking and reading in the lavatories, throwing paper, rags, quoins, type or any other articles are strictly forbidden. All electric lights must be turned out when not required: evidence that gas lighting had been replaced fairly early by electricity. And, expectedly, there is a rule against bringing into the works intoxicating liquors.

Every working day a horse-drawn van left North Street carrying the orders required for the West End publishing office. Every day magic initials would be displayed in a window appealing to a railway company to call and pick up goods: L.N.W.R. for Lancashire and Glasgow, G.W.R. for Bristol, South Wales and the West Country and G.N.R. for the West Riding, Newcastle and Edinburgh. The despatch clerk had to know his geography and his railway map. J. Curwen & Sons' books went abroad in great numbers. Surprisingly large was a consignment of three-and-a-quarter tons of Sol-fa books destined for 'Kaffirs in South Africa'. There were dispatches to most countries in the world including Russia, Burma and China. Largely through missionaries, Sol-fa books, modulators and song sheets found their way from Plaistow to propagate the Tonic Sol-fa method in many languages in many lands on every continent.

XI

SPEDDING CURWEN'S
PROBLEMS

THE Caxton Choral Society and their successes made local news. There was something endearing about a firm of music printers who were able to provide music by their own talents. The Tonic Sol-fa Press had proved they had a talent for Tonic Sol-fa sight-reading as well as for Tonic Sol-fa printing. Spedding Curwen's gift for managing without people feeling they were being managed created an almost Utopian atmosphere in labour relations. It was, it was true, a kind of Victorian paternalism but unlike much paternalism at that time the Curwen variety was free from insincere patronage and had the merit of being acceptable. By 1900 there had emerged a solid core of devoted men and women whose workmanship could be relied upon and whose loyalty to the firm was unquestioned. Apart from girls leaving to get married it was rare for anyone to hand in their notice; in industrial terminology labour turnover was negligible.

Fringe benefits in 1900 were meagre: no paid holidays, just the eagerly anticipated annual outing, the Caxton Choral Society, a sick club and, at Christmas, a box of chocolates for the boys and girls and, for the men, a pound of Ridgway's Five O'Clock tea. A punctuality bonus at the annual rate of 25s for juniors and 50s for journeymen was a reward for those with a good record of prompt starting.

Music printing was being supplemented by a local trade of general printing. This was, as has already been stated, deliberate policy on the part of Spedding in an effort to free the printing business from being entirely dependent on the publishing. Besides offering a good service in letterpress printing, there was now

Cover of *Approved Songs*, typography influenced by Art Nouveau

lithographic printing. During Spedding's management, the business of The Curwen Press, both in letterpress and lithography, was sought by large numbers of people outside musical circles who were, in the main, attracted by the high grade of the work and the responsible service. The work was technically good for the times although very dull and entirely lacking enterprise in layout and design. Influence of Art Nouveau peeps through in the cover of *Approved Songs* illustrated on the opposite page. This was the sort of typographic design which was acceptable before there was any knowledge of the Arts and Crafts Movement. Those who might be attracted to placing their work with The Curwen Press were aided and indeed urged along by Mr H. W. Jones who had been engaged by Spedding and his manager, Sidney Barras, to act as a regular traveller. Mr Jones who was a well-known Southend yachtsman seems to have given satisfaction. He remained with the firm until 1916 when he joined the Royal Navy. After the war he emigrated to Australia, much to the relief of Harold Curwen who would have been reluctant to employ him again. The customers looked after by Mr Jones were, on the whole, requiring a type of work which The Curwen Press was in the process of shedding. Plaistow and the new areas of Silvertown and Custom House which had become heavily industrialized after the opening of the first of the Royal group of docks in 1880 were the hunting ground for new work. Brown and Polson, Ingham Clark (paint manufacturers), Jeyes Sanitary Compounds, Day and Martin (boot polish), Boake, Roberts (chemicals) and Bryant and May were some of the newly acquired customers for general printing. Account books and superbly constructed ledgers, often equipped with magnificent brass locks, were in steady demand in an age which had scarcely begun to keep commercial records on card index systems. J. Curwen & Sons were manufacturers of custom-made ledgers, supplying such large organizations as the Western Electric Company, Jenson and Nicholson and West Ham Corporation Tramways. Edwin Truscott became an account-book maker of more than ordinary skill and, if these sort of things were collected, account-books by Truscott would be sought and treasured for their superb workmanship. The label pasted on the inside of front covers used up to 1914 and the Arts and Crafts inspired redesign by Harold Curwen are illustrated on page 119.

A technical stride forward was the installation in April 1906 of a 'Monotype' keyboard and caster. It was an early pattern and for a firm of the size of J. Curwen & Sons an enterprising acquisition. It meant that the firm had its own type foundry on the premises and could cast all sizes of type required for ordinary reading matter. At the time it was considered, and indeed was, a revolutionary change; however it must be said that the machines of that relatively early period were prone to continual and frustrating stoppages and lacked the mechanical perfection of the splendid 'Monotype' machines in use today. It was, however, an aid to more economic production and it was a release from drudgery to find that after pages of type had been printed they could be thrown into a bin and the metal remelted for further use. It put an end to the seemingly endless and costly business of distributing by hand each individual piece of type back into the type-cases. Henceforth only display types and typefounders' type (not cast on the premises) needed to be distributed piece by piece.

The first 'Monotype' caster had a long life and was not finally taken out of service until 1934. In twenty-eight years it must have had most of its moving parts renewed, but that it lasted so long was due to the high standards of maintenance practised at Plaistow by Mr Warne and Mr Glass who were both exceptional mechanical engineers. In 1906 the various catalogues required by the publishing side were sufficient in volume to justify the 'Monotype'. These catalogues were heavy double column settings and could be anything from 16 to 128 pages of Crown quarto. The catalogues and music setting formed a solid background of work for the composing room and made the firm able, later on, to undertake the commercial catalogues and bookwork which were eventually to rival music.

In 1906, the year in which the 'Monotype' was purchased, John Spencer Curwen was fifty-nine and Joseph Spedding fifty-six. Spencer Curwen had two daughters and one son, John Patric. It was hoped that Patric Curwen would join J. Curwen & Sons but Spencer was doomed to disappointment. Patric was determined to be an actor and towards the end of his successful career worked in broadcasting becoming famous as compere of a popular programme called 'Those were the Days'.

Spedding Curwen had three sons and a daughter. The eldest son, Kenneth, born in 1881, later directed the publishing side; the second, Robert, did not go into the business; for reasons of health he decided to live in Kenya and farmed there for the rest of his

JOHN CURWEN

JOHN SPENCER CURWEN

life. The youngest son, Harold Spedding, was born at Upton House in 1885.

Educating the young Curwen boys was a problem for Spencer and Spedding Curwen. Public schools were the training ground for the Establishment and their religious offices were that of the Church of England. Spencer and Spedding did not want their children to conform and they placed no value on the social advantages which public schools were supposed to give. J. H. Badley, the founder of Bedales School, had much to approve of in the English public school but there were weak points among which were an excessive devotion to games, a narrow range of classical curriculum little adapted, he considered, to modern needs and a training based on the traditions of a governing class.* In October 1889 Cecil Reddie opened at Rocester in Derbyshire the New School Abbotsholme. It was the first of the 'new' public schools and J. H. Badley was a member of the original staff. Abbotsholme was a daring experiment embracing very English ideals of social fairness which had the support of Edward Carpenter, a Derbyshire neighbour famous for his philosophy that brain and handwork should be combined. The school also had the enthusiastic support of Spencer and Spedding Curwen. All four young Curwens were educated at Abbotsholme. J. H. Badley writes,

The day's occupations were so well varied that no one could fail to find interest in some if not in all of them; and working together as we did, there was more comradeship than of authority and obedience. They were a fine set of boys, of less conventional type and upbringing than most of those in a public school; for only parents who thought for themselves and wanted something more than the usual training would have chosen a school in which there was so much that, in those days, was strange and untried.†

Spencer and Spedding Curwen were advocates of educational experiment and the New School Abbotsholme was exactly what they were looking for. Social pretension and worship of the Establishment had little appeal for the Curwen family. Kenneth Curwen was at Abbotsholme from 1895 to 1899. He went on to New College, Oxford and, after taking his degree in 1902, joined his father and uncle in the family business. Harold followed his brothers to Abbotsholme in 1899. He had no interest

---

*Bedales, a Pioneer School, by J. H. Badley: Methuen & Co. Ltd, 1923.
†Memories and Reflections, by J. H. Badley: George Allen & Unwin, 1955.

H

in the usual organized games which were taken so seriously in ordinary public schools. At Abbotsholme he was able to participate in a variety of practical work. He became a good cabinet-maker and metal-worker and he found it pleased him to master craft skills. The new school was steering him towards the Arts and Crafts movement and he was beginning to feel that honest workmanship and beauty in everyday life was something worthwhile. Throughout his career he was in revolt against shoddy manufacture and a dreary workshop life where not how well a thing could be done but how profitably was too often the only criterion.

William Morris was the nineteenth-century high priest of the revolt against industrial ugliness; by practical example he showed how care in design and excellence of workmanship could bring beauty to things in everyday use. Morris turned his attention to furniture making, to weaving curtains and carpets, chair coverings and wallpapers, to pottery and last of all to the printing of books.

Anything relevant to printing was of interest to Harold Curwen and he was to find inspiration and standards of quality in the work of William Morris and his disciples. Lecturing in Manchester in 1862, Morris spoke of the need in everyday life of what are called the minor arts,

the kind which we may think of as co-operative art and which when it is genuine gives your great man, be he never so great, the peaceful and beautiful surroundings, and the sympathetic audience which he justly thinks he has a right to. . . . Great minds need no slaves to rule over, but rather fellow-workmen whom they can help and be helped by. So I say that the decorative arts are as necessary to our life as civilized men as the more strictly intellectual arts are, and that which have become our end and aim—the new birth of popular art, as on the one hand it is a most arduous, so on the other it is a most worthy undertaking.

Again there is encouragement for Harold Curwen, the new recruit to the Arts and Crafts movement, in William Morris's paper on 'The Ideal Book' read before the Bibliographical Society in June 1893. It is a plea for simplicity and sensible proportion,

I lay it down, first, that a book quite unornamented can look actually and positively beautiful, and not merely un-ugly, if it be, so to say, architecturally good, which by the by need not add much to its price (since it costs no more to pick up pretty stamps than ugly ones) and the taste and forethought that goes to the proper setting, position, and so on, will soon grow into an habit if cultivated and will not take up much of the master-printer's time when taken with his other necessary business.

What Morris was preaching on popular art and printing was basically the approach of the devoted men and women in the Arts and Crafts movement and, a little later, had a powerful influence in shaping the aims of the Design and Industries Association. To a schoolboy at Abbotsholme it was an open challenge to take a hand in doing things better and turning drab manufacturing into something worthwhile. In printing it offered a chance of producing work which was utilitarian, carefully planned, pleasant to look at and informed by a well balanced judgement.

When Harold left Abbotsholme he must have felt that the printing produced at North Street had, from a design point of view, little to recommend it. It fell far short of his ideals. But he was shy and diffident and possessed of the natural modesty which seems part of the make-up of good craftsmen; it would be unthinkable to propose anything new until he had mastered all the various printing skills. It is clear that the revolution at The Curwen Press began at Abbotsholme. The extent of the revolution, the new simplicity in design, can be gauged by comparing on page 99 the front of the programme for the outing to Margate in 1905 with the front page of the outing to Rye House in 1925: the pre-Harold compared with the Harold eras.

Harold Curwen left school in 1903 and until he started full time at Plaistow the intervening years were devoted to intensive training. The school having developed his interest in good workmanship, he realized that to be a good workman, it was essential to study every aspect of his craft and get down to the grass roots. Printing was obviously going to be his field of work. Sensibly, after leaving school, he spent three years training and learning before becoming a full-time worker on the Curwen Press strength.

Although neither Spencer nor Spedding could make any personal contribution to printing design, they were ready to support new ideas and when Harold revolutionized Curwen printing giving it an entirely new look, neither father nor uncle stood in his way. Harold was lucky; he did not have to battle, as often happens in a family firm, against a built-in resistance to anything new. Provided financial prudence was not undermined and provided everyone who worked for the firm was treated with

[107]

kindness and respect, change would not be opposed. Financial prudence and thoughtfulness for others were qualities with which Harold was generously endowed.

As his first stage in training Harold spent just over a year in the various departments of the North Street works. Then in 1906 he went to Leipzig and had nearly a year with Oscar Brandstetter, the famous music printers visited by his father and elder brother in 1895. Brandstetters were a large firm and their organization and methods of production made a great impression. But they were not leaders in the field of design and were no better than the German run of the mill which was generally heavy and ugly and what was worse, in Harold's estimation, so often illegible with the common use of Fraktur, the conventional German black letter or 'Gothic'. In those days it was still a national custom for books and pamphlets to be set in German Gothic; its use as a letter form even extended to handwriting. The ability to write in Fraktur was in itself a *tour de force* but to English eyes almost indecipherable. This early German experience confirmed Harold's belief that the essential thing about printing was that it should be legible. Speaking at Derby twelve years later, he puts his views eloquently: 'Printers have a great responsibility in that with equal facility their presses can turn out well designed things which are a pleasure both to the workers who make them and to all who use them, or shoddy badly designed things which do not fulfil their purpose well and degrade everyone who makes or uses them.'

The following year, 1907, was important in Harold's educational progress: he became a student of Edward Johnston at the Central School of Arts and Crafts. Johnston taught calligraphy and brought to his students a refreshing new interest in the beauty of handwriting and type design. The influence of Edward Johnston was enormous and Harold became one of his most dedicated pupils. The lessons he learnt from his great teacher underlined the necessity of bringing simplicity and beauty into everyday printing and of giving legibility pride of place. Later Harold was to design a sans serif alphabet, in capitals and lower case which can hold its own with Edward Johnston's 'Underground' sans serif and the immensely popular Gill 'sans'. Curwen sans serif is still in the composing room and still admired and in current use.

Harold Curwen joined J. Curwen & Sons Ltd in 1908, being employed on a full time basis at the works in Plaistow. In that year there appeared in *The British Printer* an account of 'Curwens'—Music Printers. Plaistow is described as the most aggressively manufacturing suburb of London. They go on to say, with perhaps some flattery,

that the establishment is eminently self-contained and to include within its scope modern equipment and suitable accommodation for a variety of letterpress work—ranging from general jobbing, magazines and catalogues to music printing; lithography, anything from small to large; commercial bookbinding; stereotyping; and the manufacture of litho specialties, foremost being 'Liasine'.*

The composing room is similar to many others but distinctive in its music work, and it is vastly interesting to see the setting and distribution of staff notation and Sol-fa type. The members of the staff are experts and the ease with which the intricate music scores are put up, including direct transposition from one to the other system, is impressive alike to the music lover and the printer observer.

The Curwen music compositors—the elite—always attracted a visitor's attention. *The British Printer* says that they examined a variety of specimens which showed that a capital standard was maintained throughout; tastefully produced catalogues and price lists and excellent labels and small posters. It is doubtful if Harold Curwen would agree to the productions being described as tasteful and excellent. In actual fact, The Curwen Press at the time of this glowing account was going through a period which was giving Spencer and Spedding deep anxiety. Turnover was uncomfortably static and in the year ending May 1909 there was a fall in profit which while not great was nevertheless sufficent to be slightly alarming.

Spencer Curwen's second daughter, Mary, was married to Selwyn Grant, an electrical engineer and a business man concerned in important enterprises among which, it is believed, was the provision of an electric tramway system for Athens. He was asked by his father-in-law to find out how the business was doing and to suggest any changes which might be advantageous. Selwyn Grant's report is reproduced in part and shows that the problems of running a printing business in the first decade of the century are little different from those of today.

*A substance for erasing the image off lithographic stones.

31 Glenloch Road, Hampstead, N.W.
24 October 1909

Dear Father and Uncle Spedding,

I am afraid I have been sitting on the Company's accounts for a terribly long while, but I have hardly had an opportunity of giving them serious attention since our talk at Woburn Square.

You must understand in the first place that I do not claim any special knowledge of accounts, but I have some commercial experience and have thought that an entirely fresh view of the position from a source outside the Company might be of assistance to you.

The accounts are rather complicated, and I must say that it requires a good deal of study to form a clear impression of how the business is doing. I took the Profit and Loss accounts first and simplified them in my own way by putting both Berners Street and Plaistow in one account and omitting Stock entries. The latter I know it is not strictly correct to do, but, for reasons which will be explained, I think the figures thus obtained to be of some value, and accordingly give the main headings below:

Year	1903/4	1904/5	1905/6	1906/7	1907/8	1908/9
Sales at Berners St	£24,048	23,756	24,391	24,838	23,997	24,119
Printing for Customers	4,445	5,512	4,833	6,958	6,395	6,935
Hire of Band Parts and Sundries	431	500	498	532	541	764
Rentals: Berners St and Plaistow	347	224	290	162	321	329
TOTAL RECEIPTS	£29,271	29,992	30,012	32,490	31,254	32,147

From this table several things are at once obvious. The first is that the receipts are almost stationary, while expenses have increased; and the second that it is only in the last year (ending 31st May last) that there has been any marked falling-off in profits.

The table gives you a comparison of the main divisions of receipts and expenditure during the last six years. You will note especially that

1. Sales at Berners Street are where they were six years ago.
2. Printing for customers increased rapidly up to 1907 but has since remained stationary.
3. The cost of paper and materials was disproportionately high last year.
4. Wages at Plaistow and printing put out have increased very seriously without much increase in business.
5. The same applies to Advertising and Travellers.
6. Stationery and Postage &c. shows a large decrease.

[110]

Year	1903/4	1904/5	1905/6	1096/7	1907/8	1908/9
Paper and Materials	£4,199	4,983	4,173	4,929	4,783	5,276
Wages at Plaistow and printing put out	6,640	7,279	6,829	7,551	7,732	8,267
Wages and Salaries at Berners St	1,983	2,023	2,256	2,419	2,456	2,430
Stationery and Postage &c.	2,027	2,150	2,039	2,082	1,138	928
Goods bought &c.	1,649	1,278	1,345	1,493	1,372	1,484
Advertising and Travellers	1,731	1,723	1,930	2,374	2,169	2,688
Royalties on Sales	747	578	854	793	646	823
Rents, Rates and Taxes, and Repairs	1,258	1,301	1,262	1,344	1,352	1,660
Management and Directors' Fees	2,259	2,381	2,430	2,302	2,350	2,808
Sundries	721	746	813	651	731	753
TOTAL EXPENSES	£23,214	24,442	23,931	25,938	24,729	27,117
BALANCE	£6,057	5,550	6,081	6,552	6,525	5,030

I understand from Kenneth that the last item is not a saving but is to be explained by a different entry of prepaid postages in the books.

Now, what you want to do is obviously to increase receipts and keep down expenses, although I do not think that the bad results of one year are much cause for alarm, especially as that year was one of general trade depression. In respect of the receipts, all I can suggest at the moment is that special attention should be given to the Travellers. As regards expenditure, I will try to analyse some of the larger items in order to see if there is an opening for possible economies.

Before doing this I want to point out what seems to me a serious defect in your accounts, and that is that there is no way of knowing what printing for customers costs. *I consider it absolutely essential that separate accounts should be kept for this department of the business,* as if it pays, it is the one which can be most readily expanded, and, if it does not pay, you must take on less work at better prices. Further, *an accurate system of keeping works' costs should be immediately instituted,* in order to determine exactly what each and every job costs in wages and materials.

The whole system of your accounts is on the basis of Berners Street being merely a selling house, books being charged up to it at list prices less a discount (usually 45 per cent., I believe). In view of the fact that it is

Berners St which decides what is to be published, I consider this system radically wrong. It is absolutely essential that Berners St should know exactly how much or how little profit is being made on each publication, *and this can only be done by Plaistow charging up to Berners St the actual cost of production, as determined by a proper system of keeping works' costs, plus a fixed percentage for management and general charges.* I am quite sure that the results would be much better if the publishing department were in this way in closer touch with the works, as the one could no longer show a profit regardless of the other, but both would work together for the good of the business generally.

I do not propose to comment on the valuation of stock, the allowance for depreciation, or the Balance Sheet generally, as I could not do so properly without exhaustive examination of the Books.

With all diffidence, I should like to make one or two suggestions about Organization.

To start with, I was rather surprised to find that Uncle Spedding not only acts as Secretary to the Company, but also does the routine work of keeping the Books. From what I saw of the Books I believe he does this very well indeed, but, considering the interests of the Company broadly, I think it is a mistake that so much of his time should be given to work that could be done for him. I strongly believe it would be better to leave him more free to give attention to the larger interests, and especially to extend the 'Printing for Customers', which he only is qualified to do. I have already suggested verbally that you should appoint a Secretary to take some of the detail work off his shoulders, and I think you could make such an officer cost you nothing by including in his duties some of the work done by the present staff. I should have suggested Kenneth for the post, but it would probably not fit in with your intention that he should ultimately take charge of the Publishing department.

My other suggestion relates to the institution of a system of keeping works' costs. From what I hear of what Kenneth has done in the office, I believe he could do this excellently and propose that he should be transferred from the office to the works for a few weeks in order to set such a system going, which it might be part of Harold's duty to keep going. A modern card system is what you want, and Kenneth should make enquiries and read up the subject (I believe Garcke's 'Factory Accounts' is a standard book, but possibly not quite up to date).

I know too little about the organization of the business to be able to make any further suggestions, but probably all the rest is simply a question of efficient distribution of work.

Finally, I have found nothing to show that the business is not thoroughly sound and, as I have already said, do not consider one bad year to be great cause for alarm, although I think that no reason to delay making the reforms I have recommended and others which will doubtless occur to you.

I will take the first opportunity of sending back the papers to you. If you have occasion to have this letter typed I should like to have a copy.

Yours affectionately,

(sgd) SELWYN GRANT

The alarming disclosure in Selwyn Grant's report is the absence of any sound method of cost finding. It was impossible to tell what paid and what did not. For the publishing end it is clear that they paid too much for their successful editions and too little for anything issued in a small edition. It is remarkable how static the business was over the six year period: the highest total receipts being £32,490 and the lowest £29,271. It was a respectable business but scarcely a dynamic one.

Uncle Spedding is gently reproved for doing too much routine work and for acting as company secretary. And he receives advice which a line of subsequent Curwen directors have also received: he was urged to give attention to sales and exert himself to extend the 'Printing for Customers'. Selwyn Grant found the business sound but lacking in real progress. Evidently he did not consider the drop in profits for 1908–9 cause for worry.

The kind of printing done at Plaistow was to change enormously over the next fifty years. In 1906–7 music printing accounted for 76 per cent of total sales; the proportion was down to 6·5 per cent in 1956–7.

XII

ARTS AND CRAFT

HAROLD CURWEN had had, as he said, a first-class time both in and out of work hours in Leipzig. Modest and without conceit he was accepted at once by all the old faithfuls. There was indeed an agreeably easy atmosphere; the firm but genial rule of his father, Joseph Spedding, had made good nature the normal background to life at the North Street works. 'More like a printer's convalescent home' was the tersely expressed opinion of a journeyman on a visit from another firm.

The Arts and Crafts movement had a strong influence on Harold and from it he drew most of his ideas centred round the possible happiness which might come to men and women who were allowed and even encouraged to contribute towards doing good and useful work. In his opinion a printing works should be a happy place, providing a kind of second home where the day's work could be positively enjoyed. This was probably considered Utopian stuff in those days but it would be unfair to write it off. It was, indeed, forward looking and anticipated modern management where the more intelligent executives understand the value of participation and work enrichment.

There were difficulties to be overcome. Among highly skilled craftsmen, many of whom had served the firm for most of a working lifetime, there was a natural mistrust of change. Visual appreciation was almost non-existent and far from anyone being influenced by the Arts and Crafts movement, it is unlikely anybody had ever heard of it. The printing of the Kelmscott Press, the work of Emery Walker and Cobden-Sanderson at the Doves Press and the calligraphy of Edward Johnston were almost certainly, as far as Plaistow was concerned, unknown except to Harold Curwen. The training at Leipzig had made him respectful of the work of the great men of the private presses and to the beautifully formed calligraphy and lettering of Johnston. Bringing visual awareness to The Curwen Press was an uphill task needing a lot of determination. He reports to Abbotsholme Old Boys' Club that he is 'nice and busy printing music in the daytime, and after hours he devotes his time to scouting, pictorial photography and anything else that turns up'.

Scouting was a serious business and was Harold's way of following the example of his Curwen grandfather, father and uncle of actively helping less fortunate members of the community. Some present Curwen staff and pensioners recall that during the first world war the entrance lobby in North Street (then used for packing and dispatch) was appropriated on certain evenings of the week by Scoutmaster Harold Curwen and his troop. In 1911 Harold Curwen wrote in *The Old Abbotsholmian* (vol. III, no. II) an article called 'Old Abbotsholmians as Scout-masters'. It was a plea for old boys to take up scouting, claiming that the Abbotsholmian education was precisely that required for the vocation. The article takes up three pages and its earnestness would have pleased the Revd John Curwen:

Character-building, which is our chief aim, can best be achieved by example during games and work. What finer lead can you give a boy than to help him to do a kind act to somebody every day? Surely this is the essence of all religion and the firmest foundation for the building up of character. The spirit of fair play on which Englishmen pride themselves is unfortunately only too rare amongst the poorer boys, and they do not know 'how to play' and 'to play the game'. Thus, in nearly all their games, they become a shouting rabble, and finally, getting no enjoyment out of playing themselves, they give it up and devote their time instead to looking on at paid gladiators. Here is your chance; get together a number of these boys, drill them a little, but briskly, teach them hobbies, and, last but not least, teach them 'how to play'.

The collection of type faces and decorative material in the composing room before 1914 was as uninviting as could be found anywhere. Precisely what Joseph Thorp in his *Printing for Business** called a chamber of horrors. Only Monotype Old Style and the Sol-fa founts could, in default of anything better, confer some grace, however scant, on a printed page. The display types,

* *Printing for Business* by Joseph Thorp: John Hogg, 1919.

especially the fancy display founts, can only be described as grotesque. Who can identify Gresham, Victoria, Hawarden (stipple) or Edina? Specimens of these letters, which in all innocence disfigured so many pamphlets, labels, broadsides and items of stationery, are reproduced below.

Don't flatter
£&12 HIE

Don't flatter
£ & 12345

DON'T FLATTER Y
£ & 12 HIEROG

DᵒN'T FLATTᴱ & 12

Display types from J. Curwen & Sons Ltd. Type List, 1911
Reading from top, Hawarden (stipple),
Victoria, Edina and Gresham

Harold Curwen, the master craftsman and practical man, had to begin at the beginning and before devoting most of his working day to arranging printing was obliged to tackle the basic problem of finding a workable cost-finding system, a need that was strongly recommended in Selwyn Grant's report referred to in the previous chapter. The disposal of the awful collection of type would have to wait until a new costing system was seen to be effective and the firm judged to be sufficiently strong to endure a typographic revolution in its composing room.

It was proposed in the Selwyn Grant report that Kenneth Curwen should ask Harold to review the existing system of cost recording and see where it could be improved. It might even need superseding. This difficult task was handed over to Harold and by 1911 a costing system had been evolved and introduced which was not different in essentials from the system which became officially recommended by the Federation of Master Printers.

Harold made a start on his plans for improving design by redesigning the firm's letterheadings and then turned his attention to the covers of the Action Songs published by Kenneth Curwen from Berners Street. A devoted pupil of Edward Johnston, he decided that what his master called formal writing with a broad nib should replace sign-writers' commercial on Action Song covers. Formal handwriting of great beauty could be done quickly and was easy to reproduce by lithographic printing. It is difficult to date exactly when the change was made but it must have been just before the first world war. Henry Ball, a gifted calligrapher and former pupil of Johnston, was engaged to do the work and was responsible for pen-lettering all the Action Song covers for more than twenty years. Henry Ball's calligraphy was embellished by designs relevant to the song's title and various artists were employed. The cover reproduced on page 94 shows this calligraphy with an embellishment by Aldo Cosomati. The designs were often coloured by simple stencilling: this was economical as the Action Song series were usually printed in small editions of 500 to 1,000 copies. The new cover designs had the approval of Kenneth Curwen who, after the death of Spedding Curwen in November 1919, became chairman of the firm.

Although the new ideas in design had Kenneth's general support, he took no active part in their development. He had his hands full with the publishing, and his enterprise in this field brought much distinction to J. Curwen & Sons. Kenneth added

to the Curwen catalogue many works by contemporary composers and there was a continuous stream of educational music
and songs for choirs and clubs. The contribution made by the
third generation of Curwens was not entirely confined to the
printing side of the business.

Harold Curwen was made a director of the firm in 1911; he
was by then in fact, if not by official appointment, managing the
Press; the act of confirmation was deferred by Uncle Spencer
until 1914. In the decade before the first war the early endeavours
of a printing renaissance were beginning to take shape. The
renaissance, microscopic though it was, was noticed with pleasure
by the small body of admirers of fine printing which the private
presses had created. In those early days there was no career for a
professional typographer; the word was unknown and at most a
person might be recognized as being an arranger of type: to
Harold type arranging was a part, indeed an important part, of
his daily work.

There was, before 1910, little contact between the private
presses and the general printing trade. The bridging of the gulf
was due in large measure to Emery Walker.* Walker was the
man whose influence caused William Morris to start the Kelmscott Press and it was Walker who was its practical genius. After
Morris died and the Kelmscott Press came to an end, Walker
with Cobden-Sanderson founded the Doves Press. The simple
beauty and technical excellence of Doves Press books did a great
deal to make people realize that a printed book, if well made,
could be beautiful and treasured for its good workmanship.

Emery Walker was a learned, modest and generous man,
always ready to help any serious young printers by putting at their
disposal his great store of knowledge. As the real genius of
Kelmscott, partner in the Doves Press, printing consultant to St
John Hornby and the Ashendene Press, and adviser to the
German Insel Verlag, he was held in the greatest respect by the
pioneers of the printing renaissance. Harold Curwen did his best
to follow his advice which favoured close spacing between words,
the abolition of large white gaps after full stops, generous margins,
legible, unfussy type and a firm impression with stiff black ink on
decent paper. These were excellent precepts, but difficult to put

*Sir Emery Walker, 1851–1933, founder with Walter Crane of the Arts & Crafts
Society.

[118]

Redesigned label for account books.
Top 1900–11, *bottom* Harold Curwen's new style 1912

[119]

into daily practice without careful training of the composing room staff. Harold did in the end establish a routine which would have earned Emery Walker's approval, but it took time. An attractive booklet on calculating machines printed in Plaistow in about 1917 is admirable apart from the huge white spaces after full stops—the 'mutton quad' instead of the thin or mid space according to Walker principles. The result is a weakening of the page and an appearance running contrary to Harold's own belief in strong, forceful printing.

In January 1913 appeared the first issue of *The Imprint*, a journal of the printing renaissance launched by Gerard Meynell and competently printed by his Westminster Press in Harrow Road, London. It had a four man editorial team consisting of Ernest Jackson, lithographer, J. H. Mason, former compositor and pressman of the Doves Press, Edward Johnston, calligrapher and teacher at the Central School of Arts and Crafts and Gerard Meynell, master-printer and one of the pioneers in the printing revival. A special type was cut on the initiative of Gerard Meynell by the Lanston Monotype Company (later the Monotype Corporation) and was aptly christened Imprint Old Face. In their opening note the editors, after wishing subscribers and supporters a year of happiness, go on to say 'we will diligently search out things of beauty that can be printed and hope to give joy for ever thereby. We open with a bright message, which may also serve as the motto of *The Imprint*. "Glad Dawn" by Blake, is reproduced as an earnest of our ideals.' 'Glad Dawn' appears as a frontispiece, not altogether happily, to the first article graced by *The Imprint* headline beautifully written by Edward Johnston. The first article called 'Art and Workmanship' by Professor W. R. Lethaby gave enormous encouragement to those in the printing trade who were ready to hoist the flag of the renaissance. 'Art', writes Lethaby, 'is not a special sauce applied to ordinary cooking; it is the cooking itself if it is good. Most simply and generally art may be thought of as the well-doing of what needs doing.' To this kind of thinking Harold Curwen wanted to listen; it was free of fancy talk and stated the case simply; a case which many thoughtful people in industry would subscribe to today.

The Curwen Press took a full page advertisement in the first number of *The Imprint*. It is beautifully set in Caslon Old Face and might be called the Plaistow manifesto:

[120]

JOSEPH SPEDDING CURWEN

HAROLD CURWEN

OLIVER SIMON WITH HIS WIFE, RUTH

Harold Curwen of The Curwen Press has studied under one of the editors of this Magazine*, as well as under other leaders of the movement for improving the style of commercial printing. The staff of The Curwen Press has been trained so that it is able, with the present-day materials, to produce the best results in artistic and forceful Catalogues, Show Cards, Pamphlets, Labels, etc., and also in the printing and binding of beautiful books of every description. Mr Curwen requests permission to call at your address, or to send samples of his work executed at The Curwen Press, Plaistow, London, E.

Forceful and appropriate, sound and sensible were the watchwords for Harold Curwen and his Curwen Press staff. And it will be noted that the everyday needs of printing—the business printing gets pride of place. Book printing, of which the firm was capable, is mentioned almost as an afterthought. In Holbrook Jackson's view, 'one of the outstanding characteristics of the press was a recognition of the rights of all those ephemera of typography which are loosely grouped and summed up under the term "jobbing-printing". Harold Curwen abolished class distinction between the printing of books and miscellaneous printing. He said, in effect, for his pronouncements have been doing rather than saying: 'Printing is one and indivisible and it must please and serve or fail.'†

There was in the two or three years before the Great War, a stream of jobbing-printing that needed designing. The firm's stationery and labels had to show that Curwens practised what they preached. Harold explained his plans to the works and office staffs, thus making sure of their support. Without full understanding within the works and active participation, his revolution (typographic) would not have met with the success it did. Not everyone, of course, felt able to give support to new ideas in printing design which would lose the firm some of its customers and change in some degree long established routine. The manager, Sidney Barras, found he was out of sympathy with Harold Curwen; consequently he was given two months' notice, a parting gift of £300 and left the firm in November 1913. It was noted at the time that Mr Barras seemed unable to adapt himself to modern methods and lacked power in managing the staff. No new appointment was made immediately; Harold Curwen decided to take over the work himself.

*Edward Johnston.
†*The Printing of Books* by Holbrook Jackson: Cassell & Co. Ltd, 1938.

[121]

J

Long service was already a tradition before 1914. The composing room overseer, Mr Witty, died in February 1913, having started with the firm in 1867, four years after printing in North Street had begun in a cottage. His widow was paid full money for four weeks and then an annuity was bought for her to bring in £4 a year. There was, it appears, some delay in purchasing the annuity caused by Mrs Witty's sons not agreeing on how to help. In June, Mr George, the veteran binders' overseer had a cycle accident and was unable to work for six weeks; the firm continued to pay him his full money for four weeks. On 1 August 1914 Frank H. Brunwin was engaged in place of Mr Barras. He had held a similar managing appointment with Burroughs Wellcome & Co. who had their own printing department with about 200 employees. Brunwin took to Plaistow immediately and the firm took to him. He was to be their friend and wise helper for forty years; intensely loyal to The Curwen Press, he supported Harold Curwen and Oliver Simon through thick and thin and always fought hard to see that customers treated the firm with the respect which he, Brunwin, thought it deserved.

There is a laconic note by Harold Curwen dated 5 August 1914: WAR declared. War is not only written in capitals but is double underlined in red. The effect of war on industry was imponderable. As a precaution, following the advice of the Master Printers Federation, the entire staff was placed under two weeks' provisional notice. With their usual concern for the staff the directors went on to say 'our employees may rest assured that on the expiry of the said notice, we shall do what is in our power to do for them, by such measures as prudence dictates'. The uncertainty was very real and the orders for printing dropped during August by 50 per cent. Fortunately there was a steady recovery to 73 per cent by the end of October and by August 1915 the intake of work was 12·1 per cent up on the year before and Harold could report that 'in spite of war we are getting through with about 20 per cent reduction of staff quite well'. In May 1915 Brunwin asked for a reconsideration of his salary and was told that the firm was most satisfied with his work but would defer action until the accounts were out.

Rising costs were the order of the day; in November 1915 the figures in the West Ham Corporation contract were increased by 12½ per cent and by a further 7½ per cent in August 1916. The contract was for all printing needs of the West Ham Corporation

Tramways whose offices were in Greengate Street, less than five minutes walk from The Curwen Press. The tramways needed a great many kinds of printed forms, cheap fare bills, destination blinds, bound account books and, on occasions, emergency supplies of tram tickets.

In November 1916 Harold Curwen was appointed to the Union House committee of the London Master Printers Association. He was ready to give his services as he hoped to influence the establishment of a composite organization to include capital, management and labour. But nothing came of it and although always loyal to the Association he withdrew from committee work. He was, it will be seen, making an attempt to fuse into coherent co-operation the three main interests (a fourth is the customer) in manufacturing industry. It is still held to be a desirable goal by forward-looking leaders in manufacturing and commerce.

Early in 1916 H. W. Jones, the full-time traveller, left to take a commission in the Royal Navy Motor Boat Reserve. The Press was left without a regular representative during the second half of the 1914–18 war; a Calthorpe motor-cycle was purchased and used by Harold Curwen and Brunwin for dashing out to visit customers. Spencer Curwen installed himself in Harold's office on one occasion. He cross-examined Brunwin, asking if he thought the works were well-managed and efficient. Truthfulness and loyalty to Harold produced answers that were reassuring. When told of his uncle's visit, Harold commented 'he is just a silly old policeman'.

By Christmas 1917 The Curwen Press was so full of work that it was agreed to make up the two-day holiday by working the hours lost at a later date to be paid, of course, at time and a half. The war was gradually draining away the younger men. Some volunteered for army service in 1914–15 and, when the Derby scheme was launched, men of military age attested. Harold, whose attitude to war was similar to the Society of Friends, served in the Special Police and also continued with his dedicated work as a Scoutmaster.

The shortage of staff was severe but it did not stop technical progress and endeavour to increase manufacturing efficiency. A general replanning of the works began in 1916 and was completed by January 1917.

The development of offset-litho took much of Harold's time

and that of Charles Dilley* who joined the firm in 1913 as an expert in printing by the offset method. Inks gave a lot of trouble and as so many proved fugitive all ink had to be tested by controlled exposure to light. Eventually a standard range of colours emerged but not before the firm's reputation with ink makers was slightly tarnished. The Curwen Press was considered to be far too fussy. Ink for taking transfers from engraved pewter plates was found to be unsatisfactory; after much experiment a formula was arrived at by boiling a mixture of soap, mutton suet, shellac and carbon black. The smell given off was pungent and so obnoxious that boilings, after much complaining, were only allowed to take place after working hours. Even so, there was a generation who could remember the awful smell of this Plaistow brew. There is no record of what local residents thought of the smell they had to endure after the works were closed.

*Charles Dilley started at Plaistow, October 1913 and retired in November 1964.

XIII

DESIGN AND INDUSTRY

It is a revelation to find that a Ministry of Art was being advocated as early as November 1914. The Great War had brought home to many people the lead that Germany held in most branches of industrial art. Now, with the sea routes closed to Germany, it was felt it was Britain's opportunity to assert herself. In a contribution* to the Journal of the Imperial Arts League, A. Lys Baldry summarizes German progress:

they [the Germans] created a powerful association of artists, traders and officials—directors of museums, public galleries, and so on. They broke down the opposition of the commercial men, who had, as we have, an insufficient understanding of the practical importance of art . . . they initiated a regular campaign for the education of the public by means of lectures, exhibitions, lantern slide displays, and other devices by which the attention of people of all classes could be arrested. The outcome of all this activity has been an enormous growth in the efficiency and earning power of German industrial art.

Mr Baldry's warning did not fall on deaf ears.

In March 1915 an exhibition, organized by the Board of Trade was held at Goldsmith's Hall. In it was shown what was considered best in a wide range of German industrial goods. In the main they were in the group known as 'consumer durables'. 'The objects', as A. Clutton Brock pointed out in his review of the exhibition in *The Times* of 3 April 1915, 'have been carefully chosen to show that the Germans had learnt from us all that we had to teach, and had put it already to better uses than their

*Reprinted in July 1915 by the Design & Industries Association in their pamphlet *A New Body with New Aims*.

[125]

teachers have done.' In Clutton Brock's estimation, the English revival in printing had far more commercial effect in Germany than in England. This was a lamentable fact. Emery Walker and Edward Johnston had both been engaged, long before the war, to advise and give practical assistance to important firms in German publishing and printing.

A sequel to the exhibition at Goldsmith's Hall was the foundation, in May 1915, of the Design & Industries Association (D.I.A.). It was not then, and never has been, a large association and it has always been woefully short of money, but the evangelism of its members has been infectious and its influence much greater than any founding member could have imagined. The *Aims* booklet, published in August 1915, a narrow Crown octavo, unadorned and pleasantly composed in Caslon old face, was well printed by Stevens & Son of Leicester and probably done at the expense of Harry Peach, an original and untiring expounder of D.I.A. common-sense. The booklet, which bears the marks of being designed by Emery Walker and B. J. Fletcher, then principal of the Leicester School of Art, stood out above the rut of contemporary job-printing and by virtue of its good manners was the best possible advertisement for the D.I.A. cause. Its aims were very similar to the aims of Harold Curwen. Good, thoughtful design, technical excellence and economic production was the recipe for more all round satisfaction and—most important to merchants and manufacturers—for a greater volume of sales. The official D.I.A. statement put it this way: 'Sound design is not only an essential to technical excellence, but furthermore it tends towards economy in production: the first necessity of sound design is FITNESS FOR USE. Modern industrial methods, and the great possibilities in the machine, demand the best artistic no less than the best mechanical and scientific abilities.'

There were 200 foundation members of the D.I.A. and Harold Curwen was one of them. In the original membership ten printers are listed among whom was Fred P. Phillips, the founder of the Baynard Press and a man who shared closely Curwen's views. The two firms were to become friendly rivals in the provision of commercial printing which tried to be fit for its purpose. The rivalry was, indeed, so friendly that the two firms shared a stand at a Printing Exhibition held at Olympia in the early twenties.

A comforting attraction of the Design & Industries Association lay in its ability to bring together a group of artists, craftsmen, business men and industrial producers and give them an opportunity for discussion and exchange of ideas. This sort of participation was important and to it can be traced the foundation of many personal friendships. Pioneers are inclined to feel isolated and an association gives them the luxury of occasional preaching to the converted. Furthermore members were inclined to employ the talents of other members when need or opportunity arose. If a D.I.A. member wanted some cane furniture for the verandah he might go to Harry Peach; similarly for furnishing dining room or study, who better to approach than Mr (later Sir) Ambrose Heal; and for beautifully coloured, fadeless textiles there was always James Morton and his Sundour Fabrics. In printing patronage Sir Kenneth Anderson, chairman of the Orient Line, was faithful to Fred Phillips; Frank Pick, the general manager of the Underground Railways and already famous for the posters he commissioned from modern artists, favoured The Curwen Press. It was a pleasant feature of early D.I.A. days to have this mixture of loyalty and mutual aid.

It has to be remembered that the new Association was born during the Great War, a fact which prevented many becoming original members who would certainly have joined if they had been free to do so. To be able to muster as many as 200 original members shows that there was a deep dissatisfaction with industry's relations to designers and craftsmen.

Among original D.I.A. members there was one who was to have enormous influence on The Curwen Press. In the list of members published in August 1915 an entry reads: THORP, Joseph, Journalist and Printing Consultant. Either Harold invited Thorp to act as a consultant and begetter of sales or, as is more probable, it was the other way round, with Thorp taking the initiative. However it came about, it was a blood transfusion that was altogether timely; the new consultant had the ability to talk exuberantly and colourfully and expound, to all who would listen, what The Curwen Press was trying to do. Joseph Thorp was a born persuader and could also claim considerable title for offering himself to The Curwen Press. At one time Thorp had ambitions for becoming a member of a religious order, but this did not last for long. He decided on a secular career and joined the staff of the Catholic publishing firm, the Art & Book Company

[127]

of London. In 1903 Joseph Thorp was posted to Leamington Spa to help his firm's Arden Press which was going through difficult times. The printing works was managed by Bernard Newdigate. It was decided to close the press at Leamington and start a firm also called the Arden Press in Letchworth Garden City. Amongst Thorp's many friends was Emery Walker whom he introduced to Bernard Newdigate. As usual, Walker helped Newdigate most generously. Financial aid was badly needed by the Arden Press and once again Thorp's wide circle of friends and acquaintances came to the rescue. Thorp knew St John Hornby, the head of W. H. Smith & Sons, and persuaded him to take over the Arden Press. Bernard Newdigate, as a consequence, became a member of the huge W.H.S. organization and worked with them for six years until the outbreak of war in 1914. Thorp was a great help to the Arden Press and became self-appointed adviser on design to the whole of the W. H. Smith & Sons group. He had the good sense not only to talk design but to show that it was important from a sales point of view. Thorp, therefore, had real experience behind him when, as a fellow D.I.A. enthusiast, he began to help Harold Curwen and the Press to find its new and wider audience.

One of Thorp's first acts was to persuade Harold to acquire a printer's device or trademark. A unicorn was chosen. This mythical animal was supposed to have great strength and be an uncommonly hard fighter, and therefore a suitable symbol for Harold's plans for producing what he called courageous and forceful printing. On the advice of Thorp, Paul Woodroffe, a fine craftsman in stained glass and an expert in lettering, was consulted. Woodroffe had been a contemporary of Newdigate at Stonyhurst School who introduced him to the work of Emery Walker and the beauty of Caslon Old Face type. Woodroffe's work which had a distinctly Arts & Crafts Society flavour also had a 'fitness for purpose' which commended it to members of the newly established Design & Industries Association. The first unicorn commissioned by The Curwen Press was designed by Paul Woodroffe, the first of a whole species. It says much for the excellence of the first design that it is still very much alive after fifty years (see p. 196).

Harold Curwen was bound to be more and more involved in the Design & Industries Association. In February 1918 Harold Stabler, the distinguished silversmith, and director of Carter,

Stabler & Adams the potters of Poole, and Hamilton Smith for years a pillar of Heal & Son, proposed Harold for the council and he was duly elected.

More individuals and businesses were taking an interest in the appearance of their printing and this kept Harold more and more closely tied to Plaistow. He needed Joseph Thorp to expound his ideas effectively and continually. Harold felt unable to make much use of the lecture platform but when he did speak what he had to say was always an honest expression of his views. It was unaffected good sense; but unlike Thorp who was a gay and colourful speaker, Harold droned along in his flat voice which did not help to hold the attention of his listeners.

Speaking in 1919 at the opening of an Exhibition of Printing at Derby* organized by the D.I.A., Harold declared,

the Association stands for the belief that industrial unrest is largely due to the accepted aim of working for personal gain rather than to make some thing, or supply some service in the best possible way for the good of the community. Where there is scope for pride in doing a job well, there is nearly always enjoyment or, at least, absence of boredom . . . and not only this, for if the aim is to design and make a thing perfectly fitted for its intended use, almost certainly it takes on a constructional beauty more satisfying far than so-called decoration of an ill-designed and shoddy thing. I want, indeed, to press home that it is not merely beauty of sound construction for its own sake that we aim at, but also the resultant satisfaction to both maker and user.

This sort of philosophy for business was rare over fifty years ago and can easily be dismissed as too idealistic; but it is difficult for anyone who has worked in industry and has had factory-floor experience to question its validity. Sound, honest manufacture produced a happy work-team, was good for the customer and good for the profit and loss account. This last consideration was a very real one for Kenneth and Harold Curwen; it seemed clear to them that the best way to safeguard their business was to publish good music and produce honest, decently designed printing.

Curwen had to produce 'the goods' which the ebullient Joseph Thorp was to publicize. During the early years of his management at Plaistow, a good beginning had been made. There was his design of Curwen sans serif completed in 1911 but

*For full text of Curwen's speech at Derby, May 1919 see appendix A.

not cast in type until 1928. The matrices from which the type was cast were engraved by Messrs Bannerman of Wood Green. A more successful type design was the Curwen Poster type. It was completed before the end of the Great War and registered with the Patent Office on 30 May 1919 for a period of five years; an extension of copyright for a further five years was granted on 17 May 1924. It was given a first public showing in a booklet written by Joseph Thorp extolling the work of Harold Curwen and his printing press. In Curwen Poster type thin lines have been eliminated and it has the sturdy proportions needed for reading at a distance. The type is one of the best seriffed letters for poster work that has been produced. Designed by Harold Curwen with the help of H. K. Wolfenden, it is given a splendid showing on a

Curwen Poster type, designed 1918–19

pull-out sheet in the Curwen type book published in 1928. For good measure, we are also shown a 'poster border' of matching vigour designed by Enid Marx.

In 1915 there was an alarming shortage of lead in the munitions factories and a government appeal was made for the release of stocks. Harold now had his long awaited opportunity. He could sell off at a figure well above book value all the horrors which the firm had collected since its foundation. More than two hundred 'horror' faces and great quantities of printer's ornaments were got rid of. It was indeed a good riddance and the debased and often unbelievably ingenious Victorian rubbish against which Harold had been fighting was no longer there to haunt the composing room. For general work only Caslon Old Face, Monotype Old Style No. 2 and Modern Wide No. 18 remained, and Bold No. 53 was kept for the publishing side's large catalogues. To fill the gap, Monotype Imprint was acquired and for hand composition F. W. Goudy's Kennerley and Messrs Shanks's version of Plantin. These founts were sufficient for Curwen Press needs and apart from Monotype Garamond were not added to until 1923. Then the Monotype Corporation, having appointed Stanley Morison as their adviser, began its great programme of expansion. Some new type faces were purchased to meet the needs of the growing book printing business developed by Oliver Simon.

What Curwen did required considerable courage: the selling of so much familiar material alarmed some members of the staff at Plaistow. Some old hands of the firm could not perceive that a typographic revolution was taking place. Christian Barman writing in the *Penrose Annual* understandingly says,

Most people will remember Curwen as a quiet, mild-mannered, almost diffident man; not everyone realized that underneath this unassuming manner lay an inner core of extreme toughness. The gentle exterior of the sensitive artist and easily mixing craftsman concealed an iron will. The importance of this inner firmness is crucial, because the Curwen Press tradition as it has become known was not built upon it from the beginning. For Curwen did not start a new press, he inherited an old one, and it was necessary that this inheritance should be transformed at his hands.*

Barman realizes the strength that is needed to introduce new thinking into a well established concern. He concludes by

*'Harold Curwen' by Christian Barman, *Penrose Annual*, vol. 50, 1956.

quoting Francis Meynell's understanding comment that 'to recommence is much harder than to commence'.

Harold Curwen never for a moment considered himself the sole provider of good printing. If he thought about it at all, he counted himself among a group of pioneers who were trying to do good, honest work that was 'fit for its purpose' as Design & Industries Association orthodoxy put it. It is true that the war of 1914–18 caused inevitable interruption and the printing revival was obliged to mark time. Even before August 1914 things were beginning to move and there was a small group in or close to the trade who were dissatisfied with the general run of printing. *The Imprint*, the pioneer journal of the printing revival, was an outstanding achievement, and the teaching of Edward Johnston and J. H. Mason at the Central School of Arts and Crafts, was being eagerly absorbed. There were also Joseph Thorp and Bernard Newdigate, the former involved in the improvement of jobbing and the latter with decently planned book printing. Towering above them all was Francis Meynell who had, from 1911 onwards, been producing divinely inspired and modestly priced books for Burns & Oates, the Catholic publishers directed by his father, Wilfred. In 1916 the Pelican Press was started. Meynell was an authority on the history of printing types and was in no need of a Joseph Thorp to publicize Pelican work. The beauty of his work and the felicity of his writing can be appreciated in his book, printed and sold at the Pelican Press in 1923 called *Typography*; it opens with a superlative folding title page. Francis Meynell and Harold Curwen were pursuing the same objectives; their approach was parallel but, happily, different. Any Pelican printing job, just as any Curwen, could be identified without searching for the imprint.

The early workers in the printing renaissance were a happy band: they respected, and sometimes copied, each other's work but had no time for jealousy. What was more likely was a postcard from one printer to another congratulating him on some piece of jobbing printing which had caught his eye. Council members of the Design & Industries Association were expected, when called upon, to do what they could to promote the Association's aims. Harold Curwen was asked to write about printing and this gave him the opportunity to again make his declaration of faith. His essay, written in January 1918, is an excellent manufacturer's manifesto. Make well and sell well—a sensible creed and one that is likely to maintain a business in permanent good health. The essay was submitted first to Claud Lovat Fraser who proposed a few amendments. The article was headed 'Printing—Its Object'. Fraser proposed expanding it to read, 'Printing—Its Object and Ours'. A note from Lovat Fraser is pinned on to the script: 'This seems to me most admirable. Surely H.S.C. need have no qualms about his terse, nervous English. I have ventured to pencil a suggestion in the last paragraph.' Harold's testament, it is admitted, is hardly likely to appeal to that part of the business community whose sole object is to scoop as much money as possible into their own pockets. It is meant for the more civilized manufacturer and merchant who considers that, besides money, there is a service to give. Curwen writes,

In all writing on the trade betterment question I see little or no mention of what seems the most vital factor of all in the standing of a craft.

The first object of manufacturing anything is surely that it may be usable and useful to our fellow-man. That we should sell what we make is after all a secondary desirability.

The sale of any article is directly dependent on its usableness in comparison to its production cost. Those things will sell best which, whilst they fulfil every requirement of utility, are so designed and constructed as to eliminate every unnecessary and wasteful process which increases cost without increasing utility. In some articles we require ornamentation for its own sake, but directly decoration impairs utility, it is out of place. A well designed thing (i.e. one which is thoroughly usable) is of itself beautiful, for example, an aeroplane, a woodman's axe, or the 'Wrestler' statues from Herculaneum.

The point of contact between this idea and the betterment of conditions for our manual workers is this. We want to pay them higher wages. Then we must make the product of their labours more USABLE, we must design it better that is than the corresponding product of any other nation's workers. Then it will sell in greater quantity and command a higher price. By having this higher aim also their task will be vastly more interesting for they will begin to put into it more of themselves.

And to come to our own trade in particular. Printing is intended for our fellow-man to READ. If we are to improve the standing of our craft, we must think more of our PRODUCT, we must use only well designed types, we must study how to lay them out in a clear readable way and we must educate ourselves in our craft so that we may be in a position to say to our customers, 'This proof I show you is simple, clear and readable, the lettering used is well proportioned, the workmanship is good.' We must absolutely refuse to employ eight different type designs, nor yet two, in the setting of one job. I do not mean that no ornamentation must be used in print; on the contrary, certain subjects suggest a decorative treatment. But in these cases let the decoration be subservient to the wording and related to it in character. Let it help in the expression of the idea.

This is not idle talk, I have most substantially proved in our own works that to work to this higher ideal gives the workers more interest in their jobs and brings more respect and satisfaction from customers. (The few customers who kick—well let them!) and in addition, as I said at the beginning, it is the best, the most thoughtful article which gets the best price.

We are going to be 'Top Dog' commercially if our goods are FITTEST for their use and the BEST MADE. Nothing else will ensure our permanent supremacy. Here is food for the Joint Industrial Committees, for the prosperity of the individual is inseparably bound up with the prosperity of the nation.

In 1918 a leaflet was distributed to the staff at the Plaistow works. In nine paragraphs it sets out some rules to help the firm in its relations with customers. The leaflet, set in 18 point Caslon Old Face, is headed 'The Personality of The Curwen Press'. The nine sentences read:

1. Our customers are reasonable men.

2. Consider them not as customers, but as business friends whom you are anxious to help, and treat them as you would like them to treat us.

3. On the 'phone, pass a customer DIRECT to the man who will be able to complete the conversation; never waste his time; be alert and polite.

4. Give full measure, and put your best into every job.

5. Make promises carefully, and keep those you make.

6. An observant man can learn something from everybody and everything.

7. Never make the same mistake twice.

8. Don't try to put the cost of our mistakes on to our customers, and don't forget to thank anyone who gives us the chance to remedy a mistake.

9. Know your costs; ask a fair price; and stick to it.

All very sensible, especially number 9. This is precisely what the Federation of Master Printers had been, for years, trying to persuade its members to do.

XIV

JOSEPH THORP

DURING THE WAR YEARS of 1914–18 Harold Curwen shouldered most of the responsibility for the business. Spencer Curwen, long before 1914, had to put up with increasing deafness which, as time went by, became a tragic hindrance to his musical work. A nephew of Spedding's wife, Robin Rowell,* recalls that in 1908 as a boy at a preparatory school near London he remembered that Spencer Curwen was very deaf and had provided himself with an ingenious hearing aid of his own devising. It was shaped like a 'shuttlecock and battledore' bat and had some kind of thin material stretched tight within the frame: when listening he gripped half the bat between his teeth and the speaker spoke on to the other half. The effect was of a tympan transmitting sound waves on to Spencer's jawbone. It appeared to be effective and the bat was carried round on a ribbon like an eye glass. W. Stephens, who started at The Curwen Press in 1910 and retired in 1964, remembers being asked questions by Spencer Curwen and being told when replying to talk slowly and distinctly on to the tympan. Deafness obliged Spencer Curwen to withdraw gradually from active participation in the firm and from his work for the Tonic Sol-fa Association. He died in London in August 1916 at the age of sixty-nine.

Spedding Curwen also suffered from poor health. For the last seven or eight years of his life a weak heart made travelling more and more difficult. He lived in a flat in Great Russell Street opposite the British Museum and, during the war, Brunwin called there at regular intervals to present progress reports from

*Now Sir Robin Rowell, chairman from 1942–68 of the shipbuilders R. and W. Hawthorn Leslie & Co. Ltd, Hebburn-on-Tyne.

Plaistow. Spedding died at his residence in Great Russell Street in October 1919 at the age of seventy. The service at Golders Green crematorium was remembered as one of rare beauty: the prize choir from The Curwen Press augmented by the staff from the publishing office filled the gallery. Interested as he was in developing the printing and publishing business, his really deep interest was in sharing the comradeship of those who worked with him. Although neither Spencer nor Spedding Curwen could be considered rich men, they were what Edwardians called comfortably off; they belonged to a responsible middle class and were completely free of any ambition for life in grand society.

Kenneth Curwen served with distinction as an officer in the Royal Flying Corps and just as Harold had to steer into the unknown of a Britain at war in August 1914, so Kenneth had, in November 1918, to make the difficult transition from war to peace.

The Design & Industries Association was literally a lifeline for Harold Curwen. The meeting with Joseph Thorp had broken down some of Harold's diffidence. Harold could not or would not blow his own trumpet; fortunately Joseph Thorp was there to do it for him and do it with disarming exuberance.

In the year the Design & Industries Association was formed, Thorp's influence was beginning to have an effect. By a stroke of good fortune he managed to interest the artist, Claud Lovat Fraser, in the Association and Fraser became a member in the summer of 1917. This was a remarkable move for, according to Albert Rutherston, Lovat Fraser was 'not interested in groups or movements—nor was he connected with any. The Design & Industries Association is perhaps the nearest approach to any body or society advocating a common line of action in relation to aesthetic questions, in whose propaganda he showed an active interest.'* Lovat Fraser was an active member of the Design & Industries Association and sincerely supported its aims. He contributed a long letter to the Association's journal in March 1919. But more importantly, through the Association he became a close friend of Thorp who introduced him to Harold Curwen. Curwen's ideas for courageous and joyful printing appealed to Lovat Fraser and in a remarkably short time Curwen was acquiring dozens and dozens of Lovat's gay drawings and printing them

*Claud Lovat Fraser by John Drinkwater and Albert Rutherston: Heinemann, 1923.

with great understanding. Lovat Fraser and Harold Curwen worked happily together and the partnership became a central factor in Curwen's bright and daring printing.

Lovat Fraser served during the Great War as a captain in the Durham Light Infantry, fought in the battle of Loos and, shortly after, was badly gassed in the Ypres Salient; when sufficiently recovered he was sent over to England in 1916 and given home service duty. This military posting made it possible for Curwen, Fraser and Thorp to continue their pioneer work in printing well before the end of the war.

Harold was like a doctor prescribing for his patients and the deadly disease he was trying to cure was commercial drabness. It may have been reaction against the horrors of war but, whatever the reason, he was finding an encouraging number of business-men and individuals eager to accept his advice. Curwen recog-nized how much business printing, when it was appropriate, could be enriched by artists. Lovat Fraser, long before he became famous for his theatre designs, had been doing work for The Curwen Press; his range of colours was fresh and striking, heralding for the Plaistow works an era of puce, primrose yellow, viridian green and the bluest of sky blue. In 1919 this seemed daring to the point of recklessness; the dash of Lovat Fraser and the solid straightforward typography of Harold Curwen were fine weapons to use against commercial dullness. They brought ineffable charm to printing tasks of all shapes and sizes. Before meeting Lovat Fraser, Harold had been firing salvoes of advice and sound sense to buyers of printing and Joseph Thorp always insisted that Curwen was no ordinary tradesman. An elegantly engraved visiting card of about 1912 describes The Curwen Press as 'printers who take infinite pains'. A letterheading decorated at the top by a Lovat Fraser vignette has, at the foot, the battle cry 'Courageous Printing for Business & other Uses'. An early postcard, probably 1916, is headed 'Harold S. Curwen, Careful Printer' and a leaflet of the same period has the arresting heading —'Printing with a Spirit'. The leaflet goes on to affirm once again Harold's creed 'It is a great pleasure to arrange fine type, and still finer artistry to convey the spirit of your message. And work that is a pleasure is usually a success. Will you allow me to arrange and execute your Printing at The Curwen Press, Plaistow, E.13.' Never before had a message quite like this been presented to the business world. A wise note of caution is discernible in

[137]

'usually' a success. Sometimes success is impossible because customers refuse to co-operate. Clearly work that is a pleasure to produce is likely to provide good value for the customer and presupposes a new relationship where buyer and producer work in close harmony. Those who scorned or could do without a printer's help were unlikely to place orders with the works in North Street.

All kinds of practical advice was offered. About the typography of a 'statement of account' Harold suggests that a well balanced, orderly form makes for orderly work and conveys an impression of efficiency. And he comes out in favour of what is now known as house style. This is what he has to say about letterpaper for a firm of engineers in Newcastle-upon-Tyne: 'The simple, vigorous and well-proportioned type setting is in keeping with an engineering business. The company's device is usable throughout *all* the stationery of the firm, to which it gives unity and distinction.'

Most endearing and charming of all Harold's early advertisements is the 'Spirit of Joy' leaflet with Lovat Fraser's lovely and lively dancing couple. Fanciful it may be to tell hard-headed manufacturers in East London to get a spirit of joy into their printed matter! But it worked. Although Harold did not command all the custom he may have wanted, he was kept at full stretch for most of his working days. In fact there would not have been room for much more general printing in 1920 as music printing for the publishing side then took rather more than two thirds of the available output. The rare and, using a word in the 'copy', cheerily printed 'Spirit of Joy' leaflet is reproduced opposite in actual size.

At the end of the war Joseph Thorp was still hard at it expounding the virtues, as he saw them, of The Curwen Press. He wrote a booklet called *Apropos the Unicorn*, elegantly printed by Harold Curwen. Although of pocket size, it manages to show some fascinating examples of work of the 1919–20 period. The contents page is almost a roll call of early participators in the printing revival. Thorp dedicates what he calls a few candid notes to the workers at The Curwen Press whose appreciation of good work makes good work possible. *Apropos the Unicorn* has a marvellously gay cover designed by Lovat Fraser who also drew the unicorn on the title page and the satyr on the verso. The frontispiece is by Macdonald Gill and the artists contributing in

GET THE
SPIRIT OF JOY
INTO YOUR PRINTED THINGS

THE WORLD'S dead tired of drab dullness in Business Life.

GIVE your customers credit for a sense of Humour and some Understanding.

TAKE your courage in both hands and have your printing done

CHEERILY!

I arrange & make
COURAGEOUS PRINTING
At the Curwen Press
Plaistow, London, E.13
Harold Curwen

'Spirit of Joy' leaflet by Harold Curwen 1920,
decoration by C. Lovat Fraser

the text are Aldo Cosomati, Lovat Fraser, Dorothy Mulloch and Phoebe Stabler. The device printed on the last page is the original unicorn by Paul Woodroffe. In addition there is a pull-out sheet displaying business forms for 'careful clerking'. Thorp was, of course, responsible for the story. Exuberant, as might be expected, and the picture perhaps slightly exaggerated. But the dash and fun reflect the 'spirit of joy' which undoubtedly affected the Plaistow pioneers. Thorp on 'Appropriate Printing' is orthodox Design & Industries Association pleading and the 'Epilogue', although too flattering, is a deserved tribute to Harold Curwen and the staff at Plaistow.

Thorp on 'Appropriate Printing':

Good Printing must be appropriate printing. There is no formula to cover everything. I know a very distinguished press which will print a corset catalogue, historical records, and an invitation to dine with the Guild of Fishmongers, in precisely the same way. Very skilful and decorous and all that, but not appropriate; and, therefore, I would say not in the soundest sense good.

It is one of the most difficult things to avoid this cleaving to a formula, and there's much excuse and not so much harm done if it's a good formula. But it's only the beginning of good printing. The Curwen Press is always trying to meet this need for appropriateness, and to prevent settling down into the groove to which printers (who love ease as much as other men, and get less of it), being human, are subject.

If any customer find Curwen getting into a groove I would beg of him to write and tell him so. But I shall probably have done so first!—that being part of my job.

Thorp, 'Epilogue' in *Apropos the Unicorn*:

One of the queer things about the director of The Curwen Press is his pose that he needs my help and advice. Well, I am glad he is under this illusion, and perhaps two heads *are* better than one, especially if they be different kinds of heads.

All I want to say here is that I have had more pleasure, so far as my connection with fine printing is concerned, out of my work with Curwen than any other that I have done.

I know no press whose work is so *consistently* good, though I know a few whose best work is admirable. The best printing house, I am convinced, must be a relatively small house. Organization on the large scale, with its inevitable routine, kills the fine flower of 'personality' which alone gives distinction.

Of course I may be prejudiced. But after all there's plenty of evidence to support me.

Wouldn't it be a good thing, by the way, if firms when they issue their volumes of self-congratulation—on occasions of centenaries and what not—planned them on a smaller scale so that they might combine distinction with economy and put into quality what they lose in bulk? The passion for bulk dies hard in the business breast.

I have found no universal formula for printing or advertising except this: 'Always make your printing so good that no one could possibly have the heart to put it into the waste-paper basket.'

Doesn't that apply to this? I think so.

I would summarize thus: Keep your quality, both of designing and actual production, at the highest. Economize by simplification (fewer colours, reduction of size, compressed copy) and forethought (designs adaptable for various purposes, standardization of size where applicable, leisurely, not hurried planning and ordering).

Not all customers of The Curwen Press appreciated Harold's efforts to improve design. Some of the customers brought to the firm by H. W. Jones, the pre-1914 traveller, were not interested. The West Ham Corporation Tramways were furious to receive, without prior warning, their daily receipt dockets looking fresh and better arranged in Caslon type. They were accustomed to Haddon Condensed or some similar type face. As this could no longer be supplied, the Tramways held that The Curwen Press had broken their contract and abruptly closed the account. The 'spirit of joy' could not be expected to penetrate everywhere; it failed to find a welcome at the Greengate Street headquarters of the West Ham Corporation Tramways.

At the end of the war Bernard Newdigate on Thorp's suggestion joined The Curwen Press. He came in 1919 but did not stay long as he was persuaded by J. C. Squire to go to *The Field* as typographic adviser and in 1920 he was asked by Basil (now Sir Basil) Blackwell to succeed A. H. Bullen as director of the Shakespeare Head Press. In his short stay at Plaistow he was able to improve composing room practices which were to prove valuable when the business in book printing expanded. Newdigate gave a few talks to members of the composing room. The advice would certainly be sound but he was a hesitant speaker and had a habit of destroying the form of his sentences in mid-stream and starting over again: his lectures were not as effective as they might have been.

[141]

Apropos the Unicorn, cover designed by C. Lovat Fraser. The first 'house' advertising booklet issued by The Curwen Press

Joseph Thorp lectured too and he had no difficulty in holding the attention of his audience. Four lectures were delivered in November 1919 and a summary was printed under the general title 'Life and the Industrial Aim' in *Amongst Ourselves*, the house organ of J. Curwen & Sons. The war was just over and many were hoping for a better world. Thorp was among them. 'England', he declared, 'was a rotten place in many ways, but it could and would be got right by co-operation. Thank God the power had passed into their hands, and he could leave it to them, especially the younger people.' His general theme was mildly revolutionary: the ideal state would come, in his estimation, when men and women were working *with* capital and not *for* capital.

In the second lecture Thorp appeared in riding-dress and began by apologizing for his fancy dress costume. His excuse was that his work as a journalist took him into many strange quarters and he had that day been riding round with the chief of the mounted police.

Thorp was an eccentric and an entertainer. He had the gift of giving substance to the spirit of joy and to outline to war-weary audiences how a new Jerusalem could be built in England's pleasant land. Joseph Thorp was just the sort of evangelist that was needed; extravagant and extrovert he could bang the drum in the market square while Harold got on with the work of actually producing his forceful, courageous and colourful printing. According to *Amongst Ourselves* there were some satisfied customers in 1919. 'Thanks for putting through the four-page leaflet. It is faultless', writes Francis Meynell. Boake, Roberts, the large chemical manufacturers in Stratford near Bow express thanks for labels. . . . 'We much appreciate the fact you got them ready in such a short time.' Mark Webber, engineers, say how happy they are with the attention that is given to their work. Bernard Newdigate says simply he is 'very pleased with the nice posters you have done for me'. These modestly worded expressions of content with Curwen work were an encouragement. They put into proper perspective Thorp's overflowing ebullience.

The editor of *Amongst Ourselves* sums up Thorp's lectures in the January 1920 issue:

We print in this issue a brief report of Mr Thorp's lectures—quite inadequate really, but we have done our best to get down the lecturer's meteoric flow of words. As it was put to the writer one evening: 'He's like a prize fighter. You get a blow in the solar plexus, then before you can recover your wind you get a knock out, which leaves you dazed and gasping.' So there you are. For any discrepancies in our report you must blame Mr Thorp, not us.

Membership of the Design & Industries Association helped Plaistow to gain new custom for their careful, thoughtful printing. Fitness for purpose was beginning to be recognized as desirable in printing as in all other useful products. The Underground Railways, the pottery of Carter Stabler & Adams of Poole, Heal & Son and Dryad Canework were devoted followers of Harold Curwen. There were also Staples & Co. Ltd, Crittall Manufacturing Company, makers of metal windows in Braintree, the Savoy Hotel and the Comptometer Company who introduced into Britain office calculating machinery. Many other firms of all sorts and sizes brought their problems to Harold and, as may be imagined, a host of private individuals, some exceedingly fussy ones, were on his track for wedding invitations, visiting cards and private stationery. Equal care was given to everything and Harold's professional practice became so large that an extension to his drawing-board had to be fitted into his private house.

Lovat Fraser produced page after page of delightful drawings bubbling with life and dozens were acquired by Harold for Curwen Press use. A magnificent booklet describing the Savoy Hotel in thirty-two quarto pages has seventeen Lovat Fraser drawings and a specially designed cover gaily printed as an all over pattern in red and yellow. Eight fine photographs printed in half-tone complete a publication which has a freshness which makes it an early collector's piece of the printing revival. The Savoy booklet was issued in 1920.

There was so much to be done that Harold arranged to have the help of a number of artists who were prepared to spend a day each week in Plaistow. Among these were Irene Fawkes who was set to work on Staples & Co. Ltd mattress booklets and Dora Batty who designed a series of leaflets with Jane Austen looking groups for a wholesaler of watches. Phoebe Stabler was good at heraldic devices and Aldo Cosomati provided a stable companion for Paul Woodroffe's unicorn. Cosomati became a weekly visitor in 1920; he was still happily doing work for Plaistow in 1970.

Cosomati, who has over the years helped in a lot of business printing for the Press, came to England from Italy at the end of the Great War. He came for an excellent but unusual reason. He worked in Switzerland during the war and saw a great deal of the trains carrying the seriously wounded. He was deeply impressed by the stoicism and high spirits of the wounded British soldiers on their long journey home. He decided he would like to live in the country which produced such men. So he took a courageous step and settled in England permanently and for fifty years he has, as a freelance, been in contact with The Curwen Press. One day he was lunching at Gatti's in the Strand with the pianist Busoni who introduced him to Richmond Temple who was then using Curwen for his best Savoy Hotel work. Richmond Temple offered to introduce Cosomati to Harold Curwen and thus the long association began. Besides designing two unicorns, Cosomati helped with the design of a booklet issued in 1921 called *Business Printing*; it showed examples of letterheadings, circulars, catalogue covers and posters. The introductory note affirms that The Curwen Press IS ALIVE both to its duties and to its ideas. Again aims are reiterated—to supply simple and appropriate printing.

Joseph Thorp, besides telling potential customers about the sensible, appropriate work that was being done at Plaistow, had an unwritten obligation to steer orders to The Curwen Press whenever he was in a position to do so. He had considerable success but weakened his credibility by setting his sights too high. Promises of grand schemes mostly came to nothing; the staff at Plaistow found it difficult to hide their disappointment. Thorp lived gaily from hand to mouth and payments in advance were often made by Harold to help his friend. 'Would you object', writes Thorp, 'to half of the commission on Todd's Wine Book being paid to me now; one of the usual financial crises! I am rearranging my work and taking steps to do some more active canvassing.' It appears Todd's Wine Book earned Thorp £28 16s in commission and half of this was paid at once. Whether a rearranging of work ever took place it is impossible to say. Thorp's introduction to Harold first of Lovat Fraser and subsequently of Oliver Simon far outweighed any number of Todd's Wine Books: Thorp's association with Plaistow brought lasting good to The Curwen Press.

XV

THORP, LOVAT FRASER

AND OLIVER SIMON

WORK THAT is a pleasure is usually a success says a Curwen Press advertisement of 1919. Curwen was convinced that people who try to do good work are the happy ones. He managed to develop an industrial philosophy which embodied decent commercial dealing with the principles advocated by the Design & Industries Association. Fortunately a paper written in 1919 survives in which he sets out his beliefs, both spiritual and material, by which his printing press could best serve its customers and give at the same time reasonable contentment to all engaged in production.

An artist or craftsman is always striving to do a useful job: the well-made thing is always the economical thing. Applied to printing, the well made piece of reading matter, that is type easy to read, is economical of eye-sight and time. The good thing is not necessarily even the most expensive. It is the duty of each generation to produce fine, original work.

The idea that a well-trained staff devoted to doing their work as well as possible is clearly sound manufacturing sense. As every intelligent buyer of printing knows the sensibly designed piece of work fit for its purpose is nearly always the best value for money. Curwen continues,

The primary aim of industry is wrong. The aim of service to the community leads to better results both productively and socially than does the aim of individual gain. It is unsound to make work a drudge and look to off hours for enjoyment. Every worker requires to have an interest in work, to feel that the work is wanted by the community and to satisfy a natural creative

instinct. To keep the product up to the best standard the habit must be
developed of continually experimenting and comparing.

Curwen was not against profit but he was against it being the sole
or even the main motive. Industry, he perceived, existed to
produce goods or services that people wanted, and all he desired
was that the goods and services should be useful and sensibly
designed and good value for money. He broke clean away from
the Victorian 'master-worker' relationship by insisting that those
who worked for the community in the workshops should share
the satisfactions that came from doing work that is both wanted
and honest. His views on the profit motive seem to be in line with
civilized thinking in the modern industrial world. He knew
perfectly well that his works had to make a profit; profit would be
needed so that new machinery, new type and new methods could
be adequately financed. As for fostering interest among the
workers, this is a problem which continues to be a matter of
earnest and urgent study. In large organizations, job satisfaction
and job enrichment are difficult to attain. In the works in North
Street the sense of participation and work enjoyment, started in
the days of Spedding Curwen, gathered momentum under
Harold Curwen whose personal abilities and sincerity secured at
once the support of all who worked with him. Interest in work and
quality became deep rooted in the period 1920–30 and has remained, much to the advantage of all who are in the firm, an
organic part of the Plaistow outlook.

The long drawn out struggle of the 1914–18 war naturally
interrupted progress in the revival in printing. But as soon as the
country could take up civil life again the small group of printers
who had been waiting in the wings were as determined as ever to
put their ideals and ideas into practice. They were indebted to the
Design & Industries Association, which had almost miraculously
been able to continue its missionary work during the war years.
As far as The Curwen Press was concerned it was determined to
show that the aims of the Association—fitness for purpose—
were not only practical but sound business sense.

The work of 1919–21 will always be known as the Lovat
Fraser period. The vivid colours and bubbling gaiety of Lovat
Fraser's designs were something new in printing for business.
Harold Curwen and Lovat Fraser's teamwork was beginning to
be noticed. The former was responsible for type arrangement and

[147]

all the details of the printing specification and the latter cheerfully provided drawings and decorations when he was asked. Harold's practical, sensible, unpretentious work was given a 'spirit of joy' by Lovat and the results went some way to justify the almost reckless claims made on behalf of the Press by Joseph Thorp.

Fitness for purpose was, of course, never abandoned. If a piece of work in Harold's opinion required no drawing or decoration, then neither Lovat Fraser nor any other artist would be brought in. Requirements were varied and every order received its individual planning as it shuffled onto Harold's drawing-board. It was a busy life and very soon a stream of courageous printing, forceful printing and appropriate printing was being despatched, in parcels large and small, from the austere buildings in North Street. In 1920 rather more than three-quarters of Plaistow's production was music for the publishing side but a trade in catalogues, booklets and leaflets was beginning to grow. The assortment of labels, chromo-lithographs and old style job-work brought in by the former traveller, H. W. Jones, had been successfully edged out. Spedding Curwen's wish to make the printing works less dependent on orders from the publishing office had now been translated into fact and during the decade 1920–30 the proportion of output devoted to music continued to decline.

It could be said that Harold drove himself too hard. He had a great mass of work to design and supervise and he had failed to engage a full-time traveller to replace H. W. Jones. The travelling was done by Harold, assisted by his faithful manager Brunwin. In the background was Joseph Thorp with his readiness to steer work to Plaistow when opportunity occurred. Brunwin, in addition to all his other work, looked after the printing requirements of the publishing office and made a weekly call at 24 Berners Street as a matter of routine. A few publications bearing the publishing imprint on the title page of the Decoy Press, Plaistow were beginning to appear. These were special jobs engineered by Joseph Thorp. The Decoy Press never had any machinery and was just a name, the name in fact of Thorp's cottage in Sussex. It had a part-time, one man staff in the person of Joseph Thorp and the Decoy Press could be a convenience when it was impolitic for some reason to use Curwen's imprint. Thorp had too many interests and was far too mercurial to sit down and grapple with typographic detail so the task was taken on by Harold who cheerfully piled it into his already overflowing work basket. J. Curwen & Sons Ltd kindly, if unintentionally, granted extended credits.

Decoy Press publications were not numerous but they remain good examples of the early period of a struggling printing renaissance. *Change, the Beginning of a Chapter in Twelve Volumes*, edited by John Hilton and Joseph Thorp: a promise of twelve volumes is typical of the spirit of adventure which Thorp generated; as far as is known only one volume was produced and this is dated January 1919. The absence of further volumes must have been a relief to Curwen finances as it is difficult to see how the venture could have paid its way. *Change* is a pocket sized volume with the title page set in Kennerley and the text in Monotype Imprint. The printing is well done, marred only by excessive space after full-stops. Hilton and Thorp offer advice on post-war reconstruction and warn of the dangers of a wholly material outlook, and the sermonizing is made more acceptable by a generous gathering of illustration and decoration. A title device by Paul Woodroffe, woodcuts by Herbert Rooke and Robert Gibbins, three glorious illustrations in colour by Lovat Fraser, woodcuts by Philip Hagreen and, as a finale, a splendid wood engraving by Eric Gill for the printer's device of the Decoy Press.

Another Decoy Press publication of the same period is *A Book of Vision* produced for a fund raising campaign in aid of St Dunstan's in Regent's Park, in a miniature format measuring 5 inches deep by 3¾ inches wide having seventy-six pages entirely hand-set in Kennerley. No decoration apart from a wood engraving by Vivien Gribble and a fine St Dunstan's house mark by Macdonald Gill, followed overleaf by the Decoy Press device. Unlike most of Harold Curwen's work the type lacks vigour by being printed in grey ink; there may have been some reason for this but it makes the little book look precious and less easy to read. Interesting as the Decoy Press publications are for students, they were completely overshadowed by a small booklet about an office calculating machine called the Comptometer. Demy octavo and a modest sixteen pages, *A Great Step Forward* fairly sparkles with gaiety and charm generated by Lovat Fraser's magnificent illustrations in colour line. Even over generous spaces after full-stops and a tendency for the Caslon Old Face to carry too much ink cannot spoil it. It will always remain the perfect example of the 'spirit of joy' period. On the last page a short note contributed by the customer is eloquent of his appreciation—C. Lovat Fraser drew the pictures, Curwen did the printing; both are entitled to credit. We wrote the facts, and the good news thus presented is worth your attention. *A Great Step Forward* shows what can be done when there is close co-operation between customer, artist and printer.

A Curwen-Fraser triumph, worked on in 1920 and published in 1921 by Daniel O'Connor is *The Luck of the Bean Rows*. A Royal octavo of sixty-four pages generously illustrated in colour line by Lovat Fraser who also contributed a backgammon board design for the paper sides of the binding. It was advertised as the 'Catch of the Christmas Book season'. 'The drawings', wrote Bernard Newdigate, 'have been printed in colour by Mr Harold Curwen who has tried to put Fraser's own feeling into the work and has once more proved able to do so.'

Yet another beautiful book *Poems from the Works of Charles Cotton* with the poems selected and decorated by Lovat Fraser was published by the Poetry Bookshop. Demy octavo, fifty-two pages with two thoroughly enjoyable decorations on every page. No colour this time but the black printing is immaculate and an example of careful workmanship at its best. The catalogue of Curwen printed books exhibited by John & Edward Bumpus in 1929 notes *Poems from the Works of Charles Cotton* is considered by general consent to be Lovat Fraser's most successful decorated book.

There were many other distinguished pieces of printing which were the creations of Harold Curwen, the careful printer. Catalogues of sanitary ware for Doulton's of Lambeth, booklets describing London's Underground Railways, elegant brochures for the Savoy Hotel and an arresting series of Lovat Fraser patterned papers are remembered among a great heap of miscellaneous business printing which are now treasured by collectors of ephemera.

Harold was constantly dashing out on the firm's motor cycle to see customers or to discuss work with different artists and all the time he was taking a very active part in the administration of the works at Plaistow. Here was done the typographic planning, the careful assessment of proofs, choosing the appropriate paper and seeing that the quality of the printing and the colours were exactly what was intended. It was like living on the top of a volcano for it was impossible to foresee the next task or the shape

ECONOMY

WITH a Comptometer, a girl operator will do as much calculating work as three expert men in the same time. The wages of the operator, together with the cost of the machine, allowing for depreciation, interest on capital, and all incidental expenses, will be less than the wages of one of the clerks. Therefore you save more than the salaries of two clerks, plus the cost of supervision, plus the cost of providing them with office room, furniture, etc. The figures were worked out in detail in our pamphlet, 'Would a Comptometer save me £400 a year?' and you will find that the direct economy is not less than £400 per annum for every machine that can be kept busy.

But apart from this, other great savings are made possible. We are often told by our customers, for instance, how the Comptometer has enabled them to discover errors and consequently has saved them considerable sums of money, while the advantage gained by having all figure work kept up to date and all statistics presented promptly is impossible to estimate. Actually it is priceless.

Certainly it is obsolete and wasteful to do by mental processes what a machine will do at one-third the cost in one-third the time, and with absolute accuracy.

From *A Great Step Forward* decorated by C. Lovat Fraser

of the next creative explosion. The lack of any properly constituted sales staff was a serious deficiency. It made contact with customers erratic and as a result a considerable but unmeasurable amount of business must have been lost to the firm. To make matters worse, Harold suffered from bouts of forgetfulness and often important information failed to reach Brunwin's desk. There were many complaints by enraged clients wanting to know why they had not received proofs or estimates. Mercifully most of the complaints were made by telephone, and loyal Brunwin was rarely ruffled. He managed to restore a customer's confidence.

Harold Curwen and Lovat Fraser were thoroughly enjoying dealing with the many design problems which printing for business was always throwing up. They were ready to tackle a wide range of work including book illustration, book jackets, posters, pamphlets and all kinds of stationery. It was all adventure and wholly congenial. Every piece of printing, no matter how small, that Lovat Fraser and Harold Curwen designed together was an example of right making. The work had an enchantment which can never be recaptured. It was all to end tragically long before it had come to full flower. Lovat Fraser, unable to bear the strain of an emergency operation, died in June 1921 at the age of thirty-one. A memorial exhibition was held at the Leicester Galleries, Leicester Square in December 1921. Forewords to the catalogue were contributed by Gordon Craig and Walter de la Mare. There is also a note written jointly by Harold Curwen and Joseph Thorp:

Lovat was genuinely enthusiastic about this work for commercial firms, and shared our view that to put 'real beauty', sincerely felt and expressed, at the service of advertising, was, because of its wide and varied distribution, no inconsiderable privilege and opportunity . . . perhaps his best tribute is the frequency with which one now hears 'if only Lovat Fraser were here to tackle this job'. He was only at the beginning of his achievement in this as in his other work.

The real love which The Curwen Press had for Lovat Fraser and his work is made plain by the twelve pages of head-and-tail pieces, vignettes and miscellaneous ornaments printed in the *Specimen Book of Types and Ornaments** published in 1928.

**A Specimen Book of Types and Ornaments in use at The Curwen Press:* The Fleuron Ltd, 1928.

Lovat Fraser's main work was in theatre design where he had gained fame for his settings for *As You Like It* and the *Beggar's Opera*. He was a close friend of another stage designer, Albert Rutherston, who was well known in the theatre world for the work he had done for Harley Granville-Barker. Albert Rutherston was the uncle Oliver Simon consulted about a possible career in the printing trade. Uncle Albert introduced him to Lovat Fraser who passed him on to Joseph Thorp. Thorp agreed to speak to Harold about Oliver's ambition and after some false starts delightfully narrated in Oliver Simon's autobiography† he was admitted as a pupil to The Curwen Press in the late summer of 1920. Oliver's career in the printing trade was given official sanction on 15 July 1920 at a board meeting of J. Curwen & Sons Ltd when Harold Curwen reported that he had accepted Mr O. Simon as a pupil at Plaistow at a fee of £100.

Although the display of Kelmscott and Doves Press books in Sotheran's window may have reinforced his determination to enter the printing trade, Simon had already had some slight experience of the processes of printing. He took a leading part in editing and producing, with the assistance of former private soldiers, A. L. Leaver and H. Newton of Stockport, a *Record of the 53rd (Welsh) Divisional Cyclist Company. Gallipoli–Egypt– Palestine, 1915–1919*. It was competently if not elegantly printed by H. Rawson & Co., New Brown Street, Manchester. Oliver Simon became acquainted with galley proofs, page proofs, the making of numerous half-tone blocks and the selection of paper and binding. The publication required considerable editorial skill and was the first training ground for the future editor of *The Fleuron* and *Signature*. Oliver Simon's own contribution was on 'Company Cricket—1919'; it is believed that part of his war gratuity went in settlement of H. Rawson's invoice. The experience gained in producing the record of the 53rd Cyclists may have influenced Simon's choice of careers just as much as the display of Private Press books in Sotheran's window.

Oliver Simon was aware of the lucky circumstances which allowed him to become a learner among a group of skilled craftsmen and to see the printing he so much admired actually taking shape. He was given a friendly welcome by his fellow workers and for the rest of his life the noise of printing machinery and the

---

†*Printer and Playground* by Oliver Simon: Faber & Faber, 1956.

linseedy smell of printing ink reminded him of those happy days in Plaistow. Some practical factory experience was essential for Oliver; without it he could not have seen his way to the commendably high standards which he set for himself. A portrait of young Simon in his white jacket laying paper into a Victoria platen press is in existence taken when he was under instruction from Tommy Moakes. Moakes, who began work at The Curwen Press in May 1919, retiring after nearly forty years' service in 1958, was a superb craftsman, with a tremendous regard for Harold whom he felt really did know about good printing. An exacting task at this time was colour proofing Lovat Fraser's illustrations. Moakes did this work superbly well, giving entire satisfaction to both the artist and Harold Curwen. Oliver was studying alongside Moakes while this work was being done and quickly learned to appreciate the beauty of Lovat Fraser colours. The knowledge gained at this time was to prove invaluable when he received the first book printing order of his career.

Oliver Simon, as does the present writer, came from a middle-class Jewish family who came to England in the middle of the last century. Members of the family followed with some distinction careers as teachers, artists, civil servants, doctors and textile merchants. Oliver Simon was the first to go into the printing trade. The family expected high standards of work and, in general, their outlook was puritanical and they followed their careers with becoming seriousness.

When training at Plaistow, Oliver got to know Aldo Cosomati and they discussed the possibility of The Curwen Press doing book printing. Oliver's plans were clearly directed towards bookwork but he was not sure that Plaistow was the right place for it. He was aware that most book printing was done outside London and that there were seven different wage grades. The wage differential between London and the lowest grade was 25 per cent and this was partly the reason for London's decline as a centre for book printing. But Cosomati was encouraging although his estimate of Plaistow machining capacity may have been too roseate. Oliver realized that ordinary bookwork was out of the question on account of cost but he was confident that there was a fair demand for work which required special typographic skill, quality of machining and judgement in choice of materials.

Oliver finished his training at a time which could scarcely have been better chosen. Joseph Thorp felt he had contributed all he could to The Curwen Press and had decided to move on and became adviser to the *Morning Post*; he had also started on his long and distinguished career as theatre critic for *Punch*. Harold was finding it increasingly difficult to look after the works and at the same time do the lion's share of the travelling. Oliver proposed that he should be taken on at a small salary and commission and see if he could develop sales in bookwork and good quality general printing. Harold was able to tell his fellow directors in July 1921 that the year of pupilship had been completed and it was agreed to retain his (Simon's) services as an expert assistant to Harold Curwen at a salary of £5 per week. The expert assistance took the form of taking some of the load off Harold and creating bookwork sales. Harold had far too much to do but with Oliver bringing in bookwork and taking responsibility for the typography of the new custom, the designing and selling strength of the company was just about doubled. Harold took care to see that in addition to his basic salary Oliver was paid a commission on new work brought to the firm; so in the summer of 1921 Oliver became the firm's most uncommercial commercial traveller. Sensibly Oliver did not attempt what he felt he was unfitted for. Frontal attacks would, he sensed, end in failure. Infiltration were the tactics adopted; polite calls on customers and possible customers at about tea time and some interesting artists to gossip about. His belief in good work, a belief of course which he shared with Harold, was irresistible and soon built up a following of encouraging dimensions. Their plans seemed to have worked out well for, in a minute of 21 June 1922, the board specially recorded Mr Simon's success in obtaining bookwork for Plaistow.

It was a good arrangement giving Harold more time to devote to production at Plaistow and giving Oliver a chance to develop a new business based on the West End. Although it could not have been clear at the start, it soon became evident that Oliver, in his own discreet way, was as good as Joseph Thorp in getting attention directed to the admirable work that was being produced at Plaistow. It also became evident that Oliver had gifts which made him an able editor. Both as publicist and editor, he was immensely valuable to The Curwen Press.

The mere fact of Oliver's geographic positioning was a help. In printing, as in all industry, there is the element of luck. The chance of being on the spot at the right time can be crucial especially when a time factor is involved. Oliver's first success came about by his happening to be in the publishing office of Daniel O'Connor at exactly the right moment. The fairy-tale for children, *The Luck of the Bean Rows*, illustrated by Lovat Fraser had been printed by the Westminster Press. An urgent reprint was required which the Westminster Press were unable to undertake. Oliver was asked and said Curwen's could do it and at once he was on the District Railway heading for Plaistow with an order for 30,000 copies. Lovat Fraser's illustrations were in colour and Harold was able to use his experience to give the Plaistow edition some extra beauty. It was a huge order and the printing was very good indeed; unfortunately the optimism of Daniel O'Connor was not well founded and he must have been left with a mountain of unsold copies. W. Stephens* who helped to print *The Luck of the Bean Rows* describes it as quite an interesting job which caused something of a turmoil in The Curwen Press machine room; he remembers a night shift was worked for about six weeks which was a new experience for Plaistow. Stephens was understandably much offended when a copy was returned about six years later with a complaint that the pink had faded a little.

Plaistow was very much the working quarters for Harold and he never felt the need to journey to the West End unless there was a customer to call on or a project to discuss with an artist. In 1920 there was an offer of a room in the Adelphi which his brother Kenneth thought might be used as a London office. But Harold did not think the time had come to avail himself of the offer; he preferred North Street. It was rare for a customer to venture to Plaistow from the West End; it seemed a long way off and there was always the fear of being swallowed up in East London and never setting foot on North Street. Oliver, on the contrary, needed to be in the West End where all his publishers and advertising agents had their offices.

The Cloister Press of Heaton Mersey, Manchester, had been created by C. W. Hobson to produce printing of quality for the clients of his advertising agency. He had engaged Walter Lewis to manage the works and Stanley Morison was to be typographic adviser and ensure that the high quality aimed at was in fact achieved. But the times were not favourable; the Cloister Press began operating in the early part of 1920; by January 1922 Morison had had enough of Manchester and returned to Hamp-

---

*W. Stephens started at Plaistow in 1910, retiring on pension in 1964.

stead. Hobson asked Morison to look after the Cloister Press London office established at St Stephen's House, Bridge Street, Westminster. In October 1922 Hobson was obliged to sell the Cloister Press and Morison was out of a job and the office at St Stephen's House needed an occupant. On 11 October 1922 Harold Curwen suggested they should take over the office to be used, as he put it, for himself and Mr Simon for interviews with customers etc. The Curwen board agreed.

In December 1922 a calendar and diary with designs by Albert Rutherston was printed and published by Harold Curwen and Oliver Simon at The Curwen Press, Plaistow. It had for its title *The Four Seasons* and represented the first outward evidence of the printing partnership between Harold and Oliver; it was also the first employment by the firm of Albert Rutherston. In the Bumpus Exhibition catalogue *The Four Seasons* is stated to be the first book issued by The Curwen Press as an advertisement. This is not strictly accurate as it leaves out of account *Apropos the Unicorn* which was produced two years earlier. The format is pocket size (5 in. × 3¼ in.) and besides Rutherston's beautiful contribution there is a foreword which sounds like Simon composition:

By a steady growth and broadening of vision the Press has now arrived at a stage when it can confidently supply its services to those publishers, learned societies and advertisers who are wise enough to see the value of distinguished printing. Printing is an art as well as a craft; its production is by no means easy, and can only be arrived at by knowledge, judgement and good taste . . . it is not enough to be in possession of beautiful borders and initial letters; their appropriateness to subject and their appearance as a type page have to be thought of.

Rather platitudinous and serious but it needed saying and, after all, bringing beauty and common sense into printing was a serious business. *The Four Seasons* went out to customers and friends with a slip announcing that The Curwen Press had just opened a room in town on the third floor of St Stephen's House, Westminster. And the news was given that Mr Oliver Simon will be there each day and will have an interesting and ever-changing exhibition of modern English and foreign books, commercial printing and various cover and text papers. Exhibition afternoons were to be on Mondays and Thursdays.

[157]

In *The Four Seasons* there is a list of types in use at The Curwen Press. For Monotype setting Caslon, Imprint and Garamond are offered. As the calendar must have been printed in the autumn of 1922, it shows that Garamond was already available in most normal composition sizes and was indeed used in 1922 for *The Best Poems of 1922* which is the first Garamond-set book listed in the *Catalogue Raisonné* of books printed between 1920–23. The Garamond type must have been in the Monotype Corporation's programme sometime before Morison was appointed their typographic adviser in 1923. There is a page in *The Four Seasons* which sets out The Curwen Press, or more likely, Oliver Simon's views on decoration.

Many of the printers' beautiful ornaments and flowers which embellished the books and pamphlets of old are still in use, and it is to be hoped that the best will continue to survive. We have some charming old English and French printers' flowers in use at The Curwen Press. At the same time we are trying to produce flowers, ornaments, and initials of our own time, and we have a big selection, contributed by contemporary artists. We have, in fact, a collection widely chosen and continually receiving additions. Their employment adds zest to our work, and has already led to results which have been appreciated by a large number of our customers and friends. Surely each generation ought to leave its own characteristic IMPRINT.

A dedicated Simon is giving notice to customers and friends that a fine collection of proprietary ornaments and borders was going to grace the composing room at Plaistow.

The Four Seasons got as it deserved an excellent reception. The Western Electric Company wrote to say it had been admired so much by their general sales manager and supply manager and could they, please, have two more copies. Gordon Bottomley, staying at the Thackeray Hotel, Great Russell Street, thought it attractive, especially Albert Rutherston's designs, and says he has for some time followed with interest Messrs Curwen's enterprising experiments. Frank Pick at Electric Railway House was not so sure. 'May I congratulate you upon the production?', he writes in November 1922, 'I like it very much, and even like the drawings by Albert Rutherston, much as I struggle with these modern developments in art.'

Making one's way to the third floor of the grey and unremarkable office building in Bridge Street became one of the pleasures of life to the small circle interested in good printing. This London office of The Curwen Press appeared to observe an informal but regular routine. In the morning, serious work was interrupted at about eleven o'clock by an adjournment to Lyons' tea-shop. In the afternoon exhibition days on Mondays and Thursdays and on other afternoons Oliver Simon would be following his system of infiltration and be taking tea and talking about artists and printing with customers and likely supporters.

In September 1922 there appears the first trace of what eventually became *The Fleuron, a Journal of Typography*. A board minute records that Mr H. S. Curwen called attention to *Typography*, an annual to be issued in the Spring (of 1923) in which he and Mr Simon were interested. Arrangements for the printing and publishing of the work were agreed to. *Typography* was considered by many of Simon's friends a stodgy title and, it is believed, on Francis Meynell's suggestions, it was decided to call the journal *The Fleuron*. Imperceptibly the office of The Curwen Press became the office of *The Fleuron*. The idea of publishing *The Fleuron, a Journal of Typography* had Harold's warm support; he saw it as a latter day *Imprint* creating a new audience for good, decent, honest printing. For Oliver it made St Stephen's House a publishing office as well as a sales office. The Office of The Fleuron was a powerful force in the technique of sales by infiltration.

Lyons' tea-shops in the early nineteen-twenties were agreeable places; unpretentious, marble topped tables, bentwood chairs and waitresses in black serge with Nottingham lace collars. The lady dressed in black bombazine was understood to be the manageress. Any of them, in our estimation, would have made excellent models for the Camden Town group of artists. Visitors were invited to join in the fun—a cup of tea, a Bath bun and butter and the company of Oliver Simon and Stanley Morison. The latter would push his spectacles above his eyebrows and treat us to animated talks about the work of the early Italian writing masters. He had a habit of underlining his points by banging hard on the marble topped tables: it may have been to underline the seriousness of what he had to say or merely to stop our attention from wandering. The staff at Lyons did not object but treated the Morison-Simon table with reverence, as if it were the gathering place of some highly respectable club.

Morison and Simon were not always there together; Simon had his sales to attend to and the weekly visit to Plaistow while

Morison was often away at St Bride's or the British Museum laying the foundations to his scholarship in printing history which was to make him famous. There were also Morison's political pontifications to be endured: it was usual to be told that our whole way of life was wrong and there appeared, to his great sorrow, a regrettable lack of ethical standards in the business world. The young printer from Birmingham always enjoyed these tirades but felt sure that Morison was too pessimistic and that manufacturing could be carried on without exploitation.

Morison was never employed by The Curwen Press for Harold Curwen, himself a skilled typographer, was the practical man and, although he respected historical research, it really had no place in the everyday world of the commercial printing office at Plaistow.

For Oliver Simon, Morison was the ideal person with whom to share an office. Neither had any experience of business administration. They were hardly aware of costs and production problems. They could gossip freely and exchange ideas on how printing could be improved. They were in the middle of a printing revival and they were both, in their different ways, going to be influential. *The Fleuron* was endlessly discussed but it must be made clear that although Morison contributed a running critical commentary which must have been of the utmost value, yet the first four issues of *The Fleuron* were edited by Oliver Simon. The first issue of *The Fleuron* appeared in the spring of 1923 and during its preparation Morison was without regular paid employment and was in a position to give almost continuous advice to Oliver.

Morison appeared to take little interest in the business side of things and never expected there would be any profits. When Oliver suggested selling little note books covered with gay Curwen pattern papers, Morison dismissed the whole idea as frivolous. Part of the time Morison was using the office for the preparation of *Four Centuries of Printing* which Ernest Benn published in 1924. Harold Curwen hardly ever came to St Stephen's House or 101 Great Russell Street: he probably thought it best to leave bookwork under Oliver's charge and expected Oliver to come to Plaistow when technical help was required.

The move from Westminster to 101 Great Russell Street took place in June 1924. Morison had his table there until February

1925 when he moved to join Frederic Warde at the Fanfare Press at 41 Woburn Square.

In 1923 Morison was appointed typographical adviser to the Lanston Monotype Corporation and in January 1925 he was able to accept a similar part-time appointment with the Cambridge University Press.

When the Curwen office moved to 101 Great Russell Street, Bloomsbury, it remained in that part of London until it was given up altogether at the beginning of the second world war. The move meant the sacrifice of the Lyons' tea-shop but compensation was provided by a little restaurant almost next door called the Plane Tree; run by two competent, middle-aged ladies, they pleased their customers with what in truth could be called home cooking. These ladies were indirectly of great service to printing for their wholesome Scotch broth helped to restore Morison when he was recuperating from one of the serious winter ills to which he was prone.

Oliver Simon was a prudent person and at first sight it might be regarded as imprudent for a man to produce a *Catalogue Raisonné of Books Printed at The Curwen Press* when he had been little more than two years on the job. But it was evidence that he was enjoying playing a part in the printing renaissance and determined to do all he could to improve standards, especially in book printing. He also wanted the world to know that The Curwen Press were capable producers of books and the *Catalogue Raisonné* was an excellent medium for his message. As a document of Oliver's early work the catalogue is valuable; it shows the astonishing speed of his development as a master of typography.

The *Catalogue* is medium octavo ($8\frac{1}{4}$ in. × $5\frac{3}{4}$ in.) and set in Monotype Garamond which was the first of the fine series of Monotype post-war type revivals. The spacing after full-stops is still far too generous and it must have been realized soon afterwards what a defect this was for henceforward close spacing as recommended by Emery Walker became standard practice and 'white rivers' ceased to flow through Plaistow-printed pages.

Oliver Simon's editorial abilities at this time had yet to attain the scholarly care for which he was known in later years. He had not then developed the bibliographer's accuracy. Pages are often carelessly counted or not counted at all. The last entry—there were only two—for 1921 is *Autumn* by John Clare. It is stated to be seven pages which Oliver, fresh from his workshop training,

THE LUTE OF LOVE

Decorated by C. Lovat Fraser

SELWYN & BLOUNT
21 York Buildings, Adelphi
London, W.C.2

Title page *The Lute of Love* 1920. The first entry in the
Catalogue Raisonné of books printed at The Curwen Press 1920–23

should have known was an impossible unit. It is, in fact, twelve pages and is so slight that it could just as well be classified as a pamphlet as a book. As it was bound in full paper boards it was allowed to squeeze through to rank as a book. Another doubtful classification is *The Berkshire Kennet* by Richard Aldington: said to be six pages but in fact eight pages and it just seems to have scraped home as a book despite the fact it was limp bound in Batik paper wrappers. A really substantial work was *Vincent Van Gogh, a Biographical Study** by Julius Meier-Graefe in two volumes. No information about the number of pages is vouchsafed: the first volume had 16 pages of preliminaries and 144 pages text with 54 plates and a frontispiece; the second volume 10 pages of preliminaries and 110 pages text with 46 plates and a frontispiece; fine volumes, and the vigour of Monotype Imprint used to advantage. This work shows how rapidly Oliver's ability was developing. Printed slightly earlier than the Van Gogh, there is special interest in *The Best Poems of 1922*.† Interesting because it shows Oliver Simon groping for a style which was to declare itself with such confidence in Hazlitt's *A Reply to Z*:†† In the *Best Poems* Oliver uses the newly acquired Garamond for the first time but it seems he never considered either small capitals or letter spacing to improve the legibility of words set in capital letters. The book has some pleasant tail pieces by Philip Hagreen and is well machined: typographically it is Simon in the throes of his typographic apprenticeship. In a remarkably short time he found his typographic feet as is shown unmistakably in the penultimate entry in the catalogue. The classic authority, the judgement in spacing between lines and meticulous letter spacing of capitals is demonstrated in the title page of *A Reply to Z*. To begin in 1921 and to become a typographer to be reckoned with by 1923 shows the depth of his belief that printers in the trade and in the ordinary course of business could produce books that are beautiful, well constructed and legible. It is a surprise to find that the first issue of *The Fleuron* has its place in the *Catalogue Raisonné*. With Morison's help *The Fleuron* comes near to

---

**Vincent Van Gogh, a Biographical Study* by Julius Meier-Graefe: The Medici Society Ltd, 1922.

†*The Best Poems of 1922* selected by Thomas Moult, decorated by Philip Hagreen: Jonathan Cape, 1923.

††*A Reply to Z* by William Hazlitt: First Edition Club, 1923.

being a masterpiece of printing and Oliver Simon emerges with flying colours as a scholarly editor and a typographer able to work on a grand scale. The simple and charming prospectus with the striking seven-line initial letter printed in vermilion has a note by Oliver Simon. 'The principles', he concludes, 'which *The Fleuron* endeavours to promote by argument, it attempts to demonstrate by example; it is not confined within the rigid limits of commercialism. It is not merely as good as the price will permit, but as beautiful as a book can be, or if that be too high a claim, as good as its artists and workers can make it.' The Curwen Press with great generosity allowed it to be priced at 21s with an extra shilling if sent by post.

In his introduction to the *Catalogue Raisonné* Holbrook Jackson claims that 'in Harold Curwen English printing has another defender of the true typographic faith, one also who is not afraid to adventure along new paths; and in his typographer, Mr Oliver Simon, a printing artist of taste and originality'. As Harold Curwen was already a skilled designer of printing it would have been more accurate if Holbrook Jackson had described Oliver Simon as his co-typographer. Surprisingly, Holbrook Jackson accuses the private presses of actually blocking the avenues of typographical progress: this could scarcely be right as they seem to have had the very opposite effect. Those who took part in the printing revival were aware of the debt they owed to Kelmscott, Doves and Ashendene. It was true that the owners of these presses were not in 'business' in the sense they did not have to depend on printing for a living; but their workmanship was magnificent and set entirely new standards for professional work. In his foreword, Holbrook Jackson mistakenly asserts that Caxton printed from wood-type, forgetting that this was a myth for the type was cast in metal.

The *Catalogue Raisonné* drew a deserved but mild rebuke from Emery Walker:

Dear Harold Curwen, please accept my best thanks for your beautifully printed *Catalogue Raisonné*. Short of the work of those Presses which my friend Holbrook Jackson thinks blocked 'the avenue of typographical progress' I have never seen such an admirable piece of work. I am a little surprised, however, that The Curwen Press allowed themselves to father such a statement that Caxton used wooden types, *pace* Hodgkin; I thought that myth was exploded long ago. Pardon my grumbling but I could not let such a blot on a pretty book go by without protest.

[164]

'The idea that the paper, printing, and "make-up" of a book is unimportant is as absurd as the idea that it does not matter how slovenly and insanitary a house is if the tenant is honest. It would have been far better to charge sixpence or even a shilling more and have produced decent books than to have allowed this series of cheap horrors to invade an overcrowded world.' DAILY HERALD.

Poems of Emily Brontë. With an Introduction by CHARLOTTE BRONTË and decorated with arabesques by PERCY SMITH. London: Selwyn & Blount. (12s. 6d. net, demy 8vo, 93 pp., collotype frontispiece, edition limited to 500 copies on Haesbeek paper, Garamond monotype, bound in cloth back, Rizzi decorated paper boards.)

'This new edition of Emily Brontë's poems is a delightful book to look upon, both outside and in. It is bound in boards covered with a charming Italian paper and backed with buckram, and the type used is agreeable and easy to read.' THE OBSERVER.

'There must be a sufficient number of "collectors" of Emily Brontë's books to secure the speedy exhaustion of this "limited edition," which will add a very beautiful book to any library.' Mr. Clement Shorter in the SPHERE, 1st September, 1923.

The Fleuron, A Journal of Typography. No. 1. Edited by OLIVER SIMON. London, At the Office of the Fleuron. (21s. net, demy 4to, 127+vii pp. and numerous insets, edition limited to 1,000 copies on Abbey Mills Antique, Garamond monotype, bound cloth back and Michalet paper boards. There is also an édition de luxe of 110 copies on Kelmscott hand-made paper, bound in whole buckram, gilt top, and containing additional plates, £3 3s. net.)

'The first number of the "Fleuron" is a brilliant piece of book-production.' B. H. Newdigate in the LONDON MERCURY.

'Irreproachable in manner and execution, this first volume contains articles by some of the best-known authorities on printers' flowers, title-pages, initial letters, and similar matters, richly illustrated with rare examples. The book is indeed a torch to light the way for the seeker after better printing, being, unlike some books on the subject, a noble example of the art it treats of.' MANCHESTER GUARDIAN.

21

Page from *Catalogue Raisonné* edited and designed by Oliver Simon. Second item announces the first number of *The Fleuron*

On the same day, 20 February 1924, a card arrived at St Stephen's House from Francis Meynell and very welcome it must have been to young Oliver Simon: 'it is a proud achievement; itself and for what it records. *A Reply to Z* seems to me the best title page of years and years.'

XVI

DECADE

OF DEVELOPMENT

THE TEN YEARS from 1923 to 1933 take a high place in the history of the printing renaissance. It was no red-hot revolution with a great body of printers experiencing some wonderful conversion. Indeed what was being done was being done by astonishingly few. The pioneers who were out to show how modern methods and modern machinery could produce well-designed printing which was economical in cost could be counted on the fingers of both hands. They were not backward looking; they could not afford to be, for reasonable cost was rightly held to be supremely important. There was no worship of hand composition for its own sake. It was patent that mechanical composition could equal and surpass hand-set work. Printing on a hand press, mechanically not much different from that used by Gutenberg, was not reckoned a virtue; it was less costly and the impression of type on paper was more satisfactory if the printing was done on a two-revolution cylinder press in the care of a skilled minder. Modern methods for modern work was an accepted catch-phrase.

By 1923 the small band of pioneers was beginning to feel confident of a growing audience. A veteran was George W. Jones who printed at the Sign of the Dolphin in Gough Square. He was a Linotype enthusiast and his work followed—many would say too closely—the Venetian style of early Kelmscott books: the beauty lay in care in composition and a perfection of press-work. The Sign of the Dolphin earned high respect. More closely involved, and using contemporary artists like Herrick and Gregory Brown was Fred P. Phillips at the Baynard Press. Mainly working for commerce, Phillips was, like Harold Curwen, a founder member of the Design & Industries Association. The

[167]

Baynard Press supported fitness for purpose. 'His Press', Phillips said, 'which prides itself on the scholarly production of editions de luxe need not disdain to design gay and attractive biscuit labels; the same guiding principles affect both—an attention to fitness for purpose combined with good drawing and arresting colour scheme—nor should the production of striking and effective posters militate against putting forth at the same time attractive and well balanced booklets and circulars'. Fred Phillips and his Baynard Press clearly had the same all-embracing philosophy as The Curwen Press which followed Professor Lethaby with his satisfying definition that art was doing well what wants doing. There were, like at Plaistow, no class distinctions at the Baynard Press and Lethaby's applied art was part of a craftsman's everyday life.

The Nonesuch Press, founded by Francis Meynell (later Sir Francis) in 1923, had by the end of 1933 amazed the printing and publishing world by producing ninety-one books which so delighted its public that it was usual for entire editions to be taken up before publication. Francis Meynell defined his objectives in his first Nonesuch prospectus: 'to choose and make books according to a triple ideal: significance of subjects, beauty of format, and moderation of price'. The first book *The Love Poems* by John Donne was hand-set in Fell type but hand composition was exceptional and nearly all the books were Monotype set. The Nonesuch Press had no printing machinery; the books were planned in every detail by Francis Meynell whose vigilance and genial supervision allowed various presses, which were judged by him sufficiently capable, to do the printing. Nonesuch books contributed graciously and gloriously to the printing renaissance.

The Pelican Press, an earlier child of Francis Meynell's, was more concerned with printing for business. It was adventurous and never dull. The Pelican Press inset contributed to the first number of *The Fleuron* shows a distinguished advertisement setting for the Midland Bank, a programme cover for the Glasgow Orpheus Choir and a sample page from *The Builders' History* set in 14 point Monotype Garamond with Narcissus outline for the titles to chapters. To look at this inset is to appreciate the inventiveness of the Pelican Press; rarely, if ever, did it fail to produce work that was not a model of intelligent printing. The Westminster Press, the founders and printers of *The Imprint*, and Lund Humphries of Bradford, the printers and publishers of *Penrose Annual*, also played important parts in the revival which was given a great push forward in 1923 when Walter Lewis was appointed University printer at Cambridge. In 1922 the Mono-type Corporation produced Garamond as the first of a series of type face revivals. Not directly initiated by Stanley Morison, he was probably asked to give his opinion of what was being done at the Corporation's Redhill works. Morison was appointed part time typographical adviser to the Corporation in 1923 and must have supervised the fine revival of Baskerville which was made available in the year of his appointment.

Meanwhile The Curwen Press was quietly adding to printing history and was happy to be one of the small group of firms engaged in the worthwhile task of bringing a new look of freshness and simplicity of design to everyday work. Curwen Press output until 1920 was largely music printing with a sprinkling of printing for business. *The Catalogue Raisonné of Books Printed between 1920 and 1923* shows that book printing was becoming a new factor in the firm's work. The third entry for 1923, following the *Bodley Head Quartos* and *Poems of Emily Brontë* is *The Fleuron, a Journal of Typography*, no. 1, edited by Oliver Simon. In addition to working on the *Catalogue Raisonné* published in 1924, Oliver Simon had the first number of *The Fleuron* ready for launching in the early spring of 1923. Being on sale in May 1923 meant that the task of editing and putting it into type must have commenced in the previous year: this is striking evidence of Simon's rapid development for he had been working at the Press for only two years. Morison, sitting in the same room and never backward in pronouncing on the worth of any proposals, must have furnished a running commentary of a value that it is impossible to quantify. *The Fleuron* lived up to the promise of its elegant prospectus. A substantial Demy quarto (11 in. × 8½ in.), it was offered in two editions: an ordinary edition of 1,000 copies printed on Abbey Mills Antique laid, and an edition de luxe of 110 copies (100 for sale) printed on Kelmscott handmade paper—both marvels of value for money. The ordinary edition cost 21s and the de luxe edition £3 3s. The more costly edition threw in as extras a collotype portrait of T. J. Cobden-Sanderson from a drawing by William (later Sir William) Rothenstein which the artist signed, an original design by Lovat Fraser printed in five colours and a full page reproduction of a page from Fust and Schoeffer's Psalter of 1457. The de luxe edition sold out at once. After some presentation copies to the Curwen and Simon families it is

[169]

pleasing to record that George W. Jones was the first actual purchaser. He bought three copies of the de luxe edition and remained a faithful subscriber to all four issues of the journal printed at Plaistow and published from The Office of The Fleuron.

The *Manchester Guardian* of 16 May 1923 called *The Fleuron* 'a journal of typography rather in the vein of the short-lived *Imprint*. Irreproachable in manner and execution . . . richly illustrated with rare examples. So perfect is the volume in detail that a slip like Frankfürt (necessitating recourse to another fount for the wrongly modified "u") on pages 30 and 32 obtains an undeserved prominence.' Considering that European scholarship and indeed book printing was relatively new to the proof-readers at Plaistow, there are few errors and literals. Poor Moritz is misspelt Mozitz on the frontispiece to 'Printers' Flowers and Arabesques' and on the very last line of this important article Jacob Sabon becomes Jabob Sabon.

J. C. Squire reviewing *The Fleuron* in *The Observer* on 17 June 1923 sees that the new journal has spiritual as well as practical values. In a long and appreciative review he writes,

Everybody interested in book production should secure this journal, which carries on, still more sumptuously, the work which was done before the war (1913) by the *Imprint*. It is the fruit of co-operation between a number of enthusiasts who are not private printers ministering to the tastes of connoisseurs with glass-fronted book-cases and large bank balances, but commercial printers willing to expend all this art on any job which is given to them book, poster or prospectus. Every year adds to the number of commercial printing firms which are intelligently run by masters who realize how interesting this work is and by men who are taking an intelligent interest in what they do. Old firms are being regenerated, new ones are coming to birth; before long every big house will be compelled, one hopes, to adapt itself or go bankrupt.

The *Caxton Magazine* paid *The Fleuron* the compliment of changing its sub-title to 'A Journal of Inspiration'. They end their long review with an echo of Squire: '*The Fleuron*', writes the *Caxton* reviewer, 'is not likely to interest the printer who can see no satisfaction in the printing industry other than the perfect operation of his organization and satisfactory bank balance; but to all those who think of their calling as a craft, and who take pleasure and interest in its advancement, the possession of *The Fleuron* will be a source of real satisfaction.'

The Fleuron prospered in a modest way and continued to be supported by The Curwen Press and was looked upon as a valuable vehicle for encouraging a flow of books and general printing to Plaistow. The first two numbers were published from St. Stephen's House. *Fleuron* nos III and IV were issued from 101 Great Russell Street, W.C.1. After no. IV, published in 1925, *The Fleuron* was transferred to Morison and issued from Cambridge. It had previously been arranged that at some time Stanley Morison should take over the editorship. The changeover was made in 1925 and a further three numbers were published, the final volume no. VII being issued in 1930. After the change of editor, *The Fleuron* was printed at the University Press at Cambridge by Walter Lewis. There must have been some change of plan for in the list of books published at The Office of The Fleuron for 1925, *The Fleuron* (no. V) edited by Stanley Morison is announced as being 'in active preparation' and was forecast to be ready in March 1926. It may well be that Morison saw that Cambridge publishing abilities and Doubleday Doran & Co. in the United States far exceeded the limited resources of The Office of The Fleuron. *Fleuron* no. V never appeared under the Fleuron imprint: Morison assumed sole responsibility for editorship, production and publication.

The Fleuron was a declaration of faith in the new approach to printing; it was a new world in which competitors were welcomed as fellow warriors and where there was rivalry it was rivalry of how best to forward the new outlook in printing. From the start the editor of *The Fleuron* had no difficulty in getting contributions; the range and quality of the contributions are a testimony of the interest that was being shown in printing. It was eloquent of the prevailing geniality that a young editor, then almost unknown, was able to get such wholesale support. As an enterprise *The Fleuron* was a fine example of participation between Oliver Simon typographer and editor and Harold Curwen controller of production relying on the skilled staff of the Plaistow works. Plaistow, as has already been related, showed how the Tonic Sol-fa method of teaching singing was able to raise the quality of life for a large number of people, and this educational task was pursued with missionary zeal. The printing revival triggered off new missionary zeal. The general printing designed by Harold Curwen and the book printing under the typographical charge of Oliver Simon made a serious contribution to the new faith.

[171]

Very properly, in the last number of *The Fleuron* under his editorship, Oliver Simon pays tribute to two of the greatest contemporary printers: in the edition de luxe of *Fleuron* no. IV subscribers had the pleasure of receiving a collotype reproduction of a portrait of Emery Walker from a drawing by William Rothenstein and a collotype reproduction of a portrait of Bruce Rogers by F. W. Ivins.

Oliver Simon was a compulsive compiler of *catalogues raisonnés*, check lists and bibliographies. *The Curwen Press Almanack* for 1926 gives him the opportunity for more cataloguing. The calendar portion is confined to six pages, each having a finely executed drawing by Professor Randolph Schwabe. The six drawings appear again in the Curwen specimen book of 1928 as seasonal head-pieces. The agricultural sequences are portrayed with great charm especially the group of girls taking a risk in July–August by bathing in the nude with nothing but a hedge between them and a man riding on a reaper and binder. But

Seasonal head-pieces drawn by Randolph Schwabe for
The Curwen Press Almanack 1926

the calendar is really a preliminary to another *catalogue raisonné*
of books printed at The Curwen Press, 1924–5. The first entry
is the *Catalogue Raisonné of Books Printed at The Curwen Press
1920–3*. The second entry is puzzling as the *catalogues
raisonnés* claim to catalogue books where the design and choice of
materials have been freely committed to the printer. This could
not be the case for *Genesis*, the second entry, which is a Nonesuch
Press book and therefore designed in every detail by Francis
Meynell. The Curwen Press acted, it is hoped, as intelligent
interpreters of Meynell's orders. These *catalogues raisonnés*
document admirably the progress of Curwen's book printing.
Oliver Simon is still strangely unreliable in computing the
number of pages. Sixty-one pages, for example, instead of four
signatures of sixteen pages each, totalling sixty-four pages. No
reason is given why the number of text pages in the *Bodley Head*

[173]

Quartos goes unrecorded. The programme for 1924–5 shows that substantial book printing was being undertaken at Plaistow. In the second list there are no border-line cases of whether a book is a book or a pamphlet. The last entry for 1924 is *The Fleuron* no. III. For some obscure reason no mention whatever is made of *The Fleuron* no. II which must have been one of the bright stars in 1924. The omission may have been accidental or it may have been thought that enough space had already been given to *Fleurons. The Fleuron* no. IV, the last to be edited by Oliver Simon, is the sixth entry for 1925.

Fleuron no. II was, in fact, just as enthusiastically received as the first number. *The Times Literary Supplement* of 13 March 1924 speaks of 'this second number of this beautiful quarto journal of printing . . . the fascimiles and other illustrations, besides increasing the beauty of the volume, make it serviceable to students as well as to experts'. There is a contribution on the 'Planning of Printing' by D. B. Updike, the founder and owner of the famous Merrymount Press in Boston. As a consequence there is a laudatory two-column review of *Fleuron* no. II in the *Boston Evening Transcript* of 12 March 1924.

The production of all this interesting work, *Fleurons*, books and almanacks produced a new problem at Plaistow. It was discovered that a certain amount of pilfering was taking place. In November 1924 Harold felt obliged to post a notice to discourage malefactors:

I regret to notice, and to have actually seen, that certain members of the personelle [sic] are helping themselves from the printing in the works. It should hardly be necessary to point out that every sheet of paper is part of a complete saleable piece of work, and if copies are taken it makes a deduction from what we can sell to our customers. We are handling an increasingly good class of work and I must be able to rely on its safety from this theft. If anyone particularly wants to have a copy of any job, and will apply to the office, we will do our best to secure it at quite special prices.

With so much interesting work going through temptation must have been strong and some mild pilfering inevitable; but what exactly did Harold mean by quite a special price?

Six months later Harold had a more pleasant notice to pin on the board. From 25 May 1926 hours of work were rearranged so as to exclude Saturday working. The working week was reduced from forty-eight hours to forty-seven and a half, the daily working hours became nine and a half from Monday to Friday. Saturday work would be confined to emergency overtime and The Curwen Press became one of the pioneers of what is now regarded as the normal five-day week.

Well printed books have ever had their patrons and have always been the public's chief interest. It will be remembered that the fine books printed by Bulmer and Bensley were eagerly bought as they appeared in the late eighteenth and early nineteenth centuries. There was a flicker of interest in the middle of the nineteenth century when books printed by Charles Whittingham for the publisher William Pickering were esteemed and collected for the beauty of their printing. But on the whole the nineteenth century was a barren one and it was not until the end of the century that the private presses, like Kelmscott, Ashendene and Doves, began to win back once more an appreciation for book printing.

The volume of well printed books increased with the printing revival and as many of them were moderately priced, bibliophiles interested in the typography of books grew rapidly in numbers. The period 1920–30 enhanced Oliver Simon's reputation as a book designer and he could count on some staunch supporters. Although bookwork formed a relatively small part of Curwen Press production, yet it quickly made its mark and the firm was able to live up to its slightly dubious claim in its advertisement in the first number of *The Fleuron* that 'The Curwen Press is a Book House'.

Bookwork printed at Plaistow owed much to the firm's technical ability. To print with sharp impression on hand-made paper, to keep unclogged the recessed lines in wood engravings and to give unusual care to imposition and folding were in the main due to Harold Curwen who, besides insisting on high standards, could personally show how high standards could be arrived at. Curwen the careful printer was also Curwen the careful teacher.

A collector of books was unlikely to know much about the general printing trade. Printing, in common with other manufacturing, remained something of a mystery to those not in contact with it either by employment or by virtue of being a customer. The printing revival influenced general commercial printing quite as powerfully as it influenced bookwork. Books are tied to a retail selling price, but this is seldom the case for catalogues and similar commercial work. General printing could therefore afford to be more experimental and there was less need for cost restriction implicit in keeping within a fixed price.

Respect for materials was an article of faith for manufacturing members of the Design & Industries Association. Harold Curwen would have nothing to do with anything which tried to deceive. Popular at one time was a quality of book paper called Imitation Hand-Made: it had a slender chance of entering the Plaistow works. Similarly cover papers with imitation linen finish or papers simulating rhinoceros hide were barred. He preferred natural, honest materials. As paper makers seemed unable to provide the bright colours he wanted, he made his own. He took a pleasant, slightly uneven plain paper and printed on it solid, gay, bright colours. They were used extensively for Curwen printed pamphlet covers and were sold to the trade as 'Radiant Cover Papers'. Any kind of imitation deeply shocked Harold Curwen. As early as 1920 he was urging that it was his job as a trained printer-designer to assemble fine type, fine drawing and fine ink and paper. He hated anything spurious and had a healthy dislike for both deception and waste. If a piece of printing was unlikely to be useful he would advise intending customers against any expenditure.

During the decade 1920–30 Curwen gradually arrived at a set of rules for printing design which were known as his axioms. His printing had to have a sense of correct physiology, avoidance of superlatives in reading matter, simplicity of format and intimacy without impertinence; and as a final test it had to be fit for its purpose. Customers were required to play their part. They were asked to trust their typographer, writer and artist and not be afraid of adventure. A torrent of trivia and ephemera was produced by The Curwen Press during the twenties and most of it, understandably, has been forgotten; but what has remained shows how seriously all the problems were faced and the remarkable ingenuity of the designers.

It is impossible to assess the work of The Curwen Press without considering the firm's output of printing for business. By 1930 general printing accounted for well over half the output. The Curwen Press had some special advantages. Harold Curwen was an original member of the Design & Industries Association; although he would not have sought to benefit commercially by his membership, it was nevertheless natural that other members needing printing would be aware of what he was doing. Some of the firm's most valuable customers in the early years of the decade 1920–30 were, in fact, fellow members of the Association.

The importance of this connection cannot be over rated. It formed a solid foundation of important customers who, as Harold Curwen required, trusted the judgement of their typographer-printer. Another advantage was the fortunate fact that Oliver Simon's uncle, William Rothenstein, was principal of the Royal College of Art. Rothenstein, as was well known, went out of his way to help his former students and he found he could assist some by introductions to his printer nephew at The Curwen Press. Harold and Oliver were anxious to get into touch with the best of the younger generation and, by 1925, thanks to the initiative of William Rothenstein, The Curwen Press was commissioning work from a new group of young artists among whom were Edward Bawden, Eric Ravilious and Barnett Freedman. In addition they were able to enlist some members of the Royal College of Art staff. Paul Nash, who taught Bawden and Ravilious at the College, did some fine work for the firm and remained throughout his life an inspiring and loyal friend. The new artists who came to help The Curwen Press were themselves helped by Oliver Simon's persuasive recommendations when making his round of tea-time calls.

There were occasions when a trade catalogue or booklet was so splendidly arranged that what was intended to be ephemeral took on permanence. This kind of printing, if little known outside the trade, required as much skill in planning as any book and can be seen to be one of the most satisfying aspects of the printing revival. Before the seekers after good design in printing got to work, very few gave much thought to appearances and there were hardly any buyers of printing who had training or knowledge to influence design. Harold Curwen, with his practical mastery and readiness to experiment, combined with Oliver Simon's bookish and classical typography, made a responsive team. They both knew when to enlist the help of an artist and their choice of artist was rarely at fault. The atmosphere of the works at Plaistow was friendly and artists were surprised to find themselves welcome and made thoroughly at home. A manufactory that was so congenial was a great encouragement for good work. Mercifully the 'spirit of joy' of Lovat Fraser days had not deserted North Street.

Consideration of a few of the outstanding productions of the decade 1920–30 provides some idea of the contribution The Curwen Press was making. Harold Stabler, an original member of the Committee of the D.I.A., liked to find opportunities for young artists and in 1924 Edward Bawden, while still at the Royal College, was asked to design a calendar for Carter, Stabler and Adams, the well-known potters of Poole. On Harold Stabler's advice the printing was given to Harold Curwen. The calendar was Bawden's first commercial commission and his first job done at The Curwen Press. Bawden had met Harold Curwen previously, having been introduced by Oliver Simon: it was the beginning of a working partnership and friendship with Harold Curwen and Oliver Simon which produced some of the most successful and arresting examples of commercial printing of the period. Like all good work, it is impervious to fashion; what Bawden did in 1925 remains as fresh as on the day it was first proofed. Bawden found Harold Curwen's practical advice valuable and said later that Curwen took a teacher's interest in showing him how to do drawings for colour reproduction by line blocks. It was typical of Harold to take endless trouble to help artists intent on doing and enjoying good work.

After the calendar there was a booklet *Pottery Making at Poole*, with lively colour-line drawings and the text set in Monotype Garamond. Very good relatively early Curwen, but the composing room still could not be relied on to letter-space lines of capitals and reduce the unduly large white spaces after punctuation marks. In 1927–8 Bawden produced a successful series of advertisements for the Underground; simple, unfussy, slightly satiric and never without a sense of humour, his drawings could not fail to attract attention. Curwen set the series in Baskerville and the line of letter-spaced capitals formed a perfect link between Bawden's drawing and the text. The borders for the series were all designed by Bawden and show his remarkable power of invention. 'Music' in the Underground series is illustrated on the opposite page.

At the same time Bawden was providing illustrations for hundreds of advertisements for the Westminster Bank. It is difficult to realize that at that time business institutions were rarely conscious of the importance of design in industry. It was honourable that a few great enterprises like the Westminster Bank gave Harold Curwen the chance to set new standards for newspaper advertisement. Some of Bawden's drawings for the Westminster Bank are produced on page 180. These advertisements are splendid examples of the printing revival. It is chance that, like a tram ticket, they should have a short life of just a day.

[178]

MUSIC

How does the Underground train run? Legato? Allegro con brio? Prestissimo? Rallentando? There is something in the mood of the traveller. The Underground suits all moods. Music is a necessity, and London supplies all needs. Around Oxford Circus are grouped most of the principal concert halls. Here you will find the Queen's, Grotrian, Steinway, and Wigmore Halls. The Albert and Aeolian Halls are within a few minutes' walk of South Kensington and Bond Street Stations respectively. Every day of the weeks during this month there are concerts and recitals at one or more of these Halls. London has jazz too, for those who prefer it. You must seek this in the restaurants and dance halls of the West End. But whichever your choice—travel

UNDERGROUND

E1/10/28

Advertisement for the Underground, drawing and border by Edward Bawden

Drawings by Edward Bawden for press advertisements
for Westminster Bank Limited

Inevitably newspaper advertisements are fated to be ephemeral
but in the field of printing skills, they showed how simple typography combined with the work of contemporary artists could
produce what was pleasing to the eye, and just right for the job.

After Poole Pottery came Gestetner, a manufacturer of duplicating machines at Tottenham. The Gestetner booklet called *A*

Product and Its People shows the professional skill of Harold Curwen's team. The text is by E. P. Leigh-Bennett whose ability to write about other people's business was unrivalled. He and Curwen were accustomed to working together; Leigh-Bennett liked to have his work well produced and whenever he had a say in the matter Curwen would be nominated. It also worked the other way round and Curwen went about primed with Leigh-Bennett's charges which could be put forward as occasion arose; there is, indeed, abundant evidence that Curwen gave Leigh-Bennett a lot of work. The Gestetner book is brilliantly written by Leigh-Bennett and illustrated by photographs taken by Francis Bruguière who was Curwen's preferred industrial photographer. Curwen himself was responsible for the general planning and printing detail. In a period when photographs rarely came to the edge of a page and pictures were by custom boxed in by thin black surrounding frames, the cover of the Gestetner book comes as a breath of fresh air. Front and back covers are arresting photographs of the machine printed in black full out to the edges and varnished as a protection against finger marking.

The text is imaginatively set out. A rather bookish title page surrounded by a frame of rules with a 'bleed-off' picture of a Gestetner machine as a frontispiece. A foreword in Koch Kursiv and the main text in 14 point Baskerville leaded and displayed headings in Walbaum capitals. A centre spread of a montage of Bruguière's photographs taken in the factory interrupts, without severing, the text. In the vigorous and straightforward treatment of the story of an important manufacturing firm, the Gestetner book set a style from which a whole series of similar publications can trace their ancestry. Bruguière made his imaginative photographic contribution in May 1930 and was paid the reasonable fee of £75. It seems that Gestetner were satisfied. The British Soap Company asked Gestetner what they thought of Curwen's brochure. The reply in January 1931 was that of a satisfied client: 'We must say,' wrote Gestetner to British Soap, 'that this has been the most successful piece of publicity we have ever put out, and we have not only reordered another issue but we are having it translated into various languages for use in connection with our overseas organizations.' High praise for Leigh-Bennett's writing and Bruguière's photography and some can be reasonably reserved for Harold Curwen's original and sensible conception.

TO THOSE THREE

You asked me to write about your Works.
Well, this is an unadorned impression of
the job, as I see it.
When you read it I would like you to keep
in mind two things:
That very few people want to know exactly
how a duplicating machine is made.
That any stranger who visits your Works,
or anyone associated with the business, must
surely be imbued with a feeling of friend-
liness towards those in control of it.
I was. That is why I have written about it
in this way. I had to.

E. P. L.-B.

Foreword to *A Product and Its People* produced for D. Gestetner Ltd

It owed much to being shaped by a man who really understood the practice of printing.

Within a few weeks of starting the Gestetner book Curwen was asked to undertake a brochure telling the story of match manufacture in the factories of Bryant and May Ltd. It was called *Match Making* and is even more adventurous than Gestetner. The same team, the story by E. P. Leigh-Bennett, photography by Bruguière and planning by Harold Curwen. One important change was made: Paul Nash was asked to design the cover and the result was brilliantly successful. *Match Making* can hold its own in any period, defying change and the passage of time. Harold set the text in a large size of Baskerville and was ready to have minimum margins. The wide setting and the large type stood up wonderfully well to the full page splendours of Bruguière's photographs. The headings are in Harold Curwen's own sans serif capitals. Again there is the fascinating and well-informed story by Leigh-Bennett made possible by his ability to get beneath the skin of a business organization. *Match Making* with its immediate predecessor Gestetner's *A Product and Its People* are among Curwen's most impressive contributions to the revival in printing for business.

The Curwen Press have a long connection in printing for the transport industry. The first customer was the West Ham Corporation Tramways in 1905. After the trams came the long printing association with the Underground Railways. A main line railway became a customer of the Plaistow works in March 1929. On the initiative of John (later Sir John) Elliot, a quarterly journal was started and distributed to first-class season ticket holders as part of the job of making Sir Herbert Walker's immense scheme for Southern Railway electrification understood. The journal was called *Over the Points* and was so successful that it was decided to broaden the scope to take in all Southern Railway activities which might interest regular travellers. Leigh-Bennett was the author and he suggested that the design and printing should be done by Curwen. *Over the Points* is probably the first regular customer house journal that a railway company ever issued. It showed that the Southern Railway had the good sense to realize that travellers were the Company's valuable customers and their goodwill worth cultivating. Preparations for *Over the Points* began in January 1929 and on Curwen's advice the illustrations, beautifully executed in fine-line drawings, were

[183]

A Modern Canute

YOU remember that one day a king took a chair down to the sea's edge, and, sitting on it, showed his people how futile was the will of man when opposed to a law of Nature. I am reminded forcibly of Canute when I meet the Docks' engineer at Southampton: though his method and results are different. For he is doing what the reformed king knew he could not do, and is achieving complete success. But then, of course, he is armoured for his fight with highly scientific accoutrements, which even the indomitable sea cannot withstand. He is, in fact, shoving it back ruthlessly in the most authoritative manner over a very large area; and it is going to cost him millions before he can put 'paid' to the sea's bill. This is making the engineering mind think a great deal, and he must go on thinking steadily for ten vigilant years before he is through with it.

You would imagine, would you not, that to transform two miles of tidal water and four hundred acres of slithering mud into land upon which men can live, work and amuse themselves, would be a task before which even a civil engineer would quail? On the contrary, that is the work he has guaranteed joyfully to undertake, and he is deeply involved in it at this moment. This is *some* job: in his opinion the best one the

14

From *Over the Points* produced for the Southern Railway

done by T. L. Poulton. Only the most unamiable person could fail to be interested in being taken behind the scenes of a great railway company. Leigh-Bennett had a genius for telling about the other man's job.* The simple, well-arranged pages, anything from twenty to thirty-two, printed on an antique laid paper set standards which were refreshingly new. T. L. Poulton continued to illustrate *Over the Points* until March 1932 when Victor Reinganum took over the task and continued until publication came to an end in September 1939. The success of *Over the Points* lay in the fact that it was never dull. Leigh-Bennett invariably found interesting material and Harold Curwen helped greatly by personally discussing the plans for each issue with officials at Waterloo. The journal was so much appreciated that people would write and complain that they had not received their monthly *Over the Points*. They overlooked the fact that it was only a quarterly publication.

Another railway job was *East Coasting* written by Leigh-Bennett under the pseudonym of Dell Leigh. It was published in 1930 by the London and North Eastern Railway. The aim was to encourage people to holiday at places served from London by King's Cross and Liverpool Street. It is an attractive brochure. Charming and gorgeously amusing drawings by Edward Bawden fit splendidly into Harold Curwen's typographic constructions. The booklet which has sixty-four pages of text has fourteen tail-pieces or fillers that compel admiration. In his introduction, Leigh-Bennett writes, 'they said "Wander about and write." So I did. And these little studies of pleasant places in eastern England and Scotland emerged, and were set down just as they came out of the sunshine of the present and the shadows of the past. Purposely was there no set order of travel; one merely coasted carelessly, looking on at life.'

As good journalism and an example of close co-operation between artist and printer, *East Coasting* must be considered a striking success. Bawden's tail-piece to the Royal Mile in Edinburgh has been appropriated, with, it is hoped, permission of the London and North Eastern Railway, as a Curwen copyright ornament and is shown as number 122 on page 75 of the *Curwen Press Miscellany* published in 1931.

Edward Bawden clearly enjoyed working on *East Coasting*. He

---

* *The Other Man's Job* by E. P. Leigh-Bennett: George Allen & Unwin, 1937.

N

Drawing by Edward Bawden from *East Coasting* designed for the
London and North Eastern Railway

writes to Curwen in May 1930, 'it is always safe to leave things
to Curwen. That is a truth I discovered years ago and the *East
Coasting* affair ably demonstrates it. You have a masterly snip of
the scissors and a most discreet knowledge of the possibilities of
the paste-pot. I would not stop you for the world. Please continue
to snip.'

About this time Harold Curwen was concerned with the
production of a large number of catalogues and booklets for manufacturing industry. His customers sometimes express satisfaction.
'We are very pleased with the way the book [catalogue] is turned

out. It has been generally appreciated and after receiving your explanation we are quite willing to pass the account' wrote Doulton from Burslem, Stoke-on-Trent in June 1926. In the same month Marryat & Scott Ltd, lift, crane and hoist makers wrote, 'we have your invoice 31 May—£420 0s 10d. We notice one item, packing in cases £4 10s. We should like to know why this was done as we cannot trace any instruction.' After this awkward poser Marryat & Scott go on to say

With regard to the printing of this Catalogue we should like to say how particularly pleased we are with the work, and particularly with the very splendid service which you gave in connection with a complicated order. We fully appreciate your careful attention to detail from first to last and your promptness and exactitude in keeping your promises. We may also add that we fully appreciate the artistic merit of your work, and we feel that the book might have had an entirely different and less satisfactory appearance if placed in other hands.

A charming letter came from Westminster Bank Ltd. in November 1931. It was written by J. H. Arnold, the Bank's assistant secretary, who was considered by the staff at Plaistow to be the firm's perfect customer. He was ever a warm supporter and had a scholarship which made his judgements valuable. He wrote to thank Harold Curwen for doing a rush job: 'Many thanks,' writes Mr Arnold, 'for planning, printing and delivering the change of address posters, all within nineteen hours. They carry themselves with an air of positive nobility. The Curwen Press is a wonderful institution.'

XVII

'HOUSE' PUBLICATIONS

AN APPRAISAL of Curwen Press work would be incomplete without taking a look at some of the firm's own publications issued to promote goodwill and good business. There are four 'house' publications which make a contribution to printing history of the period. They show what sort of work Harold Curwen and Oliver Simon were doing and in the *Type Specimen Book* and *Miscellany* the curtain is raised on the rich storehouse of typographical material which was there for The Curwen Press to use.

In 1929 a brochure was printed with the arresting title of *How to Buy and Sell Money*. The page size measures 18 in. × 12 in. and this generous area permitted showing examples without reduction in scale. So unusually large was the format that Curwen considered, probably correctly, that few would dare to throw it aside without inspection.

The cover of *How to Buy and Sell Money* is a beautifully textured design by Edward Bawden which was originally intended as a wallpaper. Cut on linoleum, the texture of the material is preserved by finely judged transferring when making up the lithographic plates. The preface, framed in a border from the Klingspor foundry, majestically exhibits the power of Walbaum in its larger sizes. A large advertisement prepared on behalf of the Empire Marketing Board for Rhodesian Tobacco is headed by a wood engraving by John Nash which reaches near perfection in strength and beauty. Following this are a series of advertisements with drawings by Edward Bawden for the Westminster Bank, the Underground and Twinings the tea blenders. Dora Batty contributes drawings for a Flower Series for the Underground and transport is represented again by a booklet cover for the Post-

Office (London) Railway and the cover and a text page from the first issue of the Southern Railway's quarterly *Over the Points*. Like Sir Gilbert Scott's view that his hotel at St Pancras was almost too good for the Midland Railway,* it might be considered that *How to Buy and Sell Money* was almost too good for the general printing market. Never before had a jobbing printer advertised his wares in such a large format and it is likely that few, if any, have equalled or surpassed the quality of the printing.

It is sad to record that at a period when standards were low anything superior was looked at with suspicion. Good planning, simple elegance and impeccable typesetting were so uncommon and so much in advance of contemporary performance that too many possible customers concluded that Curwen printing must be expensive. It is difficult to equate expenditure with effectiveness but *How to Buy and Sell Money* seems to have done something to solve this problem. At any rate, soon after its distribution came the Gestetner and Bryant & May books, and the London & North Eastern's *East Coasting*. Frank Pick, general manager of the Underground, clearly was impressed with the Curwen effort. He said he was glad that some Underground publicity work was included in the book and declared that they still needed to come to Mr Curwen for their best settings.

Evidently *How to Buy and Sell Money* was judged a success as it was followed up two years later with the publication in 1931 of *Something to Think About*. This time a much smaller page size of 13 in. × 10 in. but again beautiful production and a remarkable testament of Harold Curwen's printing ability. A foreword handset in Kennerley italic is framed in a border specially designed for the Press by Paul Nash. Fear of the waste-paper basket is never far from Curwen's mind. We are told that roughly 97 per cent of advertising matter received through the post goes straight into the waste-paper basket. Prospective buyers are warned against employing the cheapest printer and using the lowest postal rate so as to mail the largest possible quantity. As a consequence of an over large mailing list, no funds may be available for originality of writing, careful typography and the personal goodwill generated by a closed postal packet. When quantity is everything, quality— according to Curwen's reasoning—has no chance. A college-trained printer would be likely to agree with the Curwen view.

* *Personal and Professional Recollections* by Sir George Gilbert Scott: Sampson Low, Marston, Searle & Rivington, 1879.

Quality builds goodwill and breeds loyal custom: quantity can, without quality, be merely a massive outpouring of printed rubbish. *Something to Think About* shows the Curwen philosophy translated into action.

A vigorous catalogue cover for Shell, set in Walbaum, contained within a border redrawn from an eighteenth-century pattern by Henry Ball; thanks to careful recording of transactions with artists and writers made by Elizabeth Benzing, who became Harold Curwen's secretary in 1922, the fact is disclosed that Henry Ball was paid the sum of fifteen shillings for his border. This seems an astonishingly modest sum even in 1929.

Curwen's lively use of photography is well documented. The title page of *Match Making* has a Francis Bruguière masterpiece in industrial photography; he is also represented by the Gestetner brochure cover and a harmonious arrangement of marble and granite for Fenning the stonemasons of Hammersmith. A well thought out group of pictures for Early's, the blanket makers of Witney, is the work of Harold Curwen himself. Artists were, as would be expected, well directed. Althea Willoughby is responsible for the drawings in advertisements for Witney blankets and McKnight Kauffer contributes an ultra-modern dazzlingly beautiful cover for a firm of corset makers. Edward Bawden is represented by charming drawings spiced with his gentle wit illustrating a booklet for Thos. Meadows, the shipping agents, which nobody with a grain of visual appreciation could possibly cast aside.

Transport again has a place. This time it is air transport and a page of a timetable evolved (typographically) by Harold Curwen for Imperial Airways; a careful, well considered arrangement made all the easier for travellers by the use of specially designed symbols. The advertising agent for Imperial Airways was the Stuart Advertising Agency directed by Marcus Brumwell. Brumwell had a genius for innovation and getting distinguished artists and designers to work for him. He was on Oliver Simon's list for regular tea-time calls and a close and lasting friendship had developed. Designing a timetable was a difficult task requiring exact knowledge of composing techniques. In a case like this the Curwen-Simon team's resourcefulness was put to a test: Oliver bows out after getting the order and Harold takes over the practical work.

Bawden is again responsible for the cover. Cut on linoleum and

THE
CHOICE
OF A
SHIPPING
AGENT

Drawing by Edward Bawden for a booklet issued
by Thos. Meadows & Co. Ltd, shipping agents

After the prime necessities of life nothing is more precious to us than books. The art of Typography, their creator, renders a signal service to society and lends it invaluable support, serving, as it does, to educate the citizen, to widen the field for the progress of sciences and arts, to nourish and cultivate the mind, to elevate the soul, and, generally, taking upon itself to be the messenger and interpreter of wisdom and truth.

ABCDEFGHIJKLMNO
PQRSTUVWXYZ
abcdefghijklmnopqrstuvwxyz
1234567890

Curwen sans serif designed by Harold Curwen

lightly transferred to give plenty of texture and protected with a coating of non-gloss varnish, *Something to Think About* was also well protected, it may be fairly assumed, against the dangers of the waste-paper basket.

Not everyone was won over by *Something to Think About*. Mr Pinkham, the experienced publicity manager of the General Electric Company, is clearly unmoved. He acknowledges the brochure and tells Mr Curwen he is not in the market for photography of this nature at the moment, but should he be in the future he would communicate.

Innovation is bound to create opposition and in 1930 this was plain in the printing industry as a whole. It had, however, a beneficial effect on Harold Curwen and Oliver Simon; it gave them the exhilarating feeling of fighting for a good cause. The printing revivalist, they recognized, needed plenty of faith and plenty of tenacity and they were ready to provide both. Both the 'house' publications discussed show how deeply The Curwen Press craftsmen on the shop floor were committed to Harold Curwen's belief that good work and personal happiness went together. No group of people could possibly have produced work of this quality unless they believed in what they were doing. These house publications offer the best possible proof that the printing revival was firmly established at the printing works in North Street.

While Harold was busy producing *How to Buy and Sell Money* and *Something to Think About*, Oliver Simon was busy with heavier artillery and, as with heavy guns, aim was indirect. Harold's brochures were aimed directly at getting more high quality business while the two volumes edited and produced by Oliver were based on an indirect sales approach. In 1928 The Fleuron Ltd published for The Curwen Press *A Specimen Book of Types and Ornaments in Use at The Curwen Press*. It is a beautiful book and a remarkable record of what a comparatively small printing firm can do. It establishes the fact that mechanical typesetting and modern printing presses in the hands of skilled men and women can come within measurable distance of real excellence.

In selecting type faces for the composing room, what to exclude is as important as what to stock. Nothing weakens 'house style' more than a clutter of unsuitable types. How admirably Harold Curwen and Oliver Simon exercised their discrimination is made clear in the Curwen *Type Specimen Book*. They had a flair for choosing sensibly. There was obviously a need to carry types suitable for general printing as well as bookwork; the winnowing process cannot have been easy, but it was well done.

The new type faces were Walbaum, which the Press pioneered in Britain, and Lutetia then newly designed by Jan van Krimpen. Kennerley Italic, designed in 1911 by Frederic Goudy* and in use at Plaistow as early as 1916, is shown in sizes ranging from 10 point to 24 point. Rudolf Koch's beautiful sloping calligraphic letter known as Koch Kursiv was available from 6 point to 24 point. Maximilian inlined capitals, also by Rudolf Koch, and the decorated Vesta reinforced the display types.

The book must have cost the firm a lot of money. It is surprising to find that only 135 copies were printed and a mere 95 put on sale at three guineas a copy. Either The Curwen Press had remarkably few customers or the mailing list was severely restricted. The net receipts from this noble type specimen book could not have been more than £250.

The prefatory note, written by Oliver Simon in December 1927, says

This Specimen Book was originally designed for ourselves as a guide to the type faces and typographical ornaments in current use in our own printing office. As the work proceeded, however, it became so interesting to the compiler, who saw in it something of a conspectus of modern printing tendencies, that we decided to print a few extra copies for friends of the Press. Later, when the pages of vignettes and ornaments were added, forming a unique collection of work by contemporary artists specially drawn for The Curwen Press, and probably unrivalled in any other English printing-office, we were persuaded to go a step further and to issue a limited edition to the public.

The collection was indeed unrivalled and it was a revelation to find such riches in the Plaistow storerooms.

Curwen Poster type designed by Harold Curwen with assistance from H. K. Wolfenden is gloriously displayed on a three page pull-out sheet. Percy Smith and Edward Bawden are responsible for a page of 'flowers' which were cast in metal and have subsequently been widely used. We are treated to a magnificent showing of Lovat Fraser's work and fifteen delicate vignettes by Albert Rutherston. The two pages of Curwen Press

*The rights for Goudy's Kennerley were acquired by the Caslon foundry in 1913.

CURWEN PRESS FLOWERS

DESIGNED BY PERCY SMITH

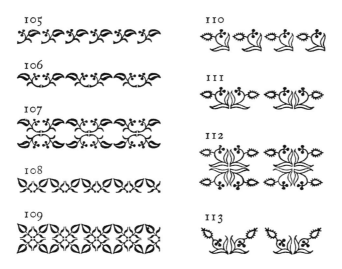

105

106

107

108

109

110

111

112

113

DESIGNED BY EDWARD BAWDEN

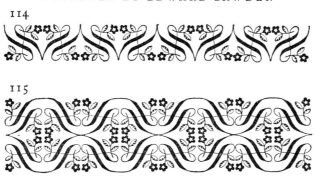

114

115

Flowers from the *Type Specimen Book*, 1928

Curwen Press unicorns
1. Paul Woodroffe, 2. Percy Smith, 3. Eric Gill
4 and 5. Lovat Fraser, 6. Aldo Cosomati

unicorns are delightful and happily still remain in elegant posture. Finally, following an inexplicable half-title saying 'Advertisement', there is a *catalogue raisonné* of books printed at The Curwen Press 1926–7. The type specimen book's even machining on hand-made paper reaches the standard expected from the firm's dedicated craftsmen. Pages from the *Type Specimen Book* are reproduced on pages 195 and 201. This handsome book is a triumph for Oliver Simon and Harold Curwen; Oliver shows his talents as editor and typographer and Harold with his printing knowledge ensures a wholly satisfactory finish to the undertaking. A copy was given to Holbrook Jackson which was acknowledged in a letter to Harold Curwen in March 1928. The distinguished bibliophile had good words to say:

I want to thank you for so generously sending me a copy of your *Specimen Book*. When I think of the few copies issued and the beauty of the book, I have to restrain this expression of appreciation lest you might think I was overdoing it. I feel sure that this is the best type specimen book ever issued in this country, and for all I know in any other country, and whilst renewing my thanks for your kindness in sending me a copy, I should like to commend this example of distinguished enterprise.

The next enterprise edited and designed by Oliver Simon was the *Curwen Press Miscellany* published on behalf of the firm by the Soncino Press in 1931. The same page size as the *Type Specimen Book*, the number printed, while still small, was nearly two and a half times greater and the edition for general sale increased from 95 to 225. All the 'house publications' in which Oliver Simon had a hand were issued in strictly limited editions. The original *Catalogue Raisonné* ran to 400 copies, *The Almanack* for 1926 to 425 copies, *The Specimen Book of Types*, as we have noted, was restricted to 135 copies and the *Specimen Book of Pattern Papers Designed For and in Use at The Curwen Press* was in an edition of 220 copies. The selling prices, in editions as small as these, bore no relation to production costs and appear to have been fixed quite arbitrarily. The *Curwen Press Miscellany* at three guineas was a bargain and, like all other Curwen 'house publications' was eagerly taken off the bookseller's shelf. The *Miscellany* shows that the Press was not resting on its laurels: there is an abundance of new acquisitions and thoughtful essays by experts. In types the larger sizes of Lutetia, from 18 point to 28 point, are

[197]

displayed and also the excellent Monotype version. Of great interest is a comprehensive display of Harold Curwen's sans serif in capitals and lower case followed by an evaluation of Curwen Sans by Harry Carter. In the essay Curwen's type is critically examined and compared with Johnston's 'Underground', Gill Sans cut by Monotype, and Cable designed by Rudolf Koch and cut by Klingspor.

Three pages are devoted to the initials designed for the Press by Jan van Krimpen. They have the authority of a master and have been much admired. A page of these initials is reproduced in the form as they appeared in the *Miscellany*. More borders are displayed: the beautifully flowing border redrawn by Henry Ball, some adventurous creations by Edward Bawden based on fine penmanship and a geometric experiment by Paul Nash which was used to frame the introduction to *Something to Think About*. The last Curwen border is by Harry Carter and for many years the Press has been grateful to him for its provision.

Edward Bawden's power of invention seems endless: in the vignette section he fills three pages, including the design which Curwen's took over from the London & North Eastern Railway. Claudia Guercio, wife of Barnett Freedman, presents two pages of flower-laden baskets and huge vases and, finally, a page of delicately drawn book-motif arrangements by Althea Willoughby.

Harold Curwen contributes a practical craftsman's essay 'On Printing "From The Wood"'. It ends with a typically Curwen plea: 'In conclusion if, as a practical man, I may dedicate this  brief article I would do so to the engravers (with a point like this on their tools) who do not merely "tickle" their blocks, and to the publisher who allows the printer to choose his paper.'

The fortunate few who received presentation copies of the *Miscellany* spoke warmly of it. Hamish Miles, a fastidious and learned bookman, was particularly kind:

It [the *Miscellany*] really would be hard to better, either in matter or manner. I have been showing my copy to three or four worthy beholders, and they have agreed without reserve that its production strengthens the position of the Press in a place of its own. I'm sure nobody can touch the quality of presswork—and in the colour stencil work, of course, you simply walk away with it.

[198]

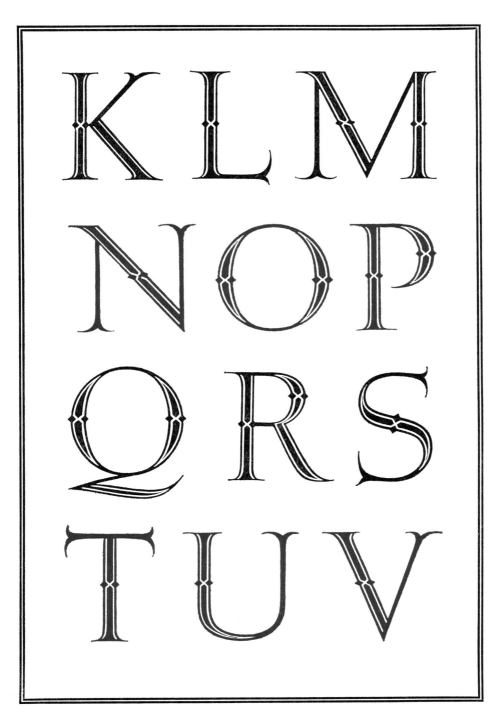

Initials designed by J. Van Krimpen

The *Miscellany* ends with another instalment of the *catalogue raisonné* of books printed at The Curwen Press from 1928 to 1930*. This valuable catalogue started in 1920 covers Oliver Simon's first decade with The Curwen Press. In this semi-final instalment no mention is made of the number of pages in the books. This may have been editorial discretion as previously when the number of pages were given, they were almost invariably wrongly counted and no thought was given to the number of pages making up a printed sheet. Oliver was persistent and a final instalment of the *catalogue raisonné* appeared in *The Curwen Press News-Letter* no. IV issued in April 1933, a month after the formation of the Press as a separate company. It carries the catalogue of Simon approved books from 1931–2, the first entry being *Sartor Resartus* for the Limited Editions Club, New York, and the last entry *An Heroic Poem in Praise of Wine* by Hilaire Belloc. The final instalment lists twenty-one titles. Again the number of pages in the books is not given.

In the last paragraph of his introduction to the *Miscellany* Oliver Simon states his objectives: 'The object of The Curwen Press is very simple. It is to give pleasure to the eventual owners of the books and, by so doing, to assure a good home for them, where they will be looked at with appreciation and taken down occasionally so that their friendliness may be felt and their pages read.' Oliver Simon was writing about bookwork and what he says has a simple, fire-side charm. But bookwork was, of course, only one facet of Curwen activity. There was music printing and general printing which had great importance for the firm and was responsible for the bulk of the output from the Plaistow works.

The four 'house publications' which form the subject of this chapter provide a fair picture of Curwen Press ability while the firm was still the manufacturing end and an integral part of J. Curwen & Sons Ltd. This pioneer of the printing revival, it is evident from its own publications, was not lacking enterprise during the whole of the decade 1920–30. These 'house publications' are fascinating productions and are good examples of the firm's advertising. The question of cost was met with disarming simplicity; they were all charged to an account labelled 'Selves Advertising', which it was hoped could be reduced by receipts from sales or failing this written off against trading profit.

---

*For *Catalogues Raisonné* from 1920–32 see appendix B.

Decorations designed by Percy Smith

XVIII

PUBLISHING

AND PRINTING

THE PREPARATION OF the first number of *The Fleuron, a Journal of Typography* was begun as soon as Harold Curwen had the blessing of the board of J. Curwen & Sons in September 1922. Before the middle of October the office at St Stephen's House, Westminster, no longer required by the Cloister Press of Heaton Mersey, had been opened as 'a room in town' for The Curwen Press. It fitted in admirably. The room in town was in fact the sales office for the new bookwork which Oliver Simon intended to develop. But to call it a sales office would have offended Oliver's susceptibilities. Rightly he considered himself more than a salesman; he was a typographer and a reliable production adviser to his customers. *The Fleuron* had to be issued from some address and to offer it from the wilds of Plaistow seemed out of the question. So the 'room in town' became The Office of The Fleuron. On the prospectus for *The Fleuron* orders are solicited from St Stephen's House. From the very moment of establishing a West End Office Oliver was able to combine sales and publishing, and The Office of The Fleuron became an important part of The Curwen Press until the Fleuron Ltd was sold to the Soncino Press in May 1930.

The first book issued at The Office of The Fleuron was *William Pickering Publisher* by Geoffrey Keynes. It is a handsome Crown quarto printed by Charles Whittingham and Griggs (the Chiswick Press) limited to 350 copies and published in 1924. It does not appear in the *catalogue raisonné* as, although it was designed by Oliver Simon, it was not printed at The Curwen Press. Books printed at Plaistow and issued from The Office of

The Fleuron did not appear until *Fleuron* no. IV, the last to be edited by Oliver Simon, was published in the spring of 1925. The first book printed at Plaistow with The Office of The Fleuron imprint was *Welchman's Hose* by Robert Graves with wood engravings by Paul Nash sold at 12s 6d in an edition limited to 520 copies. All Fleuron books until the Soncino Press took over were published from 101 Great Russell Street, Bloomsbury.

A pleasant looking eight-page catalogue with Oliver's favourite porridge paper cover appeared in 1925. It is a modest list starting with 'Art' and the announcement of a series *British Artists of Today*. Mark Gertler and John Nash start the series and The Office of The Fleuron tells prospective buyers that each is issued at the extraordinarily low price of 3s 6d so as to bring the series within the range of the most modest purse. These small books were useful introductions but Oliver Simon could not have been entirely satisfied with them as they do not qualify for inclusion in his *Catalogue Raisonné*.

The Office of The Fleuron was significant for the freedom it gave to Oliver Simon to contribute to the printing revival on his own terms. There was absolutely no customer interference and he could employ artists and use type and materials as he wished. Nothing requiring the outlay of much capital was attempted. The Fleuron books met ideally his need to produce books where the design and choice of materials was not only freely but completely committed to the printer. In this case it was Oliver Simon the publisher typographer being supported by Harold Curwen the master of printing processes.

Looking again at the 1925 catalogue of Fleuron books there is a new book of poems by Edith, Osbert and Sacheverell Sitwell with decorations by Uncle Albert Rutherston, 350 copies for sale at £2 2s. Also *Paradise Regained* decorated by Thomas Lowinsky limited to 350 copies at the unusually reasonable price of 15s. There follow two pages devoted to *The Fleuron*, no. IV is announced as ready and no. V edited by Stanley Morison is promised for March 1926, but there was a change of plan which excluded it from being an Office of The Fleuron publication. A whole page is devoted to *Fleuron* nos I–III with the proud announcement that they were all out of print. The last book in the catalogue is *William Pickering Publisher* by Geoffrey (later Sir Geoffrey) Keynes. A sad note states 'a few copies remain': sad because it is a scholarly book, and a fine example of Chiswick Press printing.

All these books, except for the *British Artists of Today* series, were limited editions and this continued to be general policy for Fleuron books. In January 1926 a financial crisis had to be faced; although Fleuron books were finding buyers, it was a slow business and the publishing machinery of the Fleuron Office was not very highly developed. Oliver was occupied in planning the books and he had, at the same time, the task of obtaining publisher's book work and general printing for the Plaistow works. It would be almost impossible to meet Plaistow's (specially cheapened) printing bills out of the slow but necessarily small revenue that the limited editions could command.

There must have been a real crisis for we find Harold Curwen outlining a scheme to the board of J. Curwen & Sons for assistance to be given to Mr Oliver Simon's venture. A scheme was approved on the condition that a small limited company be floated in which J. Curwen & Sons were to have a controlling interest and that the use of the name be clearly defined. This is understandable as J. Curwen & Sons were themselves publishers and did not wish to have another publishing branch which might need considerable capital investment or in some way engage in publishing which might not suit the manufacturing needs of The Curwen Press. There was no long delay: in September 1926 the company bought 151 shares at £1 each in the Fleuron Ltd. The shares were purchased in the name of Harold Curwen and the controlling interest was assured.

Apart from the almanacks, one for The Curwen Press in 1926 and *The Bibliophiles Almanack* for 1927 and again for 1928, the establishing of The Fleuron as a limited company produced some beautiful and even splendid books. In 1926 *Marigold: an Idyll of the Sea* by W. J. Turner, is an outstanding example of majestic typesetting. Walbaum type printed in faultless style: absurdly inexpensive at 15s—in a limited edition of 350 copies. This book has some claim to fame in the history of typography as it is the first work printed in England in Walbaum type. Founts of this handsome eighteenth-century type were purchased in Berlin in 1925 from the Berthold foundry. In 1927 there appeared another classic in Oliver Simon's typographic career: *Saint Hercules and Other Stories* by Martin Armstrong with drawings by Paul Nash, colour-stencilled with understanding by Miss Chick and the Plaistow group of stencillers. Priced at only 30s the edition was limited to 310 copies. The paper sides for the binding designed by Paul Nash would, in the estimation of some bibliophiles, be worth the 30s.

The board of J. Curwen & Sons seemed happy and in September 1929 were declaring the balance sheet of The Fleuron Ltd satisfactory. But just six months later there was a letter from the Soncino Press offering to take over the Curwen controlling shares in The Fleuron. Strangely the offer was accepted and, more strangely, the shares were transferred at their nominal value of £151.

Drawing by Stanley Spencer for Chatto & Windus almanack 1927. John and Edward Bumpus claim in 1929 that this is the one and only occasion on which the famous painter of *The Resurrection* has illustrated a book

[205]

It is likely that the Fleuron plans were too ambitious for J. Curwen & Sons and they did not want responsibility for finding the finance. But they were pleased to find that Oliver Simon had been invited to join the Soncino board and this would make it probable that some of the new, substantial work would be printed at Plaistow.

Mr John Davidson of the Soncino Press was good at selling and ready to take calculated risks which marked him out as a publisher of enterprise. An early large book was *The Anatomy of Bibliomania* by Holbrook Jackson. A small Royal octavo in two volumes, the first consisting of 432 pages and the second 448 pages—large composition and machining which Plaistow was glad to have. The first volume was issued in 1930 and the second volume in the year following. Also in 1930 Mr Davidson conceived the idea of a new critical edition of *The Haggadah* with drawings by Albert Rutherston coloured by stencil. For those who like magnificence to be on a superlative scale, this edition measured up to this kind of want. It is beautifully produced but almost too luxurious and not perhaps an advance on *Saint Hercules* which at first it seemed to be. Not cheap like other Fleuron books: 100 copies on Barcham Green's hand-made paper at £36 15s and 10 copies on Roman Vellum at £210. An interesting and much cheaper Soncino book is *Fournier on Type-founding* edited with notes by Harry Carter. A comfortable, compact volume limited to 260 copies at £4 4s.

All the books produced by Oliver Simon at The Fleuron Ltd or later at the Soncino Press are, without exception, important contributions to the printing revival. And it is gratifying to know that his work was appreciated by the directors of J. Curwen & Sons.

At the annual general meeting in November 1923 they say

Your directors would particularly like to mention Mr Oliver Simon. Mr Simon was articled to Mr Harold Curwen as a pupil and since completion of his articles has been assisting the firm in various capacities. Mr Simon has a high standing in the book production world, and activities which interlock closely with those of The Curwen Press. A joint office has been secured at St Stephen's House, Westminster, where exhibits of the firm's work are made.

Towards the end of the great decade of the printing revival

there is another annual general meeting tribute to Oliver Simon. In September 1930 they have this to say: 'On the printing side, there has been a very substantial increase in the turnover for outside customers, largely due to the book printing work brought in by Mr Oliver Simon. Each year more important works are being secured.'

Despite all the existing publishing ventures emanating from The Office of The Fleuron, Oliver Simon's main task from the view of the board of J. Curwen & Sons Ltd was to bring printing orders and especially book printing orders to Plaistow. Oliver Simon, like everyone else engaged in selling, had to keep in close contact with his customer-supporters. Few things gave him more pleasure than a tea-time call on Marcus Brumwell. They both talked the same language and held views about printing which were agreeably similar. The Stuart Advertising Agency had been started by H. Stuart Menzies and Marcus Brumwell in 1922. Unlike most advertising agencies at that time, they took a positive delight in leading their clients to appreciate work which was like a sea breeze blowing away the boring dullness and drabness current in those days. They believed in good looking printing and press advertisements and were ever eager to enlist as helpers young artists of promise. Marcus Brumwell has a vivid memory of Oliver Simon and deeply appreciated the work he was doing.

I first met Oliver Simon when he called on me from The Curwen Press though I cannot be sure in which year. I do not remember whether Stuarts and I paid him a retainer fee; he was certainly worth one and I hope we did. He did not call on us each week as a regularity, but he dropped in at least twice a month or more, generally at tea-time.

During all our association he was of the greatest help and encouragement to us. Thinking back with a happy glow I remember for instance a glorious weekend my wife and I spent with him in Dieppe which was, in those days, a favourite holiday spot for many of our artists.

Oliver's sensitivity about printing, typography and the work of applied art was outstanding, but if I were to single out one facet of his wisdom, I would choose *common sense*, in which he was unshakeable and sound. This solidity, strangely enough, went with an emotional sensitivity which was almost feminine. I have been remembering some of the books which covered grounds of our common interest such as his famous *Fleuron*, the *Curwen Press Miscellany*, *Penrose Annual* when edited by R. B. Fishenden (Consultant to Lancelot Spicer of the paper firm) and *Art in Advertising*. Oliver

[207]

gave me Updike's *Printing Types*. Then there were his excellent long series of *Signature* and the *Curwen Press Newsletter*.

Stuarts first account was Fortnum & Mason for whom we did a famous and successful mail advertising scheme lasting nearly twenty years and described by some as 'putting F & M on the map' through the issue of little booklets, mostly humorous, written by H. Stuart Menzies. Curwen Press certainly obtained some of this nice business. Then, about 1928 perhaps, C. F. Snowden Gamble brought us the Imperial Airways account (he was then publicity manager) where again much printing was required: brochures, posters, timetables. I think one of our early Curwen contacts was when Snowden Gamble asked Harold Curwen to see me about redesigning timetables, the kind of subject in which the neat and methodical Harold took so much successful interest.

In those days the famous innovationary typographer Jan Tschichold was brought to London from Switzerland by E. C. Gregory, Chairman of Percy Lund Humphries, and was the arch priest of unsymmetrical setting (i.e. chapter headings on one side instead of central etc.). The sensational artistic upsurge in Britain in those days (Moore, Nicholson, Hepworth, Herbert Read, Gabo, Mondrian, Sutherland, Moholy-Nagy, the Nash brothers, Victor Passmore, to name a few) was of course asymmetrical in spirit, while Oliver was essentially true blue traditional, and out of this contrast I remember that Ben Nicholson christened Oliver 'the archbishop'.

Among the artists Oliver was so wonderful at choosing, encouraging and helping in a practical way, were McKnight Kauffer, Bawden, Ravilious, Barnett Freedman and his wife, Michael Rothenstein, John Piper, Ardizzone, Rex Whistler and many others. Jack Beddington at Shell, Frank Pick at London Underground, were two of the most influential patrons (or customers). What a rich harvest there was and Oliver was right in the forefront of it all.

Marcus Brumwell was producing beautifully planned brochures and commercial catalogues. Many owed a great deal to Oliver Simon's typographical inventions and although the work was essential to the well being of The Curwen Press, Oliver Simon was inclined to allow some class distinction between what he called printing for business and printing for publishers. He was always on the side of good printing but his really deep interest lay in the printing of books. He was lucky to have as a customer-patron Desmond Flower who had joined Cassell in January 1930. Dr Desmond Flower, the future chairman of Cassells, appreciated Oliver Simon's work but unlike Marcus Brumwell his needs were not advertising material but book production. In a short time book production and friendship were closely bound up together.

[208]

I met Oliver Simon very soon after I joined Cassell on 1 January 1930. He came to see me for two reasons: first because of two lovely books by Arnold Bennett, *Elsie and the Child* and *Venus Rising from the Sea* (1930 and 1931) and second, because he had heard that within a few months I had decided that Cassell's typography was lamentable and that I ought to do something about it. I set about this task by redesigning the title pages of our books in proof and then pushed the matter further to designing the whole book—typographical lay-out, binding—the whole job. This brought me nearer to Oliver because, although none of these books were printed by The Curwen Press, he appreciated an enthusiastic amateur when he saw one. I must add that The Curwen Press and Cassell came to do a great deal of work together in those days, and I never sent Oliver a manuscript with wishes or instructions—he designed the book as he saw fit. I was amply fulfilling my desires by designing many other books, and who was I to question the master? And I think he was the master. Walter Lewis imposed his will at Cambridge on all and sundry and evolved the pure style which has left its indelible mark on the work which Brooke Crutchley produces today. John Johnson has not, I think, left the same legacy, but nevertheless he was a great power in his day. But Oliver was never stultified: certainly not in the early thirties. Every book was a new experiment. Although one could pick up a book and say 'that *must* be a Curwen', there was always enough vitality and originality for one to say to oneself 'well, it *could* be someone else, but I wonder who else could possibly do it?' The answer was that it was always a Curwen Press book.

I must not exaggerate Oliver's power in the middle thirties at The Curwen Press. There was Harold Curwen whom I knew very well, and I have no doubt for a moment that he performed prodigious tasks during this evolutionary period of the Press as a leader of taste at that time. But I mainly dealt with Oliver and so for me, at any rate, it is understandable that he *was* The Curwen Press.

The next book to be undertaken by us jointly was an agreeable translation by Donald Attwater of *Piers Plowman*, with woodcuts by Denis Tegetmeier, who was also a member of the Gill complex.

Then Oliver dropped his bombshell. He asked me to go to see him at his office, which was then in Great Russell Street. When I arrived he proposed to me that we should produce one of the, if not *the*, most lovely illustrated book in the history of British typography: it was to be *Urne Buriall*.

I sat on the edge of my chair. To be invited, at the age of twenty-four, to take a hand in the production of a book which, it was intended, should stand for all time was quite something. I rushed back to my office, saw my father and his senior colleague who, somewhat to my surprise, both gave me the go-ahead. Paul Nash was to be the illustrator; John Carter was to edit the text and Oliver and I were to see that the book was born. We made it for publication in 1932; it does stand as one of the greatest illustrated books ever published in any country, and its fame is due enormously to Oliver, who, with his tact and charm and firmness, was able to keep those on the job to their jobs.

After that the slump overtook us all and we did no handsome books until a limited edition of Stefan Zweig's *Buried Candelabrum*. But during this bleak period Oliver was ever more active. I am sure that many other publishers have similar memories; but he introduced me to Barnett Freedman, Eric Ravilious and Edward Bawden who did many jackets for us, all printed at The Curwen Press. When he was editing *Signature* he also introduced me to Graham Sutherland's work, with which at that time I was unacquainted. He was always exploring, with his own impeccable taste.

The centenary history of Cassells was printed for us after Oliver's death. It is a lovely book, bearing just enough of Oliver's marks to conform to tradition, since this was a history.

In addition to his great gifts as a printer and his lesser, but nevertheless welcome gifts as a cricketer, there was another side to him—the spiritual. Oliver's spirituality was something quite rare. He had almost raised his sights to a point at which he could no longer see this sordid earth. He wanted to produce better and better and more aesthetic design. He was in a phase of his life rather equivalent to Robert Graves today. Although Robert still writes great verse, quite a lot of his time is spent in cleaning and (in a sense) purifying earlier works to the point where they are crystal clear and meet his satisfaction entirely. I feel that Oliver had the same attitude but he was in a more difficult position. His works were commissioned and although I know that the customer is always right, etc., it was not always easy for him to change when he thought something had not come off. I know that *Venus Rising from the Sea* was reset three times because Oliver and Ted Kauffer could not get to the roots of the matter—but they did in the end.

Oliver Simon never found it easy to convey precisely what he was after. H. P. Schmoller, who helped most effectively on book-work after the second war, considered Oliver Simon worked by instinct and relied on his rough layouts being correctly interpreted by the skilled team of compositors who were steeped in Curwen Press traditions. He abhorred customer interference and it was sometimes carried beyond the limits of commercial prudence. The Curwen Press was in business to produce printing: it liked to hear of new accounts being opened; with Oliver Simon there was always present the danger of an announcement of an account being closed.

XIX

THE STENCIL PROCESS

A NEW DEVELOPMENT started at The Curwen Press in 1925 was the stencil process. It had a short life of only six years. The stencil process or *pochoir* printing had long been practised in France but until Harold Curwen took it up there had been no production on a commercial scale in England.

No machinery was required and it was so obviously a matter of carefully directed handwork that the mechanically minded printing trade jumped to the conclusion that it must be costly and therefore unsuitable for commercial purposes. This view, while understandable, was mistaken. Soundly organized and restricted to relatively small editions, the process could be economical and when used with proper discretion had a beauty of texture and distinction which neither letterpress, *gravure* or lithography could match. In the event the process was to benefit a small number of books, mostly in limited editions, which flourished brightly during the decade 1920–30. Limited editions were a godsend for artists and printers by providing a platform where experiment and enterprise could be happily combined; but it was all short-lived. The limited edition was almost swept off the market by the economic depression which reached its depth between 1931 and 1932.

The stencil process was a job for a craftsman organizer and if it was taken up at all it was almost inevitable that it should be taken up and developed by Harold Curwen. The early Abbotsholme school training fostered his interest in organization and method and this, combined with his mastery of printing detail, were the foundations of his success. He was aware of what was being done in France and noted that Jaconnet near Paris 'does much stencil work'. He was attracted too by a stencilled illustration done by Edna Clarke Hall in 1903.

Curwen was a thorough production man and never embarked on new techniques without careful planning. The sort of organization required for setting up a Stencil Department was examined with his professional customary approach. He knew, of course, that the stencil process was in principle no different from the child's stencilling outfits which were part of the toyshop's stock in trade. The first thing to do was to organize stencil cutting and find methods for systematic colour mixing and colour control; finally there was the training of a small group of girls who would brush or dab the colour on to the paper through the cut away portions of the protecting stencil.

A booklet called *The Stencil Process at The Curwen Press* was issued in 1927 with a short introduction by Holbrook Jackson. His essay set in the elegant Koch Kursiv has a head-piece by Edward Bawden printed in black from a line block and then stencilled in light grey and pink: very charming and very effective in showing how simple stencilling can be arranged. More elaborate work where the artist had 'designed' for stencil reproduction is to be found in *Saint Hercules and Other Stories* illustrated by Paul Nash and published by The Fleuron. In 'A Cross-Section of English Printing'* Holbrook Jackson refers to stencilling and says a trifle inaccurately that it was largely executed by girls taken almost haphazard from the bindery. Far from being taken haphazard from the bindery, Curwen took great care in selection and training. In course of time a skilled, regular and reliable team of stencillers was assembled.

Curwen taught himself how to interpret artists' work for stencilling and proceeded to cut stencils himself. The next step was to train a member of the staff to cut stencils, mix colours and generally supervise the team of bindery girls. Irene Fawkes was the first to take charge, then Lily Chick and when Miss Chick left the firm to get married, the supervising was taken on by Gertrude Temkin, who was at that time showing her remarkable ability as a typographer working within the Curwen-Simon tradition.

Curwen claimed a number of advantages for stencilling. There was a freshness of colour in using artist's pure water colour or gouache. The latter, consisting of water colour mixed with gum, was opaque and suited some illustrations better than transparent

The Printing of Books by Holbrook Jackson: Cassell, 1938.

[212]

water colour. There was thus always the choice of transparent or opaque colours. Mattness of texture was another advantage, for the surface of the paper was not rendered shiny. Further there was the pleasant texture naturally made by brush marks and sponging: colour-line letterpress in printing ink from blocks was, by contrast, flat and lifeless.

Stencilling, Curwen suggested, was suitable for moderate quantities. For the finest results illustrations specially planned for stencil reproduction by artists experienced in the medium was desirable. That the process had not been used in England before seemed to Curwen a specially good reason for offering it as a commercially viable enterprise. What The Curwen Press was able to do between 1926 and 1932 proves that Harold Curwen's judgement was right. It was poor reward and bad luck that the world-wide financial distress of the early 1930s brought the fine pioneering work to an abrupt end. Fortunately, Gertrude Temkin's memory of stencilling is vivid and her narrative is full and delightful. She must be allowed to tell her own story,

When I arrived on The Curwen Press scene, stencilling was a going concern. I do not know who cut the stencils, perhaps Irene Fawkes, or Harold Curwen himself. They were cut on oiled board, such as is still sold in stencil sets, and proper stencil brushes were used. They used water colour mixed up in little pots and dabbled small quantities into a dish, a saucer probably, and dabbed the colour on with the stencil brush. They had a hand coloured picture as a guide.

When I came along Harold Curwen was experimenting with copper stencils. He had some Japanese ones—cut with unbelievable skill and of an incredible intricacy, and my first task in the stencil effort was to try and cut through the copper. This I found impossible, although Harold Curwen would demonstrate the ease with which *he* could cut it. If you can imagine the strength in his enormous hands and my trembling, terrified efforts, you will realize that he often became short tempered over this operation! Happily, he discovered that the copper discoloured the paint and went on to experiment with celluloid. This turned out to be workable, although it stretched—the day of stable material hadn't yet arrived—which meant recutting. It had the great advantage of being transparent, so that any smudging, or bad fit, could be seen easily and quickly. We used to *paste* (with gloy!) a thin paper pull of the key block onto the celluloid and cut through it. I developed quite a skill in breaking down the originals into the component colours—and also took over the actual colour mixing—I have a very true eye for colour and of course had been taught to paint, and so enjoyed this

[213]

part of the procedure immensely. When it came to register, Harold Curwen invented a wooden stand with a true right angle; the individual sheets would be stacked so that they fitted into the right-angled corner; the stencils were cut to the same register, that is, the key pulls were positioned exactly to the same lay. This worked for single plates; sometimes there was sheet work and for this we made register marks—part of a line or another illustration. I do not remember this clearly but whatever it was, it worked. Hardly anything was smudged, but occasionally the colour would bead up under the edges of the stencil and they would have to stop and clean up. The sheets would be spread out over the bench and then, when dry, knocked up and stacked.

Ordinary stencil brushes were used for all the work, in varying sizes, according to the area to be covered. Stencil brushes are short-haired, thick-stemmed, stubby things, the coarse hair all cut to the same length; the size variations were in the diameter of the tuft and the length of the tuft increased with the diameter, but was never longer than about half an inch. I used to enjoy trying to achieve a 'textured' look and experimented a lot. Some of the illustrations called for this sort of thing and I had to get some sort of technique worked out before passing it on. The girls were very good and picked up these tricks very quickly. They also used small sponges to get a stippled effect, sometimes with one colour over another. I also had a lovely time working out a sort of splatter effect with a toothbrush. I used to 'pass' each colour when wanted, also demonstrate the sponging and stippling. I never did any actual stencilling and should have loved a go but the girls were all from the bindery, set to work as required!

I remember having aching hands from gripping the stencil cutting knife too hard, and Harold Curwen would come along and cut up the stuff like cheese! I think he bought the knives from Germany: they had removable blades which slotted into a bulbous sort of handle, and he taught me to sharpen them on an oilstone.

Apart from the stencilling, Harold Curwen taught me a great deal about printing and paper and all that goes with it, and I am eternally grateful to have had the opportunity—frightened as I was for years!

The stencil department staff was small but they were all skilled and bubbling with enthusiasm. The little pots of colour made a gay show and brushing or dabbing the paper was utterly remote from machine printing. There was an atmosphere that produced once again the 'spirit of joy' which Joseph Thorp had noted at Plaistow ten years earlier.

Stencil cutting when not done by Harold Curwen was carried out by Irene Fawkes and later by Gertrude Temkin. They were also responsible for mixing colour and, until she got married, Lily Chick acted as supervisor. The bindery team consisted of

Myrtle Griggs, Alice Cook and Doris Hardman. Alice Cook started at Plaistow in 1918 and Doris Hardman in 1926; they are both still active and contribute daily to the well-being of The Curwen Press.

The books printed and stencilled at Plaistow were a mere handful but they had beauty and even, some would say, magnificence. The two artists who seemed to understand best what the stencil process had to offer were E. McKnight Kauffer and Paul Nash. It is true that Albert Rutherston, Edward Bawden and Barnett Freedman all did some fine stencilled illustrations: but Rutherston did not get far away from the boundaries of colour-line and Bawden seemed more closely attached to lino cutting. For Barnett Freedman, hand drawn lithography was his preferred technique. Kauffer and Paul Nash succeeded in getting most out of the process.

Elsie and the Child by Arnold Bennett was illustrated by McKnight Kauffer and was stencilled with opaque gouache colours. The result has a depth of colour and a brilliance which could hardly have been achieved by any other printing method. *Elsie and the Child* was published by Cassell & Co. in 1929. The same firm published in 1931 *Venus Rising from the Sea* by Arnold Bennett and again illustrated by McKnight Kauffer. This time the artist chose transparent water colour and the illustrations are beautiful in their delicacy and almost ethereal realism. *Elsie and the Child* was printed and stencilled in a limited edition of 750 copies; two years later we find *Venus Rising from the Sea* limited to 350 copies. Sad evidence of the economic difficulties which were paralysing so many good things in our daily life. McKnight Kauffer was appreciative of the production. Writing to Harold Curwen in October 1931 about *Venus Rising from the Sea* he said 'I enclose placement of illustrations for A.B's book. I am sure they are quite clear and I have avoided placing them in between pages but at sections which I assume is easier for binding. Your part of the job has again been done with superb artistry. The colours are lovely, the texture of the wash is better than the originals. Personally I feel indebted to you for having lifted these illustrations up 80 per cent. The high praise was merited: for Harold Curwen for his sensitive workmanship and for Oliver Simon for his vision as a typographer and his powers of persuasion. Desmond Flower, at that time a junior director of Cassell, was the responsible publisher. For splendid books in strictly limited editions, they seem to have been sold at bargain prices. Two guineas for *Elsie and the Child* and five guineas for *Venus*.

Paul Nash illustrated the last book printed and stencilled at Plaistow. Many consider it the best. *Urne Buriall, and the Garden of Cyrus* by Sir Thomas Browne, with thirty drawings by Paul Nash, was published by Cassell & Co. in 1932 in an edition of 270 copies. It was moderately priced at £15 15s but it came out when the depression had left its scars and book collectors were unable to give it the reception it deserved. Paul Nash, who was never lavish in giving praise, wrote a letter in January 1933 which gave Harold Curwen pleasure. Writing from New House, Rye, he says what he thinks of the stencilling in *Urne Buriall*:

Now you will hardly credit it, but I have only just recently been able to compare the plates (stencilled) you did with my original coloured proofs. I should like to tell you how very good I think the stencil work is. Mostly, it is quite astonishing for accuracy of interpretation. Considering how insensitive the collotypes are and that you were obliged to slightly strengthen my colours (which alarmed me to contemplate) I must say I think your people surpassed themselves in their understanding of the problem.

The only plate that was wrong was the 'Vegetable Creation' where they got the colours too hot and just somehow *not* mine. Otherwise I have little to complain of. In fact, my belated, but warmest congratulations.

A nice letter to receive but it shows that very high standards were expected of The Curwen Press. The firm did its best, but not always successfully, to live up to the high standards expected and often exacted. Whatever the percentage of success achieved it was largely due to the devoted, sustained search after perfection on the part of Harold Curwen and Oliver Simon. When Paul Nash says 'your people surpassed themselves' he was giving praise to Gertrude Temkin, Alice Cook and Doris Hardman who brought astonishing care, born of real love, to their stencil work.

Nash was perfectly justified in expressing dissatisfaction with the full page plate 'Vegetable Creation'. A large area of buff colour had been stencilled in a tone slightly deeper than the colour in the proof. The difference is not great but is sufficient to make the illustration look quite wrong. It shows how much care had to be taken; to be successful with twenty-nine out of the thirty illustrations in *Urne Buriall* is quite good and underlines the competence of The Curwen Press stencilling team.

The Stencil Department at Plaistow was able to be of service to the Nonesuch Press. The first book stencilled at The Curwen Press was *The Anatomy of Melancholy* by Robert Burton illustrated by E. McKnight Kauffer and published by Nonesuch in December 1925. Beautifully designed by Francis Meynell, it was the first large scale stencil work that had been undertaken. Kauffer's illustrations are superb and were, as it turned out, the beginning of a happy and close association between artist and printer. McKnight Kauffer was quick to recognize the value of Harold Curwen's judgement as an interpreter.

The Nonesuch Press kept the Curwen stencillers busy. Most of the work must have come up to Francis Meynell's high standards. There was Harold Curwen's careful overseeing and his sensitive feeling for colour and texture which were exactly what Nonesuch was seeking.

The Nonesuch work, after Burton and Herman Melville's *Benito Cereno*, went on until the autumn of 1930. A frontispiece for Cobbett's *Peter Porcupine* in 1927, five full page illustrations to Bunyan's *Pilgrim's Progress* in 1928 and in 1929 aid for three books. Nine drawings by T. L. Poulton for Izaak Walton's *Compleat Works*, twelve illustrations by Jacquier stencilled in colour for *Graziella* by A. de Lamartine and *A Plurality of Worlds* by Bernarde de Fontenelle with eight decorations by T. L. Poulton. This work is unusual for being without a 'key' printing for the stencilling: the whole decoration is stencilled.

The last Nonesuch book to make use of the Curwen Stencil Department was the great two-volume edition of *Don Quixote* by Cervantes with twenty-one illustrations in colour by E. McKnight Kauffer published in December 1930. The Curwen Press must have felt honoured to be concerned in the making of one of the finest Nonesuch books. Cambridge University Press did the letterpress printing and although the Curwen contribution was far smaller it helped significantly to the success of the whole.

After 1932 no more stencilling was done at Plaistow. According to Brunwin the French were quoting absurd (i.e. low) prices. Brunwin had little regard for French industrial production and was of the opinion that their low prices were only possible by the extensive use of ill paid outworkers. This may have been true, although there is no evidence that The Curwen Press undertook any investigation. But the usage of cheap labour was believed to be an established fact and was clearly something that Harold Curwen would not consider tolerating.

[217]

XX

PROFIT AND LOSS

MUCH HAS BEEN SAID about the sort of printing The Curwen Press was doing in the years between 1920 and 1930. But how much of a financial help was it to J. Curwen & Sons Ltd? Looking at the 'house' publications and the admirable Fleuron books it would be easy to overlook the fact that The Curwen Press was a part, and until 1930 the lesser part, of the music publishing business. There is scarcely a reference by Plaistow to J. Curwen & Sons Ltd yet The Curwen Press had no board of directors until printing and publishing became separate companies in March 1933. The directors of J. Curwen & Sons Ltd were Kenneth Curwen who was chairman and in charge of publishing, and his brother Harold Curwen who looked after the printing side. Selwyn Grant, son-in-law of Spencer Curwen, was a non-executive member of the board with special responsibility for finance.

At the beginning of the century the printing works traded as either the Tonic Sol-fa Press or J. Curwen & Sons Ltd. It was not until the advent of Joseph Thorp in 1915 that the printing part of the firm regularly called itself The Curwen Press. Seen from the publishing office at Berners Street, the main function of the works at Plaistow was to meet the firm's own printing requirements: it was encouraged as a secondary task to engage in general printing as a means of reducing music printing costs and perhaps contributing to profits.

Selwyn Grant's knowledge of printing was minimal but he had very considerable business experience. His report to his father-in-law and Uncle Spedding in October 1909 makes this clear. He saw at once the absurdity of charging printing to the publishing side on the basis of 45 per cent of the publication's selling price when the calculation was made on a selling price which the printer had no part in fixing. It was all pure guesswork and the wonder is that The Curwen Press managed to survive. Proper costing and charges based on known costs as recommended by Selwyn Grant were introduced by Harold Curwen in his early days at Plaistow and by the time he was made a director in 1911 the reorganization had been largely completed.

The accounting year for J. Curwen & Sons Ltd went from the beginning of June to the end of May. Table I shows the publishing and printing sales and the respective departmental profits for eleven years from the year ending 31 May 1920 to the year ending 31 May 1930.

TABLE I

Year to 31 May	Publishing sales £	Printing sales £	Publishing profit £	Printing profit £
1920	67,000	45,600	667	6,136
1921	72,000	45,400	5,014	3,367
1922	56,700	40,700	4,200	608
1923	56,300	42,900	5,844	3,143
1924	56,500	38,600	4,174	460
1925	57,400	47,100	1,842	5,660
1926	57,200	43,000	4,128	2,766
1927	59,000	43,100	2,750	2,083
1928	54,000	38,700	4,315	426
1929	48,100	42,800	1,590	2,108
1930	45,800	45,600	4,452	2,590

Publishing sales exceed printing sales during the whole period although by 1930 they were only marginally ahead. Publishing enjoyed a regular 'over the counter' sale of about £7,000 a year and there was a steady sale of musical instruments. Kenneth Curwen had started in 1911 a new department at Berners Street for the importation and wholesale distribution of musical instruments of all kinds. Apart from a brief upsurge in 1919–21 following the end of the Great War publishing sales remained very stable. A decline in the popularity of community singing about 1926–7 was thought to be responsible for the small decline in 1928; the decline was accelerated alarmingly by the financial collapse in 1929 which caused a sudden drop in American sales.

[219]

The publishing turnover during the eleven years to May 1930 averaged £57,250; the average for printing over the same period was £43,000. There was never a year without the publishing and printing making profits although in 1922, 1924 and 1928 printing came dangerously near to being loss makers. On the whole profits were quite evenly distributed with the publishing profits being, as a rule, greater. Average departmental profit for publishing over the eleven year period was £3,500 and for printing £2,600. Profit figures shown in Table I are exclusive of director's fees and the cost of servicing debentures. The debentures cannot have been a heavy burden. The first debentures were extinguished in October 1927 and six months later the second debentures were paid off.

The decline in printing profits in 1922, 1924 and 1928 reflect severe variations in demand in a trade where there is little or no opportunity of making for stock. All firms in the general printing trade have to cope with periods of different degrees of activity. The problem defies solution. It is obviously impossible to persuade customers to place orders to suit a printer's convenience. It has been established that the poor results in 1928 were due not only to a fall in turnover but also to great variations in the degree of activity in the different departments. The works were either too busy or too slack and if it had been possible to arrange for a steady even flow, better profits would have been made.

TABLE II

Year to 31 May	Sales to publishing	Sales to general customers	'Selves' printing (included in general customer sales)
	£	£	£
1920	26,880	19,080	5,495
1921	25,420	20,190	4,463
1922	20,080	21,560	2,737
1923	17,300	25,560	2,380
1924	15,300	22,650	1,940
1925	15,990	31,240	5,004
1926	13,480	29,580	5,319
1927	18,480	24,490	4,717
1928	14,040	24,940	3,480
1929	12,600	30,120	3,137
1930	10,700	34,770	2,409

No allowance has been made for small variations in work in progress.

Table II shows the value of Curwen Press sales to the publishing side and to general customers. The period covered is again the eleven years from the period ending 31 May 1920 to the end of May 1930. It shows clearly that the content of printing sales were very different at the beginning of the period than at the end. In 1920 music printing exceeded general printing by £7,800. At the end of May 1930 the position had been reversed: general printing sales exceeded music printing by £24,000. During the whole of the eleven years, with the exception of a small revival in 1927–8, music printing declined. In contrast, except for a wobble in 1927–8, general printing increased. Average music printing sales over the eleven years were £17,300 and for general customers the average was £25,800.

A business man may wonder why with all the new custom for bookwork and elaborately constructed catalogues and brochures the volume of general work remained so surprisingly static. The answer is probably to be found in the weakness of having no regular sales staff. Selling, apart from music printing, was mainly done by Harold Curwen and Oliver Simon. The more successful they were the more they were entangled in design and typographic detail and the less time was available for keeping in touch with customers. The system also made it difficult to find time to cultivate new sources of custom. Oliver Simon in his autobiography is clearly aware of the problem: 'I soon ceased to be', he writes, 'a traveller, for typography and the personal supervision of the printing and binding of the books we were producing began to take more and more of my time.'* Both Harold and Oliver were greatly assisted by Brunwin the manager and F. H. Riches who was engaged as assistant manager in December 1923. They were always ready to go out and visit customers and ready to investigate the inevitable complaints which cropped up from time to time. But it was sporadic effort and the problem of steady, continuous selling remained unsolved until Herbert Marsh devoted his entire energies to the task in 1952. As a result of the lack of continuity there is little doubt that many promising accounts just withered away. Harold Curwen was as successful as Oliver Simon in producing good orders but he too had little time for regular contact. Work such as the Gestetner brochure, Bryant and May's *Match Making* and the fine catalogues for

---

* *Printer and Playground* by Oliver Simon: Faber & Faber, 1956, p. 19.

[221]

Crittall's metal windows and Doulton's sanitary ware made enormous demands on his time and creative energy. He appears not to have realized that a selling organization would have had a stabilizing effect and may have been the proper way to counter the steady decline in music printing. F. H. Riches, who worked with the firm from 1923 until his death forty-four years later, made up in some degree for the lack of regular contact by taking over interviews with customers as often as possible. He was very helpful to Oliver Simon and more and more acted as his understudy when a publisher customer wanted to see someone about a book jacket or had some tiresome commercial detail which needed settling. Riches loved books and was an ardent and discriminating reader. Nobody at Plaistow was more delighted than he was to see the growing business in well printed bookwork.

Oliver Simon was an artist or, more exactly, an artist-typographer with a gift for cultivating business. But he was no good at figures and was unable to trust himself with even sums of simple addition. Balance sheets were a nightmare and he was never sure who were the debtors and who the creditors. As for calculating the amount of paper needed for a book he would have considered this to be in the realms of higher mathematics. Riches was aware of these shortcomings and with great devotion helped him over every stile. Indeed Riches made a special point of seeing that every book produced under Oliver's care was under his care as well.

A new and important appointment was made in December 1926. Harold Curwen realized that he was so occupied in producing printing which had the then unusual quality of being fit for its purpose and was so busy initiating and supervising various techniques of production that he had little time to spare for keeping in touch with cost accounting. O. R. G. Williams was engaged to look after cost accounting and to see that the cost system was properly applied. He spent forty years at Plaistow retiring in December 1966. They were forty happy and fruitful years although he admits he took the job in the first place because The Curwen Press worked a five-day week thus enabling him to play 'away' games on Saturdays for his beloved rugby football team. He helped the sales side of the business a great deal although his influence was indirect. One of his first tasks at Plaistow was to overhaul the costing system and see that it was structurally as fair as possible. Fair apportioning of cost made for fair charges to a customer. A satisfied customer, especially if he were satisfied with the economic side of the transaction, was the most valuable kind of customer. The firm had plenty of them: but they would have had a lot more if some sales follow up had been available.

Another problem confronting Williams was the question of a special (low) rate for composition to be charged on book work. Oliver Simon was aware that wage rates in London put him at a disadvantage compared with rates paid in provincial towns which were graded lower. He pressed, therefore, that Plaistow should lower the bookwork rates to meet this competition. The suggestion aroused a good deal of controversy. Why, it was asked, should bookwork be treated differently from other work? If we were unable to show we could give value for money was there justification for going on? Harold was unenthusiastic about a special rate. In his view there was only one proper cost rate and anything else would be self-deception. But here the mastery of costing that Williams possessed settled what might have been an awkward unresolved problem. He was able to show Kenneth and Harold Curwen that the much greater number of words which would be handled daily in the composing room with bookwork orders reduced unit cost significantly. Kenneth, the chairman, was convinced and the new bookwork rates were adopted. It did not appear to have an adverse effect on profits and it certainly encouraged bookwork sales. Again, if there had been a sales staff, sales and profits would have almost certainly risen much more.

In Table II the right hand column shows the amount spent each year on 'selves' printing. The work was either advertising or publications which the firm had underwritten.

The years 1920–1 had to take in Joseph Thorp's splendid advertising booklet *Apropos the Unicorn* and various Decoy Press ventures including the plea for a better and fairer post-war society which was the aim of *Change*. The 'selves' printing had in it an element of manufacturing for stock and if properly controlled could help in maintaining an even flow of work. In 1925–6 the Fleuron books accounted for much of the expenditure. Some, if not all, paid their way and even if they did not they were looked on as generators of more work from publishers. From 1927 until 1931 the 'selves' account had to shoulder *How to Buy and Sell Money*, *The Type Specimen Book*, *We Have so Much to Spend* and the *Curwen Miscellany*. O. R. G. Williams was able to find an orderly method for dealing with all these publications; his accounting system had full approval of the board of J. Curwen & Sons, including a blessing from the formidable Selwyn Grant. Williams was only defeated in one field: he had to admit that he could find no way of recovering the cost of experimental work which was sometimes quite a heavy burden.

The general sales show up well for 1929 and 1930 and the profit remained firm. These years benefited from the success Harold Curwen had with the work for Gestetner and Bryant & May. The autumn of 1929 also saw the beginning of the Southern Railway's *Over the Points*. Oliver Simon, in these years, had to his credit the regular work, first a monthly and later a quarterly, of *Life and Letters* and the highly successful *Legion Book*. This book produced by Captain Cotton Minchin with valuable editorial help from Simon, was published to raise money for the British Legion. H.R.H. The Prince of Wales took a personal interest in it. It was an enormous success and became the most substantial bookwork order Plaistow had ever undertaken. *The Legion Book* made the printing sales for 1930 look good. There was a very special edition of 100 copies held in the gift of the Prince of Wales, a special edition of 600 copies on mould-made paper and an unlimited edition called the 'Abridged Popular Edition'. It was very popular and deserved to be. In the autumn of 1929 the popular edition was reprinted three times. Captain Cotton Minchin, the editor, leaned heavily on Oliver Simon. A study of the contents clearly shows that Cotton Minchin was glad to receive and take the advice offered. *The Legion Book* is a fine example of Curwen bookwork and the Lutetia type in which it is set is of great beauty and dignity.

In December 1929 Harold Curwen celebrated the successful printing of *The Legion Book* by presenting twelve copies to members of the firm. The recipients were:

*Miss Craddock (forelady, bindery)
†Mr Brunwin (manager)
†Mr Williams (chief accountant)
†Mr Herbert Wakeling (overseer, composing)
*Mr Ben Smith (compositor)
  Mr Chapman (head reader)
*Mr Dixon (overseer, letterpress printing)
†Mr George Wakeling (letterpress printer)
*Mr Barnes (letterpress printer)

*Mr Campbell (letterpress and expert printer on hand-made
    paper)
*Mr Ginbey (in charge of imposition)
*Mr Truscott (overseer, bindery)

By 1930 music printing had become far less important to The
Curwen Press than it had been a quarter of a century earlier. In
1907 Selwyn Grant's report showed that music accounted for
over 75 per cent of printing revenue but by 1930 the proportion
of music printing had dropped steeply and accounted for only 24
per cent of total sales. Reliance on captive work, work which came
to Plaistow without soliciting, was by 1930 no longer an expecta-
tion to be automatically counted on.

How did the shift in sales to general customers affect the works
at Plaistow? The answer seems to be that the problems it was
creating received little attention. In 1900 the enormous stock-
room was filled to capacity, but thirty years later less than a third
of the shelf space was holding printed stock.

Capital expenditure was not greatly affected although it may
have been better if more definite plans had been made to purchase
capital goods to deal effectively with the changed content of
sales. During the ten years from 1920–30 the composing room
added to its stock a number of new types and a collection of
proprietary borders and ornaments. These additions were very
valuable but being spread over several years the capital expenditure seemed negligible. The heavy machinery remained much the
same and was of a kind specially suited to music printing. The
machine room could boast of three two-revolution letterpress
printing machines by 1930 and, modern as these were, they were
not equipped with automatic feeders for the paper nor for deep
stacking at the delivery end and as a consequence hourly output
was less than it might have been. Most of the printing machinery,
and particularly the lithographic machines, were unsuited for the
type of general work that was being undertaken. The directors of
J. Curwen & Sons did not deny their printing side capital expenditure but they appear to have been slow to appreciate the
changes that had taken place and did not feel obliged to study the
question of modernization. Decline in demand for music printing

*More than fifty years' service.
†More than forty years' service.

R

merely meant to the publishing side a decline in importance to them of their printing department. Kenneth Curwen was a publisher with a gift for musical appreciation and naturally his main concern was with building up a good book and sheet music catalogue. Interest in printing came second and he was scarcely aware of the excitements of the printing revival.

Music publishing was severely hit by the alarming economic decline following the American collapse in 1929. By chance at that time Kenneth Curwen and Selwyn Grant had decided to back a new invention which synchronized sound, by means of a kind of long-playing gramophone record, to cinematograph film. The success of the new invention, called Synchrophone, seemed imminent. Unfortunately, unknown to the inventor, experiments had just been successfully concluded in adding a sound track to the film itself. This was the system that was universally adopted and Synchrophone never came on the market. The capital cost of development was substantial and unfortunately came to nothing. Ill luck played a part but the venture was outside the firm's experience and development costs were far heavier than expected. Added to this, the declining importance of the printing works to the music side prompted an investigation into the structure of J. Curwen & Sons. Accountants were called in and the opinion given that the publishing and printing sides should part company and work as separate businesses.

Expert valuation was made and a satisfactory form of separation devised acceptable to both businesses. It is surprising that the valuers put no price on goodwill which must have been considerable. Both the printing and publishing, it could be argued, contributed to goodwill but it is unlikely that the values would be identical for both sides of the business. However, there were no regrets and it was recognized that the time had come for the two sides of the business to work separately. On 1 March 1933 the Plaistow works of J. Curwen & Sons Ltd became The Curwen Press Limited. For the first time the printing works had its own responsible directors. The first directors were Harold Curwen and the brothers Oliver and Herbert Simon. The company secretary was O. R. G. Williams.

XXI

EPILOGUE

THE LEGAL SEPARATION of the printing from the music publishing made it in some ways easier for the newly established
Curwen Press Limited to contribute even more vigorously to the
printing revival. Apron strings can be comforting and often
necessary and from the earliest days to the end of the Great War,
some lightly tied strings were appropriately attached. Until
Plaistow developed its own strong trade, the manufacture of
printing was bound to take second place to the publishing of
music.

J. Curwen & Sons were generous in support of their printing
division but their publishing investments came first, which made
it inevitable that the printing plant was not quite as modern as it
might have been: the use of the floor space available at the factory
lacked the regular reviews which would have been beneficial.

The new company brought in a new broom and new brooms
are expected to do some effective sweeping. The one imported
from Birmingham was no exception. Several sweeping changes
were made, on the whole advantageous to the firm and mostly of a
kind that came naturally to a fresh pair of eyes. The policy of The
Curwen Press remained the policy of Harold Curwen and Oliver
Simon: the provision of good, appropriate printing that should
give satisfaction both to the customer and the producers. The
rider now added was that quality should remain unchanged or be
improved but that by better use of floor space and the employment of advanced equipment more could be undertaken at less
cost to the customer and at reasonable profit to the company.

The new broom found that the largest single building, the store
for music, was largely occupied by empty or sparsely filled shelv-
ing. A space of about a sixth of the existing area was found

sufficient to store the printed music. The huge room that was released was converted into a bindery and warehouse. This involved the purchase of more folding, sewing, stitching machinery and guillotines so that runs of well over 100,000 copies of pamphlets, timetables and similar items could be handled with ease and speed. Previously the larger finishing work was only able to be done with outside help.

It was, of course, obvious that the machine room had been equipped to print sheet music and publications in relatively small editions as cheaply as possible. Most of the machines were unsuitable either for long runs, good quality halftone work or bookwork. Agreement was obtained for scrapping the older machines, fitting the more modern plant with automatic paper feeders, adding some new high-speed presses and, most important of all, buying two large book printing presses which enabled the department to print thirty-two pages of a normal sized book instead of sixteen pages at a time.

The works were then recosted by the company secretary and, rather to the alarm of Oliver Simon, cost rate distinctions between bookwork and general printing were abolished. He need not have worried: the saving in cost through the use of more modern equipment, the larger sheets that could now be printed and the economy the new bindery offered on the binding of limited editions made far larger and ambitious books a new field for his talents. The same boost was given to general printing and Harold had no need to be disconcerted when the Southern Railway ordered a bumper number of *Over the Points*.

The ability of Harold Curwen to produce printing that was both a pleasure to behold and fit for its purpose remained as effective as ever. It is well exemplified in a small publication given to visitors arriving in England by Southern Railway services for the Royal Jubilee celebrations in 1935. Nothing grand, but just charming: *Thrice Welcome* pocket sized with simple readable pages beautifully adorned with wood engravings by Eric Ravilious.

General printing grew rapidly: some of the work had that special distinction which Harold Curwen brought out with seemingly limitless powers of invention. There were a fine group of booklets for Austin Reed, numerous jobs where every detail of composition had been thoughtfully worked out and resulting in many useful and profitable hours for the printing machines and bindery. Especially appreciative were the Westminster Bank, some of the pioneers in the new unit trust movement and a mass of beautiful brochures and timetables for Imperial Airways, the forerunner of what became British Overseas Airways Corporation. It still remained true that the origin of Plaistow printed work rarely needed confirmation by a search for the imprint. In addition there was a group of work from some Midland manufacturers who insisted with admirable loyalty of having their printing looked after by the new broom. As most of these firms were in the Black Country, this valuable addition to the firm's output became known at Plaistow as the Staffordshire Knot.

THE BEAUTY
OF SOUTHERN ENGLAND

By S. P. B. MAIS

I lay stress upon that word beauty, because man's craving for beauty is the primary urge of his being. It is in search of beauty that he sets out on his travels, or he is no true traveller. And he is right to set his face towards England, for in this country he will find beauty in abundance.

But it is well to remember that England is small, and her beauties are on a Lilliputian scale. The hills of the South Country are smooth, rounded, green knolls, inspiring serenity but never awe. They bear no resemblance to the

Wood engraving by Eric Ravilious for *Thrice Welcome*
produced for the Southern Railway in 1935

Bookwork gained greater and greater importance. More efficient manufacture brought, as it deserved, the reward of more custom. Oliver Simon was at the height of his typographic power. Among much attractive work some deserve, as the military have it, to be mentioned in dispatches. Three larger jobs speak for themselves. In 1936 Oliver undertook for the Limited Editions Club of New York a two-volume edition of George Borrow's *Lavengro*. The page size is 9 in.× 5½ in. and both the first and second volumes are 400 pages in length. The type is Monotype Walbaum and there is almost perfection in the simplicity of the pages and the sure handling of the prelims and chapter headings carrying a synopsis of content. And to enhance it all there are sixteen hand-drawn lithographs by Barnett Freedman that master-craftsman of drawing on stone and also some fine-line illustrations which are printed with just the right amount of ink.

Following closely is *The Westminster Bank through a Century* by Professor T. E. Gregory, published by Oxford University Press in 1936. The page size is 9¾ in. × 6 in., the first volume occupies 408 pages and the second volume 364. Set in Monotype Baskerville and so careful in every detail that the reader is presented with an atmosphere which is calm and unfussy. There are numerous tables, a difficult genealogical tree and a series of graphs which are all handled in a way that fits perfectly into the book's general pattern. It is a work that would be appreciated for its technical command by anyone who is professionally engaged as a top-line compositor.

The third book for special mention is Boswell's *Life of Samuel Johnson* printed for the Limited Editions Club in 1938. The page size is 9¾ in. × 6⅛ in. and is set in Monotype Baskerville. It is a large work, the first volume running to 532 pages, the second volume 496 pages and the third volume 484 pages. It is the sort of book which requires numerous decisions concerning exactly how the vagaries of the text are to be handled. Oliver Simon deals with all this with an astonishing sureness. Besides the main text which is frequently broken by letters, quotations and footnotes, the typographic scheme had to accommodate in the margins the comments and markings made by Mrs Thrale Piozzi. It is all done with such feeling and scholarly wisdom that the book is not only comely but has the merit of being comfortable for the reader.

An important event in Oliver Simon's life as a mature typographer and editor was the publication of *Signature*. It was described as a quadrimestrial of typography and graphic arts. The first number appeared in November 1935 and continued for fifteen issues until war-time conditions brought it to an end in December 1940. It was revived in July 1946 and called *Signature* New Series but it ended after eighteen issues in 1954. In the final issue a serene adieu is contributed to Oliver Simon from Edmund Blunden.

Signature was the private property of Oliver Simon and Plaistow helped by charging less than half the real cost of the work. It was a substantial subsidy but at the time and certainly in retrospect it was considered money well spent. *Signature* like so many of The Fleuron publications was offered far too cheaply. The initial series was a mere 3s per number (postage 4d) and it could have sold equally successfully for four times the price. *Signature* New Series was sold at 4s 6d despite the fact that the cost of printing had by then risen by more than twice pre-war prices. Oliver Simon knew very little about costing and if he had known the real extent of the subsidy he was receiving he might have set his selling price at a more realistic figure. But *Signature* has been worth all that was put into it. It lived worthily up to the promise in its original prospectus where it proclaimed an endeavour to keep its readers informed of the main current typographic events. The relatively small number of subscribers is evidence that the typographic revivalist still had hard work to do and that conversion to the appreciation of good work was a slow business.

And so it goes on. A relatively small firm in Plaistow still has its ideals and the spark of the 'spirit of joy' kindled by Harold Curwen has not been extinguished. There are, as the firm well knows, other printers doing fine work but The Curwen Press is probably the only survivor of the pioneering days which can be dated from the foundation of the Design & Industries Association in 1915.

It was felt at Plaistow to be significant that the only part of the works which survived the devastation of the last war in recognizable condition was the original Independent Chapel to which John Curwen was appointed pastor in 1844.

APPENDIX A

Harold Curwen's address at the opening of an exhibition of printing at Derby organized by the Design & Industries Association, 14 May 1919.

In the first place it should be made clear that the Design & Industries Association is not an association of people and firms for the object of self-advancement. It is an organization rather for those who want to see better standards of life and more joy in the accomplishment of everyday occupations. It is an association to put work into not merely to draw advantage from.

The association stands for the belief that industrial unrest is largely due to the accepted aim of working for personal gain rather than to make some thing or supply some service in the best possible way for the good of the community.

Where there is scope for pride in doing a job well, there is nearly always enjoyment or at least absence of boredom. And even if the job has been rendered so mechanical by modern contrivances that no intelligence of the operative can make the product either worse or better, still if the thing being made is designed to be of the utmost usefulness, and if it is a thing which is actually required, the mere knowledge of these conditions makes for satisfaction to the workers.

And not only this, but if the aim is to design and make a thing so that it may be perfectly fit for the use for which it is intended, almost certainly it takes on a constructional beauty far more satisfying than any so called decoration of an ill-designed and shoddy thing.

I want to press home that it is not merely this beauty of sound construction for its own sake that we aim at but the satisfaction to both maker and user which it brings about.

Again, the well made thing by lasting longer will prove the more economical and if the aim of manufacture is service rather than personal gain, the natural tendency will be to make things primarily to last rather than to sell. Some do not want certain things to last too long, preferring a change, but I believe that one of the sure tests of fitness for use is that we do not get tired of a good thing.

[232]

The application of these principles to printing is comparatively easy.

Since the introduction of more accurate machinery and photo process reproductions we have come to think merely of mechanical excellence when we talk of good printing, but this mechanical excellence although important matters much less than sound arrangement.

To start with the alphabet, whether in typeset reading matter or in larger 'displayed' or drawn lettering. The capitals which were at their best 2,000 years ago, as seen in the old inscriptions, are the soundest model. They were clearly designed with a view to fitness for use, that is readableness. They are an instance of a good thing proving its worth by our fidelity to it.

Whereas every letter should have a clear characteristic of its own and be as different from its fellows as possible, the tendency in nearly all types in general use now is to reduce all letters to one approximate width, and owing to our apparent complete lack of any knowledge of good lettering on the part of the perpetrators, to lose the special characteristics.

So many of the types in use now look to have been constructed by an engineer's draftsman rather than by a lettering artist who loved his subject. Indeed I believe (incredible as it will seem to anyone here who is not a printer) there is not one British Typefounder who has even a consultative connection with one of the really first rate lettering craftsmen of whom there are several in England today.

In the arrangement of typeset matter in book form, line length and margin apportionment are of vital importance. Lines should contain from eight to ten words: more cause a difficulty in carrying the eye back, and fewer make necessary the wide and irregular spacing between words which obstructs the regular unconscious swing of the eye in reading.

In larger so called 'displayed' pieces of lettering it is difficult in a few words to say what constitutes a good arrangement. Concise grouping of the essential facts, the use of uniform style of lettering and the avoidance of great varieties of sizes in consecutive matter are some of the most vital points.

There is also what I might call pictorial printing, as opposed to pure typography. Into this class come all kinds of drawn work, labels, showcards, posters, book illustrations, etc.

This should be either frankly an illustration, in which case probably the photo-mechanical process is the best, or if a realistic illustration is not the object, a courageous representation, correct in fundamentals, is more satisfying than elaboration of detail with no constructional idea.

A muddy photographic style is not effective. In work which from the nature of it gives only a brief impression, detail has no value. It is the strong silhouetted design which tells.

For purely decorative purposes, do not attempt to reproduce but rather receive inspiration from the subject and endeavour to convey the spirit of the model. As for instance, in making a decorative representation of flowers, do not attempt to give all the modelling and fine texture, but rather get the essential gay cheerfulness into the design in a broad way. Fine detail drawing in this case would destroy the impression aimed at. It is well to keep wording and picture entirely separate, but both must be related in character.

Printers have a great responsibility in that their presses can turn out with equal facility either well designed things which are a pleasure to both the workers who make them, and to all who use or see them, or shoddy, badly designed things which do not well fulfil their purpose and which degrade everyone who either makes or uses them.

In closing, I would strongly urge master printers to take a much keener interest in the sound design and fitness for use of the output of their presses, thinking not solely of the mechanical excellence and high finish, but of the more important fundamental soundness of the work, many ideas of which are shown by the exhibits. And also I would urge all users of printed matter to demand this sound constructional fitness for use in work done for them.

APPENDIX B

CATALOGUE RAISONNÉ OF
BOOKS PRINTED AT THE CURWEN PRESS
1920–1932

PRINTER'S NOTE to *catalogue raisonné* 1920–1923: The items in the following list are not to be understood as a complete record of the Press's work in the field of book production, but as a catalogue of Books where the design and choice of materials has been freely committed to the printer.

PRINTED IN 1920

The Lute of Love, An Anthology
Decorated by C. LOVAT FRASER.

1921

The Luck of the Bean-Rows
By CH. NODIER. Decorated by C. LOVAT FRASER.

Autumn
By JOHN CLARE. London, Privately printed for Oliver and Herbert Simon, Esqq. (demy 8vo, 7 pp., edition limited to 80 copies on Haesbeek paper. Caslon, bound in all-decorative paper boards.)

1922

Shah Abdul Latif
By M. M. GIDVANI. London, The India Society. (7s. 6d. net, demy 8vo, 48 pp., edition limited to 500 copies, Caslon monotype, bound in cloth boards, lettering by PERCY J. SMITH.)

Four Comedies
By CARLO GOLDONI. Translated by MARGUERITE TRACY, HERBERT & ELEANOR FARJEON and by the editor, CLIFFORD BAX. London, CECIL PALMER. (25s. net, demy 8vo, 320 + xiv pp., photogravure frontispiece, edition limited to 500 copies on Abbey Mills Antique Laid. Caslon monotype, bound in linen back, Michalet boards.)
The edition is beautifully printed. W. J. Turner, in LONDON MERCURY.

[235]

A Long Spoon and the Devil
By HENRY SAVAGE. London, CECIL PALMER. (6s. net, crown 8vo, 56 pp., Imprint, bound in cloth back, decorated paper boards.)

The Woodcutter's Dog
By CH. NODIER. Decorated by C. LOVAT FRASER.

Letters and Journals of Anne Chalmers
Edited by HER DAUGHTER. London, The Chelsea Publishing Company. (Privately printed, demy 8vo, 201 pp., edition limited to 200 copies on Haesbeek paper, Caslon monotype, bound in linen back, Michalet paper boards.)

Poems from the Works of Charles Cotton
Decorated by C. LOVAT FRASER.

Catalogue of the First Exhibition of Books and Manuscripts held by the First Edition Club
London, The First Edition Club. (£2 2s. net, demy 8vo, 178 pp., edition limited to 500 copies on Haesbeek paper, Caslon monotype, bound in buckram back, paper boards.)

The catalogue of the collection is in itself a remarkable work, finely printed on perfect paper, so as to be truly the first and enduring imprint of the club, and to be coveted as such by collectors in the future. DAILY TELEGRAPH, *December 6th, 1922.*

The bibliographical catalogue deserves a word in passing to itself. This is work which only patience and love of books could have produced. It is admirably done, and was printed privately. The edition is limited to five hundred copies. It should become a useful book of reference. THE TIMES, *December 8th, 1922.*

. . . . It was printed privately, and the edition is limited to five hundred copies. As a book it is a good specimen of fine binding and printing, and as a catalogue it has qualities that should make it of permanent value. THE TIMES LITERARY SUPPLEMENT, *December 14th, 1922.*

A Collection of Nursery Rhymes
Decorated by C. LOVAT FRASER.

The Best Poems of 1922
Selected by THOMAS MOULT, decorated by PHILIP HAGREEN. London, Jonathan Cape. (6s. net, crown 8vo, 145 + xiii pp., Garamond monotype, bound in Batik paper boards.)

The Four Seasons
Decorated by ALBERT RUTHERSTON.

Vincent Van Gogh, A Biographical Study
By JULIUS MEIER-GRAEFE. Translated by JOHN HOLROYD REECE. London, The Medici Society Ltd. (£3 3s. net, demy 4to, 2 vols., Imprint monotype, bound cloth back, paper boards. There is also an édition de luxe limited to 100 copies on hand-made paper, bound in vellum, £10 10s. net.)
. ˙ . The book contains 102 full-page collotypes.
The type and aspect of the book are of the finest. MANCHESTER GUARDIAN.

1923

The Bodley Head Quartos
Edited by G. B. HARRISON. A series of reprints of Elizabethan and Jacobean Pamphlets, Plays, etc. London, John Lane, The Bodley Head Ltd. (2s. 6d. net, 7 × 4¾, Caslon monotype. Each volume bound in a different coloured paper wrapper, hand dyed at The Curwen Press.)

ROBERT GREENE
I *A Notable Discovery of Coosnage* (1591)
  Conny Catching Part II (1592)
III *Conny Catching* Part III (1592)
  A Disputation between a Hee Conny Catcher and a Shee Conny Catcher (1592)
VI *The Groatsworth of Witte Bought with a Million of Repentance* (1592)
  The Repentance of Robert Greene Maister of Artes (1592)

GABRIEL HARVEY
II *Foure Letters . . . Especially touching Robert Greene* (1592)

BEN JONSON
V *Discoveries* (first printed 1640)
  Notes of Conversations with Drummond of Hawthornden (1619)

THOMAS NASHE
  Pierce Penilesse his Supplication to the Divell (1592)

WILLIAM SHAKESPEARE
  The Tragicall Historie of Hamlet Prince of Denmarke (1603)
. . . clearly printed and easy to hold. TIMES LITERARY SUPPLEMENT.
These neat and scholarly reprints. . . . MANCHESTER GUARDIAN.
No better series of reprints has appeared in our time. TO-DAY.
. . . . Mr. Harrison's work comes out of this test, for the most part, with flying colours, and he would no doubt attribute part of the credit to the Curwen Press, his printers, who have turned out delightful little books. SATURDAY WESTMINSTER.
It is extraordinary that wealthy publishers like Messrs. Hutchinson should not take more pride in their books. We advise whoever is responsible for their 'Library of Standard Lives' to have a look at Mr. John Lane's Bodley Head Quartos, printed by the Curwen Press. No man or woman could take up one of those books without wanting to buy it. Beside them any one of the 'Library of Standard Lives' looks, and is, an abominable eyesore. But the bad print, bad paper, and tasteless format are not due to low price. They are due to ignorance and lack of taste on the part of those responsible for the production and publication of the books, and these defects will seriously affect their sale.
The idea that the paper, printing, and 'make-up' of a book is unimportant is as absurd as the idea that it does not matter how slovenly and insanitary a house is if the tenant is honest. It would have been far better to charge sixpence or even a shilling more and have produced decent books than to have allowed this series of cheap horrors to invade an overcrowded world. DAILY HERALD.

Poems of Emily Brontë
With an Introduction by CHARLOTTE BRONTË and decorated with arabesques by PERCY SMITH. London: Selwyn & Blount. (12s. 6d. net,

demy 8vo, 93 pp., collotype frontispiece, edition limited to 500 copies on Haesbeek paper, Garamond monotype, bound in cloth back, Rizzi decorated paper boards.)

This new edition of Emily Brontë's poems is a delightful book to look upon, both outside and in. It is bound in boards covered with a charming Italian paper and backed with buckram, and the type used is agreeable and easy to read. THE OBSERVER.

There must be a sufficient number of 'collectors' of Emily Brontë's books to secure the speedy exhaustion of this 'limited edition', which will add a very beautiful book to any library. Mr. Clement Shorter in the SPHERE, *1st September, 1923.*

The Fleuron, A Journal of Typography. No. 1
Edited by OLIVER SIMON. London, At the Office of the Fleuron. (21s. net, demy 4to, 127+vii pp. and numerous insets, edition limited to 1,000 copies on Abbey Mills Antique, Garamond monotype, bound cloth back and Michalet paper boards. There is also an édition de luxe of 110 copies on Kelmscott hand-made paper, bound in whole buckram, gilt top, and containing additional plates, £3 3s. net.)

The first number of the 'Fleuron' is a brilliant piece of book-production. B. H. Newdigate in the LONDON MERCURY.

Irreproachable in manner and execution, this first volume contains articles by some of the best-known authorities on printers' flowers, title-pages, initial letters, and similar matters, richly illustrated with rare examples. The book is indeed a torch to light the way for the seeker after better printing, being, unlike some books on the subject, a noble example of the art it treats of. MANCHESTER GUARDIAN.

Claud Lovat Fraser
By JOHN DRINKWATER and ALBERT RUTHERSTON. London, William Heinemann. (£6 6s. net, royal 4to, 39 pp.+8 pp. colour collotypes, 18 pp. monochrome collotypes, and 13 pp. line drawings. The edition is limited to 430 copies on hand-made paper, Imprint monotype, bound in whole black buckram, gilt top.)

A Garland of Elizabethan Sonnets
London, Leonard Parsons. (7s. 6d. net, 7½×5⅝, 34 pp., edition limited to 500 copies on Zanders hand-made paper, Garamond monotype, bound in cloth back, Rizzi decorated paper boards.)

Let it be said that the format in which they are presented is correspondingly adequate in taste and workmanship. The book is a thing of beauty, the sonnets—a joy for ever. BOOKMAN'S JOURNAL.

The book is published in a limited edition of 500 copies, and is irreproachable in format. The exquisite rightness of the printing of the Curwen Press, Plaistow, merits a word of praise for itself. EDINBURGH EVENING NEWS.

Odes
By JOHN KEATS. Decorated by VIVIEN GRIBBLE. London, Duckworth & Co. (10s. 6d. net, 10×6, 20 pp., edition limited to 170 copies on hand-made unbleached Arnold paper, Caslon, bound in linen back, brown Japanese paper boards. There is also a popular edition, demy 8vo, bound all paper boards, 2s. 6d. net.)

I have never seen a more charming piece of cheap, good printing than Messrs. Duckworth's edition of Keats' Odes. The Curwen Press are the printers of the delightful decorations by Miss Vivien Gribble. The more expensive edition has hand-made paper, a better binding and larger margins; it would please anybody to whom it was given. J. C. Squire, the LONDON MERCURY.

A Box of Paints
By GEOFFREY SCOTT. Decorated by ALBERT RUTHERSTON.

The Berkshire Kennet
By RICHARD ALDINGTON. London, privately printed for Holbrook Jackson (6 × 4¼, 6 pp., Garamond, edition limited to fifty copies on Van Gelder hand-made paper, bound in Batik paper wrappers).

A Reply to Z
By WILLIAM HAZLITT, with an introduction by CHARLES WHIBLEY. London, The First Edition Club. (£1 1s. net, 10 × 6⅜, 40 pp., edition limited to 300 copies on Zanders' hand-made paper, Baskerville monotype, bound cloth boards, gilt top.)

Meditative Ode on Vision
By RICHARD HUGHES. London, privately printed at The Curwen Press. (6 pp., edition limited to 75 copies of which 25 are for sale. Zanders' hand-made paper, Caslon monotype, bound in dyed Japanese paper wrappers.)

1924

Catalogue Raisonné of Books Printed at The Curwen Press 1920–1923
With an introduction by HOLBROOK JACKSON. London: The Medici Society. (5s. net. Demy 8vo. 27 pp. + 9 illustrations. Edition limited to 400 copies on Haesbeek paper. Garamond monotype. Bound full paper boards.)

Genesis
Twelve woodcuts by PAUL NASH, with the first chapter of *Genesis* in the Authorised Version. London: The Nonesuch Press. (£1 1s. net. 10½″ × 7½″. 28 pp. [unnumbered]. Edition limited to 375 copies on Zanders' hand-made paper. Neuland type. Bound full paper boards.)

The Discovery
A comedy in five acts, written by MRS. FRANCES SHERIDAN. Adapted for the modern stage by ALDOUS HUXLEY. London: Chatto & Windus. (5s. net. Crown 8vo. vii + 121 pp. Caslon monotype. Bound cloth back, paper boards. There is also a special edition of 210 copies on Italian hand-made paper. Bound cloth back, and decorated paper boards designed by C. Lovat Fraser. 10s. 6d. net.)

Ding Dong Bell
By WALTER DE LA MARE. London: Selwyn & Blount. (5s. net. Crown 8vo. ix + 76 pp. Caslon monotype. Bound full cloth boards. There is also

an édition de luxe of 300 copies on Zanders' hand-made paper. Bound linen back, paper boards. £1 10s. net.)

A Bibliography of the First Editions of Books by William Butler Yeats
Compiled by A. J. A. SYMONS. London: The First Edition Club. (7s. 6d. net. Post 8vo. viii+46 pp. Edition limited to 500 copies on Japon paper. Garamond monotype. Bound full paper boards.)

Walt Whitman
A study and a selection by GERALD BULLETT. London: Grant Richards. (15s. net. Royal 8vo. 166 pp. Edition limited to 750 copies on English mould-made paper. Imprint monotype. Bound cloth back. Batik paper boards.)

Nothing or The Bookplate
By EDWARD GORDON CRAIG. With a handlist by E. CARRICK. London: Chatto & Windus. (£3 3s. net. Super royal 8vo. Edition limited to 280 copies on Zanders' hand-made paper. 26 pp. 51 reproductions in colour and in black and white. Imprint monotype, bound full buckram.)

Claud Lovat Fraser
Sixty-three unpublished designs. With an introduction by HOLBROOK JACKSON. London: The First Edition Club. (10s. net. 6″×4½″. Edition limited to 500 copies on yellow French Ingres paper, hand-dyed at The Curwen Press. Caslon monotype [introduction]. Bound cloth back, decorated paper boards designed by C. Lovat Fraser.)

A. C. Benson, Selected Poems
London: John Lane, The Bodley Head. (6s. net. Crown 8vo. xiii+185 pp. Caslon monotype. Bound full buckram.)

The Fleuron: No. III
Edited by OLIVER SIMON. London: The Office of The Fleuron. (£1 1s. net. Demy 4to. 135 pp. Printed on Abbey Mill antique laid. Caslon mono-type. Bound full cloth. There is also an édition de luxe of 125 copies on Kelmscott hand-made paper containing additional plates. Bound whole buckram, gilt top. £3 3s.)

1925

Bibliographical Catalogue of First Editions, Proof Copies and Manuscripts of Books by Lord Byron exhibited at the Fourth Exhibition held by The First Edition Club, January 1925
London: The First Edition Club. (£1 10s. net. Crown 4to. xvii+97 pp. Edition limited to 500 copies on Van Gelder paper. Caslon monotype. Bound full cloth boards, gilt top.)

G. B. Bodoni's Preface to The Manuale Tipografico of 1818
Now first translated into English, with an introduction by H. V. MARROT.

London: Elkin Mathews Ltd. (15s. net. Foolscap 4to. 57 pp. Edition limited to 310 copies on Van Gelder Simili Japon paper. Bodoni monotype. Bound full paper boards. There is also a special edition of 25 copies printed on Japanese vellum, bound full paper boards.)

True Dialogues of the Dead
Compiled by FRANCIS BICKLEY. London: Guy Chapman. (6s. net. Crown 8vo. 150 pp. Imprint monotype. Bound cloth back, paper boards. There is also an édition de luxe of 200 copies printed on Van Gelder paper, with design by Albert Rutherston on the title-page in red, bound full cloth boards, gilt top.)

Ten Tales by Ambrose Bierce
With an introduction by A. J. A. SYMONS. London: The First Edition Club. (15s. net. Demy 8vo. xiv+136 pp. Edition limited to 500 copies on Dutch mould-made paper. Caslon monotype. Bound full cloth boards, gilt top.)

The Espalier
By SYLVIA TOWNSEND WARNER. London: Chatto & Windus. (5s. net. Pott 4to. 103 pp. Caslon monotype. Bound full cloth boards.)

The Fleuron: No. IV
Edited by OLIVER SIMON. London: The Office of the Fleuron. (21s. net. Demy 4to. 164 pp. Printed on Abbey Mill antique laid. Caslon monotype. Bound full cloth. There is also an édition de luxe of 120 copies on Kelmscott hand-made paper containing additional plates. Bound whole buckram, gilt top. £3 3s. net.)

Welchman's Hose
By ROBERT GRAVES, with wood engravings by PAUL NASH. London: The Office of The Fleuron. (12s. 6d. net. Pott 4to. 61 pp. Edition limited to 525 copies on Italian mould-made paper. Imprint monotype. Bound cloth back, and paper boards designed by Paul Nash.)

Poor Young People
By EDITH, OSBERT, and SACHEVERELL SITWELL, with drawings by ALBERT RUTHERSTON. London: The Office of The Fleuron. (£2 2s. net. Crown 4to. 60 pp. Edition limited to 375 copies on Van Gelder paper. Caslon monotype. Bound full cloth boards.)

Sandro Botticelli
By YUKIO YASHIRO. 266 collotype plates. London: The Medici Society. (£15 15s. net. Super royal 4to. 3 vols. Vol. I, xxix+267 pp. Vols. II and III, collotype plates. Edition limited to 630 copies on Dutch mould-made paper. Caslon monotype. Initial letters by Percy Smith. Bound full buckram).

The Fairy Doll
By JEAN-GALLI DE BIBIENA. Translated by H. B. V. with an introduction by SHANE LESLIE. London: Chapman & Hall. (£1 1s. net. Demy 8vo.
xv+153 pp. Edition limited to 1000 copies on 'Ellerslie' paper. Garamond
monotype. Bound cloth back, decorated paper boards designed by Albert
Rutherston, gilt top.)

The Opportunities of a Night
By M. DE CRÉBILLON LE FILS. Translated by ERIC SUTTON. With an
introduction by ALDOUS HUXLEY. London: Chapman & Hall. (£1 1s. net.
Demy 8vo. xxv+188 pp. Edition limited to 1000 copies on 'Ellerslie'
paper. Garamond monotype. Bound cloth back, decorated paper boards
designed by Albert Rutherston, gilt top.)

Nothing or The Bookplate
By EDWARD GORDON CRAIG. With a handlist by E. CARRICK. London:
Chatto & Windus. (7s. 6d. net. Royal 8vo. 26 pp. 25 reproductions in colour
and black and white. Imprint monotype. Bound cloth back, paper boards.)

Hymns
Selected for use at Abberley Hall by L. W. GREENWOOD. (Privately
printed. Foolscap 8vo. 92 pp. Edition limited to 400 copies on Japon paper.
Garamond monotype. Bound full cloth boards.)

A Chatto & Windus Almanack, 1926
London: Chatto & Windus. (1s. net. Crown 8vo. 151 pp. Imprint monotype.
Paper wrappers. There is also an édition de luxe of 250 copies on Perusia
[*sic*] hand-made paper. Bound cloth back, paper boards.)

The Bodley Head Quartos
A series of reprints of Elizabethan and Jacobean Pamphlets, Plays, etc.
Edited by G. B. HARRISON. London: John Lane, The Bodley Head Ltd.
(2s. 6d. net. 7″×4¾″. Caslon monotype. Each volume bound in a coloured
paper wrapper, hand dyed at The Curwen Press.)

 IV HENRIE CHETTLE
  Kind-Hartes Dreame (1592)
  WILLIAM KEMPE
  Nine Daies Wonder (1600)

 VII WILLIAM SHAKESPEARE
  The Tragicall Historie of Hamlet Prince of Denmarke (1603)

 VIII THOMAS DEKKER
  The Vvonderfull Yeare, 1603
  Wherein is shewed a picture of *London* lying sicke of the Plague.

 IX KING JAMES THE FIRST
  Daemonologie (1597)

Newes from Scotland declaring the Damnable Life and death of Doctor Fian, a notable Sorcerer who was burned at Edenbrough in Ianuarie last. (1591).

X ROBERT GREENE
The Blacke Bookes Messenger (1592)
Cuthbert Conny Catcher: The Defence of Conny Catching (1592)

XI THOMAS NASHE
Pierce Penilesse, his Svpplication to the Divell (1592)

XII ANTHONY MUNDAY
The English Romayne Lyfe (1582)

XIII JOHN MARSTON. (With an introduction by the Editor.)
The Scourge of Villainie (1599)

XIV SAMUEL DANIEL
A Defence of Ryme (1603)
THOMAS CAMPION
Observations in the Art of English Poesie (1602)

1926

The Curwen Press Almanack for 1926
London: The Fleuron. 5s. net. Crown 8vo. 39 pp.+8 pp. illustrations. Edition limited to 425 copies. Italian wove paper. Caslon. Bound cloth back, paper boards.

Nine Poems
By LORD ALFRED DOUGLAS. Privately printed for A. J. A. Symons. $7\frac{1}{4}'' \times 5\frac{1}{4}''$. 13 pp. Edition limited to 50 copies. Italian wove paper. Caslon Monotype. Bound full paper boards.

Stendhal
By ANATOLE FRANCE. Translated by J. LEWIS MAY. Privately printed for Holbrook Jackson. Crown 8vo. 24 pp. Edition limited to 110 copies Italian wove paper. Garamond Monotype. Bound paper wrappers.

Horati Carminum Libri IV
London: Peter Davies. 30s. net. Demy 8vo. 141 pp. Edition limited to 500 copies. 'Ellerslie' mould-made paper. Koch Kursiv. Bound full cloth.

Sailing Ships and Barges of the Western Mediterranean and Adriatic Seas
A series of copper plates engraved in the line manner by EDWARD WADSWORTH and coloured by hand, with an Introduction and Brief Descriptions by BERNARD WINDELER. London: Frederick Etchells & Hugh Macdonald. £3 15s. net. Large Imperial 8vo. 79 pp. + copper engraved Frontispiece, map, and imprint. Edition limited to 450 copies. Zanders' hand-made paper. Koch Kursiv. Bound full cloth.

Anacreon: 29 Odes
Rendered into English verse by DORIS LANGLEY. London: Gerald Howe.
5s. net. Pott 4to. 45 pp. (unnumbered). Italian wove paper. Garamond
Monotype. Bound full cloth.

A Bill for the Better Promotion of Oppression on the Sabbath Day
By THOMAS LOVE PEACOCK. London: Privately printed for H. V.
Marrot. Foolscap 8vo. 8 pp. (unnumbered). Green Czecho-Slovak hand-
made paper. Imprint Monotype. Bound full paper boards.

A Chatto & Windus Almanack for 1927
With designs by STANLEY SPENCER. London: Chatto & Windus. 1s. net.
6½″ × 5″. 202 pp. Caslon Monotype. Bound paper wrappers. There is also a
special edition de luxe on Italian wove paper limited to 250 copies at
10s. 6d. net. Bound linen back, paper boards.

The Bibliophile's Almanack for 1927
Edited by OLIVER SIMON and HAROLD CHILD. London: The Fleuron.
2s. 6d. net. Crown 8vo. 68 pp. + 11 pp. of advertisements. Caslon Monotype.
Bound paper wrappers. There is also an édition de luxe of 325 copies on
English wove mould-made paper. Bound buckram back, paper boards. 6s. net.

Marigold: an Idyll of The Sea
By W. J. TURNER. London: The Fleuron. 15s. net. Large Imperial 8vo.
34 pp. Edition limited to 350 copies. Italian wove paper. Walbaum. Bound
full cloth.

Exalt the Eglantine and Other Poems
By SACHEVERELL SITWELL. Decorated by THOMAS LOWINSKY.
London: The Fleuron. 21s net. Foolscap 4to. 37 pp. Edition limited to 350
copies. Kelmscott hand-made paper. Baskerville Monotype. Bound full
cloth.

1926–1927

XVIII Century French Romances
Edited by VYVYAN HOLLAND. London: Chapman & Hall. 21s. net each.
Demy 8vo. Each book is of different length and set in a different body type,
or a different size of body type. The edition is limited to 1000 copies of each
book. 'Ellerslie' mould-made paper. Bound cloth back, paper boards.
TITLES: *Angola: An Eastern Tale*; *The Queen of Golconda*; *Rameau's
Nephew*; *The Prophet's Cousin*; *The Masked Lady*; *All the Better for
Her!*; *The Coachman's Story*; *Spleen*; *A Thousand and One Nights*.

1927

Marino Faliero
By JACK LINDSAY. London: The Fanfrolico Press. 30s. net. 104 pp.

Crown 4to. Edition limited to 450 copies on English wove mould-made paper. Walbaum. Bound full paper boards.

The Woodcut: An Annual. No. I
Edited by HERBERT FURST. London: The Fleuron. 12s. 6d. net. Imperial 8vo. 75 pp. Baskerville Monotype. Bound cloth back, paper boards. There is also an edition de luxe on Zanders' hand-made paper limited to 75 copies at £2 2s. net. Bound full buckram.

Frederick Baron Corvo
By A. J. A. SYMONS. London: Privately printed for the Sette of Odd Volumes. $5\frac{3}{4}'' \times 4\frac{1}{2}''$. 40 pp. Imprint Monotype. Edition limited to 109 copies on English wove mould-made paper. Bound paper wrappers.

Robert Eyres Landor
A biographical and critical sketch by ERIC PARTRIDGE. London: The Fanfrolico Press. 10s. 6d. net. Demy 8vo. 108 pp. Caslon Monotype. Abbey Mills antique laid paper. Bound cloth back, paper boards.

Selections from Robert Landor
Edited by ERIC PARTRIDGE. London: The Fanfrolico Press. 7s. 6d. net. Demy 8vo. 176 pp. Caslon Monotype. Abbey Mills antique laid paper. Bound cloth back, paper boards.

Poisonous Plants
Engraved on wood, with an Introduction by JOHN NASH. London: Frederick Etchells & Hugh Macdonald. £2 12s. 6d. Large Imperial 8vo. 85 pp. Walbaum. Edition limited to 350 copies on Renker's Ingres paper. Bound full cloth.

Edward Thomas: Two Poems
London: Ingpen & Grant. 21s. net. $7\frac{1}{2}'' \times 5\frac{5}{8}''$. 12 pp. (unnumbered). Caslon. Edition limited to 85 copies on Zanders' hand-made paper. Bound paper boards.

Saint Hercules and Other Stories
By MARTIN ARMSTRONG, with drawings by PAUL NASH. London: The Fleuron. 30s. net. Large Imperial 8vo. 65 pp. Baskerville Monotype. Edition limited to 310 copies on Zanders' hand-made paper. Bound cloth back, paper boards.

The Bibliophile's Almanack for 1928
Edited by OLIVER SIMON and HAROLD CHILD. London: The Fleuron. 5s. net. Crown 8vo. 85 pp. +advertisements. Imprint Monotype. Bound cloth back, paper boards. There is also an edition de luxe of 120 copies printed on hand-made paper, 10s. 6d. net. Bound buckram back, paper boards.

1928

The Buck in the Snow
By EDNA ST. VINCENT MILLAY. Harper & Brothers. Crown 8vo. Full cloth. 5s.

Emin: The Governor of Equatoria
By A. J. A. SYMONS. The Fleuron. Foolscap 4to. Cloth back, paper boards. 300 copies. 12s. 6d.

Never Again! and Other Stories
By CLAUDE-JOSEPH DORAT. Translated by ERIC SUTTON, with an Introduction by VYVYAN HOLLAND. Chapman & Hall. Demy 8vo. Cloth back, paper boards. £1 1s. [The last of a series of Twelve French Romances.]

Music of The Italian Renaissance
By NESTA DE ROBECK. The Medici Society. Small Crown 4to. Full cloth. 18s.

Nine Poems by V
With an Introduction on MRS. ARCHER CLIVE. The Scholartis Press. Demy 8vo. Cloth, paper boards. 225 copies. 5s. 6d. Also 45 copies on 'Etruria' hand-made paper. Full buckram. 15s.

The Old Bailey
By GEOFFREY DORLING ROBERTS. Opusculum 86, privately printed for Ye Sette of Odd Volumes. $6\frac{1}{16}'' \times 4\frac{3}{4}''$, paper wrappers. 133 copies.

Printing of To-day
Edited by OLIVER SIMON and JULIUS RODENBERG, with an Introduction by ALDOUS HUXLEY. Peter Davies. Elephant 4to. Cloth back, paper boards. £1 1s. Also 300 copies on hand-made paper. Full buckram. £3 3s.

A Specimen Book of Pattern Papers Designed for and in use at The Curwen Press
With an Introduction by PAUL NASH. Published for The Curwen Press by The Fleuron. Super Royal 4to. Full buckram. 220 copies. £2 2s.

The Ravenna Journal
By GEORGE GORDON BYRON, SIXTH LORD BYRON. With an Introduction by LORD ERNLE. The First Edition Club. Demy 8vo. Full cloth. 15s.

Sitwelliana 1915–1927
Compiled by THOMAS BALSTON. Three portraits of the authors by ALBERT RUTHERSTON. Duckworth. Crown 8vo. Paper boards. 2s. 6d.

A Specimen Book of Types and Ornaments in use at The Curwen Press
Published for The Curwen Press by The Fleuron. Imperial 8vo. Full cloth. 135 copies on hand-made paper. £3 3s.

The Woodcut No. II
Edited by HERBERT FURST. The Fleuron. Imperial 8vo. Cloth back, paper boards. 12s. 6d. Also 80 copies on hand-made paper. Full buckram. £2 2s.

Francis Unwin: Etcher and Draughtsman
Edited by JOHN NASH, with a Memoir by CAMPBELL DODGSON. The Fleuron. Crown 4to. Cloth back, paper boards. 300 copies. £1 1s.

1929

The Apocrypha
With wood-engravings by BLAIR HUGHES-STANTON, GERTRUDE HERMES, LEON UNDERWOOD, STEPHEN GOODEN, RENÉ BEN SUSSAN, M. E. GROOM, ERIC JONES, WLADISLAW SKOCZYLAS, HESTER SAINSBURY, FRANK MEDWORTH, ERIC KENNINGTON, ERIC RAVILIOUS, JOHN NASH, and D. GALANIS. The Cresset Press. Foolscap folio. Full parchment. 450 copies. £6 6s. Also 30 copies on hand-made paper. Full black vellum (hand-sewn, flexible cords, laced in boards). £21.

Book Clubs and Printing Societies of Great Britain and Ireland
By HAROLD WILLIAMS. The First Edition Club. Small Crown 4to. Full cloth. 18s.

Beyond the Threshold
By PAUL RAYMOND. Translated from the French, and illustrated by CHARLES RICKETTS. Privately printed. Narrow Crown 4to. Full morocco. 150 copies.

The Bull against the Enemy of the Anglican Race
By FREDERICK BARON CORVO. Imperial 8vo. Paper wrappers. 50 copies privately printed for A. J. A. SYMONS.

William Bulmer and Thomas Bensley
A Study in Transition, by H. V. MARROT. The Fleuron. Crown 4to. Full cloth. 300 copies. £2 2s. Also 25 copies on hand-made paper. Full hard grain morocco (hand-sewn, laced in boards). £5 5s.

The Woodcut No. III
Edited by HERBERT FURST. The Fleuron. Imperial 8vo. Cloth back, paper boards. 12s. 6d. Also 75 copies on hand-made paper. Full buckram. £2 2s.

The Legion Book
Edited by CAPTAIN COTTON MINCHIN. Privately printed. Royal 4to. Full vellumized pigskin (hand-sewn flexible covers, laced in boards). 100 copies held in the gift of H.R.H. The Prince of Wales. Also an abridged

edition of 600 copies privately printed (for the British Legion) on mould-made paper. Full buckram. £5 5s.

The Legion Book
(Abridged Popular Edition.) Edited by CAPTAIN COTTON MINCHIN. Cassell & Company. Demy 4to. Full cloth. 21s.

Catulli Carmina
The Poems of Catullus, with complete verse translation and Notes by F. C. W. HILEY, M.A., and illustrations by VÉRA WILLOUGHBY. The Piazza Press. Small pott 4to. Full parchment. 500 copies. £2 2s.

The Casale Pilgrim
A Sixteenth-century illustrated guide to the Holy Places, reproduced in facsimile, with Introduction, translation, and Notes by CECIL ROTH. The Soncino Press. Crown 4to. Full vellum (hand-sewn). £3 3s. Also 48 copies on hand-made paper. Full hard grain morocco (hand-sewn, laced in boards). £6 6s.

The Diary of a Madman
By NICHOLAS GOGOL. Translated by PRINCE MIRSKY, illustrated with aquatints by A. ALEXEIEFF. The Cresset Press. $10\frac{3}{4}'' \times 8''$. Full cloth. £3 3s. Also 30 copies printed on hand-made paper. £9 9s.

Elena
By WILLIAM HARRISON WOODWARD. The Medici Society. Demy 8vo. Full cloth. 10s. 6d.

Ash Wednesday
By T. S. ELIOT. London: Faber & Faber. New York: The Fountain Press. $8'' \times 5\frac{3}{4}''$. Full cloth. £1 11s. 6d.

Elsie and the Child
By ARNOLD BENNETT, with drawings by E. MCKNIGHT KAUFFER. Cassell & Company. Crown 4to. Full cloth. £2 2s.

Holy Face and Other Essays
By ALDOUS HUXLEY, with drawings by ALBERT RUTHERSTON. The Fleuron. Full buckram. 300 copies. £3 3s.

A Brief History of Moscovia
By JOHN MILTON. Introduction by PRINCE MIRSKY, with illustrations by A. BRODOVITCH. The Blackamore Press. Narrow Crown 4to. Full cloth. £1 10s.

The Lady who Loved Insects
Translated from the Japanese by ARTHUR WALEY. Dry-points by HERMINE DAVID. The Blackamore Press. Small foolscap 4to. Full cloth. 500 copies. £1 1s. Also 50 copies printed on hand-made paper. Full cloth. £3 3s.

The Night Jaw
A Play in Three Acts by E. B. BROWN. Williams & Norgate. Crown 8vo.
Paper wrappers. 2s. 6d.

Pomegranate Flower
By MARGARET MAITLAND RADFORD. The Scholartis Press. Demy 8vo.
265 copies. 7s. 6d. Also 25 copies on hand-made paper. Full buckram. £1 1s.

'Rhenish'
By HENRY EDGAR VAUX HUGGETT. O.V. LXXXVIII, privately printed
for Ye Sette of Odd Volumes. $6\frac{1}{16}'' \times 4\frac{3}{4}''$. Paper wrappers. 199 copies.

Seven Sciagraphical Poems
By W. J. TURNER. Privately printed by HAROLD CURWEN and OLIVER
SIMON for members of the Double Crown Club. Pott 8vo. Full cloth. 65
copies.

Second Journal to Eliza
By LAURENCE STERNE, with an Introduction by MARGARET R. B.
SHAW and a Foreword by CHARLES WHIBLEY. G. Bell & Sons. Demy
8vo. Full cloth. £1 1s.

Introduction to the Method of Leonardo da Vinci
Translated from the French of PAUL VALÉRY by THOMAS MCGREEVY.
John Rodker. Imperial 8vo. Cloth back, paper boards. 18s. Also 50 copies
printed on hand-made paper, parchment back, paper sides. £2 2s.

1930

The Woodcut No. IV
Edited by HERBERT FURST. The Fleuron. Imperial 8vo. Cloth back,
paper boards. 12s. 6d. Also 75 copies on hand-made paper. Full buckram.
£2 2s.

Ash Wednesday
By T. S. ELIOT. Faber & Faber. Crown 8vo. Full cloth. 3s. 6d.

Sixteen Drypoints and Etchings
A record of the Great War, by PERCY SMITH, with a Foreword by
WILLIAM ROTHENSTEIN and an Introduction by H. M. TOMLINSON.
The Soncino Press. Royal 4to. Full cloth. 145 copies. £1 5s. Also 22 copies
on hand-made paper. Full buckram. £6 6s.

Historical Records of the Middlesex Yeomanry 1797–1927
By CHARLES STONHAM, C.M.G., and BENSON FREEMAN, O.B.E.,
F.R.HIST.S. Edited by J. S. JUDD. Privately printed for the Regimental
Committee. Demy 8vo. Full cloth.

Les Sonnets a Philis
Par VINCENT MUSELLI. J. E. Pouterman, Paris. Foolscap 4to. Paper wrappers. 380 copies.

Sixteen Letters from Oscar Wilde
Edited and with Notes by JOHN ROTHENSTEIN. Faber & Faber. Pott 4to. Full cloth. £1 1s.

A Facsimile Reproduction of a Unique Catalogue of Laurence Sterne's Library
With a Preface by CHARLES WHIBLEY. James Tregaskis & Son. Demy 8vo. Cloth back, paper sides. 330 copies. £1 1s.

Theme and Variations
By JAMES STEPHENS. The Fountain Press, New York. Narrow Crown 8vo. Full cloth. $10.00.

How to Write a Village History
By A. L. HUMPHREYS. Privately printed for the Author. Demy 8vo. Paper boards. 1s.

The Haggadah
A New Critical Edition with English translation, Introduction and Notes Literary, Historical, and Archæological, by CECIL ROTH, with drawings by ALBERT RUTHERSTON. The Soncino Press. Royal 4to. Full levant morocco (hand-sewn, flexible laced in boards). 100 copies. £36 15s. Also 10 copies on Roman vellum. Full levant morocco (hand-sewn, flexible laced in boards). £210. [This book is printed in Hebrew and English.]

Advice to Young Men and (incidentally) to Young Women
By WILLIAM COBBETT. With illustrations after Gillray, and edited with a Preface by EARL E. FISK. Alfred A. Knopf. Crown 4to. Full buckram. £3 3s.

The Modern Library Collected by Viscount Esher at Watlington Park
Privately printed. Crown 4to. Full buckram. 100 copies.

Fournier on Typefounding
The text of the *Manuel Typographique* (1764–1766) translated into English and edited with Notes by HARRY CARTER. The Soncino Press. Crown 8vo. Full buckram. 260 copies. £4 4s.

The Anatomy of Bibliomania (Vol. I)
By HOLBROOK JACKSON. The Soncino Press. Medium 8vo. Full buckram. 28s. Also 48 copies printed on hand-made paper. Full hard grain morocco (hand-sewn, laced in boards). £6 6s.

About Zionism
Speeches and Letters by PROFESSOR ALBERT EINSTEIN. Translated and edited with an Introduction by LEON SIMON. The Soncino Press. Foolscap 4to. Full cloth. 5s.

The Vision of William concerning Piers the Plowman
A version by DONALD ATTWATER, with woodcuts by DENIS TEGET-
MEIER. Cassell & Company. Imperial 8vo. Cloth back, paper boards. 200
copies. £3 3s. Also 25 copies bound in full hard grain morocco (hand-sewn,
laced in boards), with the woodcuts hand-coloured by the artist. £10 10s.

Credo
By F. M. HEYWOOD. Decorated by ELIZABETH CORSELLIS. Privately
printed. Foolscap 4to. Full cloth.

Facets
A Book of Poems and six illustrations by EDNA CLARKE HALL. Elkin
Mathews & Marrot. Crown folio. Full cloth. 300 copies. £2 12s. 6d.

King Lear
By WILLIAM SHAKESPEARE. Illustrated by YUNGE, with an Introduction
by G. K. CHESTERTON. David Magee, San Francisco. Full buckram.
Super Royal 4to. 240 copies. $15.

The Labyrinth
By JAMES W. MILLS. Illustrations by RAYMOND MCGRATH. Williams
& Norgate. Foolscap 4to. Cloth back, paper boards. 7s. 6d. Also 50 copies
printed on hand-made paper. Full buckram. £1 1s.

Love among the Haystacks
By D. H. LAWRENCE. With a reminiscence by DAVID GARNETT. The
Nonesuch Press. Medium 8vo. Full buckram. 15s.

A Life of Gaudier-Brzeska
By H. S. EDE. William Heinemann. Super Royal 4to. Full buckram. 350
copies. £15 15s.

1931

Sartor Resartus
By THOMAS CARLYLE, with the Preface of RALPH WALDO EMERSON,
and an Introduction by BLISS PERRY. The Limited Editions Club, New
York. Narrow Crown 8vo, full cloth. $10.

Wine in Shakespeare's Day and Shakespeare's Plays
By ANDRÉ LOUIS SIMON, O.V. XCIII. Privately printed Opuscula of the
Sette of Odd Volumes. $5\frac{7}{8}$ in. $\times 4\frac{1}{2}$ in. Paper wrappers. 199 copies.

Venus Rising from the Sea
By ARNOLD BENNETT. With twelve drawings by E. MCKNIGHT
KAUFFER. Cassell & Company. Crown 4to, full cloth. 350 copies. £5 5s.

Plato's Banquet
Translated from the Greek. A Discourse on the manners of the ancient
Greeks relative to the subject of Love, also a Preface to the Banquet by

PERCY BYSSHE SHELLEY. Revised and enlarged by ROGER INGPEN from MSS. in the possession of Sir John C. E. Shelley-Rolls, Bart. Printed for private circulation. Demy 8vo, full cloth. 100 copies.

Men's Gods
A fragment from an unfinished pageant by EDWARD CHARLES. Joiner & Steele. Foolscap 4to, full canvas. 150 copies. £1 1s.

The Curwen Press Miscellany
Edited by OLIVER SIMON. Published for The Curwen Press by The Soncino Press [Publishers]. Imperial 8vo, full cloth. 275 copies. £3 3s.

The Child
By RABINDRANATH TAGORE. George Allen & Unwin. Crown 8vo, full paper boards. 2s. 6d.

Catalogue of Books, Manuscripts, Maps and Documents in the William Inglis Morse Collection, 1926–1931
Privately printed. Demy 8vo, full cloth.

The Zohar, Vol. I
Translated by HARRY SPERLING and MAURICE SIMON. With an Introduction by DR. J. ABELSON. The Soncino Press. Medium 8vo, full buckram. £1 1s. Also 35 copies printed on hand-made paper, bound full leather, £3 3s.

1932

On Love
Freely adapted from the Tibetan by A. R. ORAGE. The Unicorn Press. Crown 8vo, full cloth. 2s. 6d. Also 150 copies printed on hand-made paper, bound in full leather, £1 1s.

The Zohar, Vol. II
Translated by HARRY SPERLING and MAURICE SIMON. The Soncino Press. Medium 8vo, full buckram. £1 1s. per vol. Also 35 copies printed on hand-made paper, bound full leather, £3 3s.

Johnson and Queeney: Letters from Dr. Johnson to Queeney Thrale from the Bowood Papers
Edited with an Introduction by the MARQUIS OF LANSDOWNE. Cassell & Company. Demy 8vo, leather back, cloth sides. 500 copies. £2 5s.

A Family Record
[By LADY WEMYSS.] Privately printed. Medium 8vo, full cloth.

The Fear of Books
By HOLBROOK JACKSON. The Soncino Press. Medium 8vo, full buckram. £1 1s. Also 48 copies printed on hand-made paper, bound in full leather, £4 4s.

Broadcasting House
The British Broadcasting Corporation. Crown 4to, full cloth. 5s.

The Land of the New Adventure
[The Georgian Era in Nova Scotia.] By WILLIAM INGLIS MORSE. Quaritch. Demy 8vo. 325 copies. £2 15s. net. 25 copies, bound in full leather, £15 15s. net.

Peckover: The Abbotscourt Papers, 1904–1931
Edited by C. R. ASHBEE. Illustrated by REGINALD SAVAGE. The Astolat Press. Royal 4to, vellum back, paper boards. 350 copies. £3 3s.

The Anatomy of Bibliomania
By HOLBROOK JACKSON. The Soncino Press. Medium 8vo, full buckram, £1 1s. [Complete in one volume.]

Lovely Laughter
An Anthology of Seventeenth-Century Love Lyrics. Edited by EARL E. FISK. Decorated by VÉRA WILLOUGHBY. Cassell & Company and Alfred Knopf, New York. Royal 8vo, vellum back, paper boards. 500 copies. £1 5s.

Urne Buriall and The Garden of Cyrus
By SIR THOMAS BROWNE. With thirty drawings by PAUL NASH. Edited with an Introduction by JOHN CARTER. Cassell & Company. Royal 4to, vellum back, leather sides. 215 copies. £15 15s.

An Heroic Poem in Praise of Wine
By HILAIRE BELLOC. Peter Davies. Demy 4to, paper boards. 100 copies. £1 1s.

INDEX

T